Pedro Pérez Zeledón

Argument on the Question of the Validity of the Treaty of Limits Between Costa Rica and Nicaragua

and Other Supplementary Points Connected With It

Pedro Pérez Zeledón

Argument on the Question of the Validity of the Treaty of Limits Between Costa Rica and Nicaragua
and Other Supplementary Points Connected With It

ISBN/EAN: 9783337071547

Printed in Europe, USA, Canada, Australia, Japan

Cover: Foto ©ninafisch / pixelio.de

More available books at **www.hansebooks.com**

ARGUMENT

ON THE QUESTION OF THE VALIDITY OF THE TREATY OF LIMITS BETWEEN COSTA RICA AND NICARAGUA

AND

OTHER SUPPLEMENTARY POINTS CONNECTED WITH IT,

SUBMITTED TO THE

Arbitration of the President of the United States of America,

FILED ON BEHALF OF THE GOVERNMENT OF COSTA RICA

BY

PEDRO PÉREZ ZELEDÓN,

Its Envoy Extraordinary and Minister Plenipotentiary
in the United States.

(Translated into English by J. I. Rodriguez.)

WASHINGTON:
Gibson Bros., Printers and Bookbinders.
1887.

CONTENTS.

ANTECEDENTS.

	PAGE.
Treaty of Guatemala establishing the basis of the arbitration	5
Points which, according to the Government of Nicaragua, are doubtful and require interpretation,	9

INTRODUCTION, ... 15

FIRST PART.—HISTORICAL PRELIMINARIES.

CHAPTER I.
Nicoya; its annexation to Costa Rica, ... 21

CHAPTER II.
The San Juan river during the Spanish rule, . 30

CHAPTER III.
The San Juan river from 1821 to the date of the treaty of 1858, . 36

CHAPTER IV.
Negotiations for the settlement of the question of limits from the dissolution of the Republic of Central America to the year 1858, 45

CHAPTER V.
Continuation of the subject of the foregoing chapter, . . . 51

SECOND PART.—ELUCIDATION OF THE PRINCIPAL POINT.

CHAPTER I.
Exposition of the arguments made by Nicaragua in support of the idea that the treaty of 1858 is not valid, ... 61

CHAPTER II.
The treaty of limits was not made under the sway of any constitution, but under a Government temporarily endowed with unlimited powers, ... 65

CHAPTER III.
The consideration of the exceptional regime existing in Nicaragua in 1858 continued, ... 70

CHAPTER IV.
The treaty of limits does not imply any reform or amendment of the Nicaraguan Constitution of 1838, ... 77

CHAPTER V.
The treaty of limits was ratified, not once or twice, but on several repeated occasions by the Nicaraguan Legislatures, . . . 82

CHAPTER VI.
    The public law of Nicaragua recognizes the principle that the Republic is bound by an international treaty whatever the importance thereof may be, ... 89

CHAPTER VII.
    The whole of the present controversy rests substantially upon the use of a certain word.—Validity of the treaty in good faith, . 93

CHAPTER VIII.
    Repeated acknowledgments of the validity of the treaty by different Nicaraguan administrations, ... 97

CHAPTER IX.
    Costa Rica has never admitted that the treaty of limits required for its validity further ratifications, ... 104

CHAPTER X.
    The second alleged cause of the nullity of the treaty of limits, which is the want of ratification by Salvador, examined in general, ... 108

CHAPTER XI.
    Whether the treaty of 1858 was, or was not, the result of violence used against Nicaragua by the Administration of Don Juan Rafael Mora, President of Costa Rica, ... 111

CHAPTER XII.
    The Government of Salvador was not an essential party to the treaty of limits, ... 115

CHAPTER XIII.
    The Government of Salvador was, primarily, a fraternal mediator, and subsequently, and in regard to only one secondary clause of the treaty, guaranteeing party of the execution of the said clause, ... 120

CHAPTER XIV.
    The guarantee cannot be construed as a condition of the treaty, . 127

CHAPTER XV.
    Examination of the latter reasons alleged by Nicaragua in support of her theory that the treaty of limits is invalid, . . . 134

THIRD PART.—ANSWER TO THE QUESTIONS PROPOUNDED BY NICARAGUA IN REGARD TO THE RIGHT CONSTRUCTION OF THE TREATY OF LIMITS.

CHAPTER I.
    Whether the starting-point of the border line is movable as the waters of the river, or whether the Colorado river is the limit

of Nicaragua, and whether the waters of the San Juan river can be deviated without the consent of Costa Rica, . . 139

CHAPTER II.
Whether men-of-war or revenue cutters of Costa Rica can navigate on the San Juan river, ... 155

CHAPTER III.
Whether Costa Rica is bound to co-operate in the preservation and improvement of the San Juan river and the Bay of San Juan, and in what manner; and whether Nicaragua can undertake any work without considering the injury which may result to Costa Rica, ... 162

CHAPTER IV.
Which is the centre of the Salinas Bay ?—Is Costa Rica a party to the grants of interoceanic canal which Nicaragua might make? What are, in this respect, the rights of Costa Rica ? . . 169

CONCLUSION, ... 179

DOCUMENTS.

No. 1.
Treaty of limits between Costa Rica and Nicaragua concluded April 15, 1858, ... 185

No. 2.
Decree of the Federal Congress of Central America in 1825 approving the annexation of Nicoya to Costa Rica, . . . 192

No. 3.
The state of things existing at the time of the labors of the Constituent Assembly is declared to be an extraordinary regime, wherein the constitutional rules in force under regular circumstances could be laid aside, ... 193

No. 4.
Communication from the Costa Rican Secretary of State.—It shows the ardent desire of Costa Rica to settle finally, and forever, the questions pending between it and Nicaragua, even at the sacrifice of its own rights and its national pride, . . 195

No. 5.
Communication showing the spirit of conciliation and fraternity which prevailed in the making of the treaty of limits.—The limits between Nicaragua and Costa Rica are, more than anything else, internal or domestic jurisdictional boundaries, . 197

No. 6.
Congratulation by the United States Minister for the near settlement of the differences between Costa Rica and Nicaragua.—

		PAGE.
	Speech of Gen. Mirabeau B. Lamar, Envoy Extraordinary and Minister Plenipotentiary of the United States in Nicaragua,	199
No. 7.		
	Note of the Costa Rican Secretary of State showing the peaceful disposition of Costa Rica in regard to the question of limits,	200
No. 8.		
	Communication from the Secretary of State of Costa Rica showing that the initiation of the treaty of 1858 was due to the friendly mediation of the Government of Salvador and to overtures made by Nicaragua subsequent to the repudiation made by the latter of the treaty of 1858, which Costa Rica had approved of,	202
No. 9.		
	Act of exchange of the ratifications of the treaty of limits,	204
No. 10.		
	Editorial of the official newspaper of Nicaragua on the conclusion of the treaty.—It shows the spirit of conciliation and fraternity of Costa Rica and Nicaragua.—Thanks given to the Government of Salvador for its friendly mediation,	205
No. 11.		
	Leave-taking of President Mora,	207
No. 12.		
	Leave-taking of Señor Negrete,	209
No. 13.		
	Answer to the letter of leave-taking of Col. Negrete.—He is called Apostle of Peace.—Solemn and effusive expression of gratitude tendered to Salvador,	211
No. 14.		
	Editorial of the "Gaceta de Nicaragua" subsequent to the official leave-taking of Señores Don Juan Rafael Mora and Col. Negrete.—The latter is promoted to the rank of General as a reward for his services.—The Nicaraguan people feel jubilant for the friendly relations between Costa Rica and Nicaragua,	213
No. 15.		
	Spirit of concord which presided over the treaty.—Evident necessity and advisability that it should be concluded.—Faculties of the Government to approve it.—Final character of the treaty.—Identical position of Costa Rica and Nicaragua,	214
No. 16.		
	The treaty of April 15, 1858, is communicated to the friendly Governments as a happy termination of the protracted differences between Costa Rica and Nicaragua,	217

No. 17.
    Validity of the Treaty, ... 220
No. 18.
    The Constitution of Nicaragua declares that the Nicaraguan territory borders on the south by the Republic of Costa Rica.— The Treaty of Limits is raised to the character of fundamental law, ... 222
No. 19.
    The value and force of the Treaty of Limits is recognized, and one of its provisions is thus carried into effect, . . . 223
No. 20.
    Costa Rica is recognized as a party to the contract of the Interoceanic Canal, and its acquiescence is asked to make certain modifications in it, ... 224
No. 21.
    Official despatch acknowledging that the Nicaraguan territory ends at the Salinas Bay as declared by the Treaty of Limits of 1858, ... 226
No. 22.
    The Nicaraguan Chambers direct Article VIII of the Treaty of Limits of April 15, 1858, to be complied with, and the Executive Power carries their decision into effect, . . . 227
No. 23.
    Official despatch showing the validity and strength of the Treaty of Limits and the execution thereof by both Republics, . . 228
No. 24.
    Costa Rica a party to the contract of Interoceanic Canal approves modifications made thereto, ... 229
No. 25.
    Despatch showing the validity and strength of the Treaty of Limits, and its execution, ... 230
No. 26.
    The Government of Nicaragua asks that of Costa Rica to remove its custom officers from the La Flor river, its former frontier, to the new limit fixed by the treaty of April 15, 1858, . . 231
No. 27.
    The Government of Costa Rica is invited to assist that of Nicaragua in improving the port of San Juan del Norte, almost destroyed by the deviation of the waters of the San Juan river into the bed of the Colorado river, ... 233
No. 28.
    Nicaragua reminds Costa Rica of the duty imposed upon her by the treaty of April 15, 1858, to defend her frontiers at San Juan and the Bolarios Bay, ... 235

PAGE.

No. 29.
    Execution of the Treaty of Limits, ... 237

No. 30.
    The Nicaraguan Chambers direct the Executive to comply with Art. VIII of the Treaty of Limits of April 15, 1858, . . . 238

No. 31.
    The strict compliance with the Treaty of Limits demonstrated.—The Government of Costa Rica asks the rights vested in it by Article VI of a contract of transit to be expressly secured, . 239

No. 32.
    ·The Government of Nicaragua asks for some forces to be situated at Sarapiquí (a confluent of the San Juan river, on the right bank), ... 242

No. 33.
    The Nicaraguan Chambers order one of the provisions of the Treaty of Limits of 1858 to be complied with, ... 244

No. 34.
    Validity and force of the Treaty of Limits.—Costa Rica does not accede to situate forces at Sarapiquí on the ground that it is unnecessary, ... 245

No. 35.
    Costa Rica protests against the occupation and deterioration of the Colorado river, ... 247

No. 36.
    The Government of Nicaragua recognizes that the Colorado river and its mouth are in Costa Rican territory and belong to Costa Rica, and cannot be closed against the will of the latter, . . 248

No. 37.
    Nicaragua recognizes still more solemnly that the Colorado river and the right bank of the San Juan river are Costa Rican territory, ... 250

No. 38.
    The Minister of Nicaragua in Washington solemnly declares before the American Government that the Republic of Costa Rica borders on the interior waters of Nicaragua, and that its flag is the only one which, in union with the Nicaraguan flag, can float on said waters, ... 251

No. 39.
    The Government of Nicaragua approves the declaration of its Minister at Washington, and commends him for his zeal and fidelity, ... 252

No. 40.
    The action of Don Luis Molina, Minister of Nicaragua in Washington, is approved and commended.—Executive order reward-

ing the important services of Don Luis Molina, Minister Plenipotentiary of Nicaragua in the United States, and Mr. Mandeville Carlisle and Don Fernando Guzman, ... 253

No. 41.
Validity and strength of the treaty of April 15, 1858, . . . 254

No. 42.
Validity and strength of the Treaty of Limits, . . . 256

No. 43.
The Government of Costa Rica orders an exploration to be made of its lands bordering on the San Juan river, ... 257

No. 44.
New expeditions to the banks of the San Juan river, . . 258

No. 45.
Nicaragua acknowledges that Costa Rica borders on the San Juan river, ... 259

No. 46.
Nicaragua promises that the interests of Costa Rica will be respected, and that its rights will suffer no detriment, . . 260

No. 47.
Costa Rica protests against the deviation of the waters of the Colorado river belonging to that Republic, ... 261

No. 48.
Despatch stating that a sanitary cordon of Costa Rica has trespassed on the Nicaraguan frontier as established by the treaty of 1858, ... 262

No. 49.
Nicaragua asks that a sanitary cordon be moved back to the frontier established by the treaty of 1858, ... 263

No. 50.
The Government of Costa Rica consents to move back its sanitary cordon to a point indisputably located within the limits established by the treaty of April 15, 1858, ... 264

No. 51.
Costa Rica shows her disposition to enter into arrangements with Nicaragua to determine by mutual agreement what should be done in regard to communications on the Atlantic side, . . 265

No. 52.
Contract Ayón-Chevalier.—Costa Rica is an essential party to the interoceanic canal.—The contract will be void if Costa Rica does not accept it.—Costa Rica will be invited to make in favor of the grantee such concessions in the Costa Rican territory as Nicaragua makes in her own, ... 266

No. 53.
    Editorial of the Nicaraguan "Gaceta" on the Ayón-Chevalier canal contract.—The San Juan river explicitly declared to be (1869) in great part the frontier of Costa Rica.—The adherence of Costa Rica to the contract recognized to be indispensable.—Costa Rica is asked to grant in her territory what Nicaragua has granted in hers.—All of this presupposes the acknowledged validity of the Treaty of Limits, ... 268

No. 54.
    The Government of Nicaragua asks the Government of Costa Rica to request the National Constituent Convention to modify certain articles of a treaty between the two Republics for the digging of an interoceanic canal, ... 270

No. 55.
    Project of a road from San José de Costa Rica to San Carlos for the export of coffee through San Juan del Norte.—Costa Rica earnestly invited to co-operate in the restoration of the port of San Juan by uniting the waters of the Colorado river with those of the San Juan river, ... 271

No. 56.
    Remarks made by the Government of Costa Rica to the Government of Nicaragua when the latter submitted to the Nicaraguan Congress its so-called doubts in regard to the validity of the Treaty of Limits of 1858, ... 274

No. 57.
    Remarks of the Government of Costa Rica in refutation of the doubts entertained by the Government of Nicaragua on the validity of the Treaty of Limits, ... 279

No. 58.
    Costa Rica declares that it will keep its custom-houses and maintain its sovereignty over the whole territory which, according to the treaty of 1858, belongs to it unless other limits are not established by mutual agreement or arbitral decision, . . . 290

No. 59.
    Costa Rica protests against the non-compliance on the part of Nicaragua of Article VIII of the Treaty of Limits, . . . 291

No. 60.
    The explanations of Nicaragua as to the non-compliance with Article VIII of the Treaty of Limits are accepted, . . . 294

No. 61.
    Opinion of the historian of Central America, Dr. Don Lorenzo Montufar, at present the Secretary of State of the Republic of Guatemala, in regard to the Treaty of Limits between Costa Rica and Nicaragua, ... 296

No. 62.
 Extracts from the "History of Nicaragua from the Remotest Times to the year 1852," written by order of General Don Joaquin Zavala, President of the Republic, by Señor Dr. Don Tomas Ayón. Vol. I. Granada: Printing office of El Centro Americano, 1882.—The author of said history gives the name of Desaguadero to the San Juan de Nicaragua river, . . 305

No. 63.
 Organic laws of Costa Rica in regard to limits with Nicaragua, . 308

No. 64.
 Failure of Canal Negotiations with the Government of the United States owing to the fact that Nicaragua refused Costa Rica intervention in it, ... 316

ANTECEDENTS.

ANTECEDENTS.

Legation of Costa Rica,
Washington, D. C., *July* 30, 1887.

Sir: I have the honor to enclose a copy of the treaty signed at the city of Guatemala on the 24th of December, 1886, by plenipotentiaries of Costa Rica and Nicaragua with the friendly mediation of the Guatemalan Government, in which it was stipulated that both contracting parties should submit to the arbitration of the President of the United States of America the question whether the treaty of limits celebrated by them on the 15th of April, 1858, is or is not valid.

In the name and under special instructions of the Government of Costa Rica I request you to interpose your good and valuable offices with His Excellency the President in order that he may consent to render to my country the eminent service above referred to.

My Government hopes that such a marked favor will be obtained by it, and grounds its expectations upon the benevolent friendship shown to it by your Government and on the traditional interest that this great nation has always felt for the peace, tranquility, and welfare of the other nations of America which are its sisters.

With protestations of my highest consideration, I am, your most obedient servant,

PEDRO PEREZ Z.

To the Honorable Thomas F. Bayard,
Secretary of State, &c., &c., &c.

LEGATION OF COSTA RICA,
WASHINGTON, D. C., *July* 31, 1887.

SIR: I have been favored by your estimable communication, dated yesterday, in which you were pleased to inform me that His Excellency the President has been pleased to consent to be arbitrator to decide the controversy between Costa Rica and Nicaragua on the validity or invalidity of the treaty of April 15, 1858, celebrated by the two Republics for the final settlement of their questions about territorial limits.

It is with great satisfaction that I have received this pleasant information, which I hastened to transmit by cable to my Government. Indeed, I never apprehended that the illustrious Chief Magistrate of this great nation would refuse Costa Rica the inestimable service of adjusting its differences with its neighboring sister, the Republic of Nicaragua.

I comply with a very gratifying duty in giving to His Excellency the President and to you yourself, for your own part in the premises, my most expressive thanks for this new testimony of friendship given to my Government. And in so doing I comply, also, with special recommendations of my Government.

I shall have the honor to submit to the high consideration of His Excellency the President, within the period marked by the treaty, the grounds and reasons which, in the opinion of the Government of Costa Rica, rendered the validity of the treaty of 1858 evident and irrefutable.

With feelings of high esteem, I am, your very obedient servant,

PEDRO PEREZ Z.

To the Hon. THOMAS F. BAYARD,
Secretary of State, &c., &c., &c.

Treaty of Guatemala Establishing the Basis of the Arbitration.

Convention between the Governments of Nicaragua and Costa Rica to submit to the arbitration of the Government of the United States the question in regard to the validity of the treaty of 15 April, 1858.

The Governments of the Republics of Nicaragua and Costa Rica desiring to terminate the question debated by them since 1871, to wit:

Whether the treaty, signed by both on the 15th day of April, 1858, is or is not valid, have named, respectively, as plenipotentiaries, Señor Don José Antonio Roman, envoy extraordinary and minister plenipotentiary of Nicaragua, near the Government of Guatemala, and Señor Don Ascension Esquivel, envoy extraordinary and minister plenipotentiary of Costa Rica, near the same Government, who having communicated their full powers, found to be in due form, and conferred with each other, with the mediation of the minister for foreign affairs for the Republic of Guatemala, Doctor Don Fernando Cruz, designated to interpose the good offices of his Government, generously offered to the contending parties and by them gratefully accepted, have agreed to the following articles:

(1) The question pending between the contracting Governments, in regard to the validity of the treaty of limits of the 15th of April, 1858, shall be submitted to arbitration.

(2) The arbitrator of that question shall be the President of the United States of America. Within sixty days following the exchange of ratifications of the present convention, the contracting Governments shall solicit of the appointed arbitrator his acceptance of the charge.

(3) In the unexpected event that the President of the United States should not be pleased to accept, the parties shall name, as arbitrator, the President of the Republic of Chili, whose acceptance shall be solicited by the contracting Governments within ninety days from the date upon which the President of the United States may give notice to both Governments, or to their representatives in Washington, of his declination.

(4) If, unfortunately, the President of Chili should also be unable to lend to the parties the eminent service of accepting the charge, both Governments shall come to an agreement for the purpose of electing two other arbitrators within ninety days, counting from the day on which the President of Chili may give notice to both Governments or their representatives, in Santiago, of his non-acceptance.

(5) The proceedings and terms to which the decisions of the arbitrator are limited shall be the following:

Within ninety days, counting from the notification to the parties of the acceptance of the arbitrator, the parties shall present to him their allegations and documents. The arbitrator will communicate to the representative of each Government, within eight days after their presentation, the allegations of the opposing party, in order that the opposing party may be able to answer them within the thirty days following that upon which the same shall have been communicated.

The arbitrator's decision, to be held valid, must be pronounced within six months, counting from the date upon which the term allowed for the answers to the allegations shall have expired, whether the same shall or shall not have been presented.

The arbitrator may delegate his powers, provided that he does not fail to intervene directly in the pronunciation of the final decision.

(6) If the arbitrator's award should determine that the treaty is valid, the same award shall also declare whether Costa Rica has the right of navigation of the river San Juan with vessels of war or of the revenue service. In the same manner he shall decide, in case of the validity of the treaty, upon all the other points of doubtful interpretation which either of the parties may find in the treaty, and shall communicate to the other party within thirty days after the exchange of the ratifications of the present convention.

(7) The decision of the arbitrator, whichsoever it may be, shall be held as a perfect treaty and binding between the contracting parties. No recourse whatever shall be admitted, and it shall begin to have effect thirty days after it shall have been notified to both Governments or to their representatives.

(8) If the invalidity of the treaty should be declared, both Governments, within one year, counting from the notification of the award of the arbitrator, shall come to an agreement to fix the dividing line between their respective territories. If that agreement should not be possible, they shall, in the following year, enter into a convention to submit the question of boundaries between the two Republics to the decision of a friendly Government.

From the time the treaty shall be declared null, and during the time there may be no agreement between the parties, or no decision given fixing difinitely the rights of both countries, the rights established by the treaty of the 15th of April, 1858, shall be provisionally respected.

(9) As long as the question as to the validity of the treaty is not decided, the Government of Costa Rica consents to suspend the observance of the decree of the 16th of March last as regards the navigation of the river San Juan by a national vessel.

(10) In case the award of the arbitrators should decide that the treaty of limits is valid, the contracting Govern-

ments, within ninety days following that upon which they may be notified of the decision, shall appoint four commissioners, two each, who shall make the corresponding measurements of the dividing line, as provided for by Article 2 of the referred to treaty of 15th April, 1858.

These measurements and the corresponding landmarks shall be made within thirty months, counting from the day upon which the commissioners shall be appointed. The commissioners shall have the power to deviate the distance of one mile from the line fixed by the treaty, for the purpose of finding natural limits or others more distinguishable. But this deviation shall be made only when all of the commissioners shall have agreed upon the point or points that are to substitute the line.

(11) This treaty shall be submitted to the approval of the Executive and Congress of each of the contracting Republics, and their ratifications shall be exchanged at Managua or San José de Costa Rica on the 30th of June next, or sooner if possible.

In testimony of which the plenipotentiaries and the minister of foreign affairs of Guatemala have hereunto signed and sealed with their private seals, in the city of Guatemala, this 24th day of December, 1886.

ASCENSION ESQUIVEL.
J. ANTONIO ROMÁN.
FERNANDO CRUZ.

Points Which, According to the Government of Nicaragua, are Doubtful and Require Interpretation.

Department of
Foreign Relations of Nicaragua,
Managua, *June* 22, 1887.

Sir: By order of the President and in pursuance of Article VI of the Convention of Arbitration, concluded at Guatemala, between Costa Rica and Nicaragua, I have the honor to communicate to the Government of Your Excellency the points of doubtful interpretation found in the treaty of April 15, 1858, which, in the event foreseen by that Article, this Government proposes to submit to the decision of the arbitrator.

FIRST.

1. Punta de Castilla point having been designated as the beginning of the border line on the Atlantic side, and finding itself, according to the same treaty, at the mouth of the San Juan river; now that the mouth of the river has been changed, from where shall the boundary start?

2. How shall the central point of the Salinas Bay, which is the other end of the dividing line, be fixed?

3. Whether by that central point we are to understand the centre of the figure; and, as it is necessary for its determination to fix the limit of the Bay towards the ocean, what shall that limit be?

SECOND.

4. Nicaragua consented, by Article IV, that the Bay of San Juan, which always exclusively belonged to her and over which she exercised exclusive jurisdiction, should be

common to both Republics; and by Article VI she consented, also, that Costa Rica should have, in the waters of the river, from its mouth on the Atlantic up to three English miles before reaching Castillo Viejo, the perpetual right of free navigation for purposes of commerce. Is Costa Rica bound to concur with Nicaragua in the expense necessary to prevent the Bay from being obstructed, to keep the navigation of the river and port free and unembarrassed, and to improve it for the common benefit? If so,

5. In what proportion must Costa Rica contribute? In case she has to contribute nothing—

6. Can Costa Rica prevent Nicaragua from executing, at her own expense, the works of improvement? Or, shall she have any right to demand indemnification for the places belonging to her on the right bank, which may be necessary to occupy, or for the lands on the same bank which may be flooded or damaged in any other way in consequence of the said works?

THIRD.

7. If, in view of Article V of the treaty, the branch of the San Juan river known as the Colorado river must be considered as the limit between Nicaragua and Costa Rica, from its origin to its mouth on the Atlantic?

FOURTH.

8. If Costa Rica, who, according to Article VI of the treaty, has only the right of free navigation for the purposes of commerce in the waters of the San Juan river, can also navigate with men-of-war or revenue cutters in the same waters?

FIFTH.

9. The eminent domain over the San Juan river from its origin in the Lake and down to its mouth on the Atlantic,

belonging to Nicaragua according to the text of the treaty, can Costa Rica reasonably deny her the right of deviating those waters?

SIXTH.

10. If, considering that the reasons of the stipulation contained in Article VIII of the treaty have disappeared, does Nicaragua, nevertheless, remain bound not to make any grants for canal purposes across her territory without first asking the opinion of Costa Rica, as therein provided? Which are, in this respect, the natural rights of Costa Rica alluded to by this stipulation, and in what cases must they be deemed injured?

SEVENTH.

11. Whether the treaty of April 15, 1858, gives Costa Rica any right to be a party to the grants of inter-oceanic canal which Nicaragua may make, or to share the profits that Nicaragua should reserve for herself as sovereign of the territory and waters, and in compensation of the valuable favors and privileges she may have conceded?

In transmitting the above to Your Excellency, and requesting Your Excellency to acknowledge the receipt thereof, it is pleasing to me to reiterate the assurances of my respect and consideration.

FERNANDO GUZMAN.

To His Excellency THE MINISTER OF FOREIGN RELATIONS of the Government of Costa Rica.

INTRODUCTION.

INTRODUCTION.

WHAT is the question submitted by the Republics of Costa Rica and Nicaragua to the impartial and final decision of the President of the United States of America?

It is simply:

Whether the treaty of limits concluded by both Republics at San José of Costa Rica on the 15th day of April, 1858, is or is not valid?

This, and nothing else, forms the subject of the debate.

If, as I confidently hope, the question is decided in an affirmative sense, then some other points, of secondary or accessory character, depending upon the subject-matter, and referring to the proper construction to be placed upon the treaty, shall be also considered.

If, on the contrary—what in my judgment is little less than an impossibility—the question is decided in a negative sense, then the discussion about limits, which was closed and disposed of in 1858 by the treaty, so adjudged to be invalid, shall be reopened and restored to the condition in which it was at that time; but the determination of the boundaries between the two Republics will not, in any way whatever, be included within the scope of the arbitration. This important subject is left to be disposed of by subsequent negotiation between the two Governments; and if it should happen that no agreement can be reached within the period of one year, then another arbitration, the terms of which will then be discussed and agreed upon, should be resorted to to settle and set at rest the dispute.

These are substantially, and as far as the fixing of the subject of the controversy is concerned, the provisions of the treaty of Guatemala of December 2, 1886, which established the basis of the present arbitration.

Under these circumstances it is clear that I must not occupy myself at all, unless incidentally, with anything which refers to limits between one country and the other, because this is not, by any means, the point to be discussed ; and that, therefore, my argument must be directed to show that the treaty of April 15, 1858, is perfectly valid ; that it cannot but be valid in the light of international law ; that it has been always recognized as valid by Costa Rica and other nations equally friendly to the two neighboring Republics ; and that Nicaragua herself, for many years, did also recognize its validity.

But, in order to illustrate in such a manner as is desirable and proper this only subject of the debate, it seems to me unavoidable to preface my work by some historical remarks and refer therein to the ancient boundaries of Costa Rica, which were the San Juan river through the whole of its course, the great Lake, and the La Flor river. But this I will endeavor to do as briefly and concisely as permitted by the purpose I have in view, which is to show how far Costa Rica was carried by its spirit of conciliation and true fraternity when it consented to the treaty of 1858, which deprived her of her historical, as well as natural and legitimate, boundaries—thus leaving beyond a doubt that if Costa Rica has always acted with proper firmness in defending and asserting its rights in regard to the treaty in question, it is not because the said treaty is in any way or manner whatsoever advantageous to Costa Rica, but because the Costa Rican Government and people have always desired, as they do now desire, that a perfect international agreement be respected and complied with.

I will, therefore, begin by making a statement of the questions which the treaty of limits, now under discussion, set at rest and decided, and were, on the one side, the annexation to Costa Rica of the Nicoya district, which took place in

1824, when the States forming the Federal Republic of Central America were organized and defined, and on the other side the different claims set forth by both bordering nations on the outlet (el " Desaguadero ") of the Lake of Nicaragua or San Juan river. Subsequently I will explain the circumstances which preceded the treaty of 1858. And then I will proceed to examine and refute such arguments as have been made by Nicaragua in opposition to that treaty and for the purpose of invalidating or rescinding it.

FIRST PART.

FIRST PART.

HISTORICAL PRELIMINARIES.

Chapter I.

NICOYA—ITS ANNEXATION TO COSTA RICA.

THE Province of Costa Rica, now the Republic of the same name, was created by Emperor Charles V in the year 1540, under the name of "Government of Cartago or Costa Rica," in that part of the Province of Veragua which the Crown reserved for itself, west of the Dukedom of Veragua, granted in 1537 to the descendants of Christopher Columbus.

The limits of this Government extended from sea to sea in latitude, while in longitude they ran along the Caribbean Sea from the Zarabaro or Almirante Bay (Lake of Chiriqui) to the Rio Grande river, now called Aguan or Roman river, west of Cape Camaron, embracing the whole Central American littoral between the 9th and 16th parallels of north latitude.[1]

This demarcation expressly included within the jurisdiction of Costa Rica, and as a principal part of this Province, the territory of the mouths of the outlet (Desaguadero), or San Juan river, and a great part of its course, following it up to within fifteen leagues of the Lake of Nicaragua, and running from there toward the north, always at a distance of fifteen leagues from the coast, up to the banks of the Rio Grande river. Therefore the whole of the Atlantic coast of Nicaragua and a part of that of Honduras belonged to Costa Rica.

---

[1] TORRES DE MENDOZA. "*Colección de documentos ineditos de Indias publicada bajo los auspicios del Gobierno Español.*"
PERALTA. "Costa Rica, Nicaragua y Panamá, en el siglo xvi, Madrid, 1883," pp. 101, 113, 741 to 754. LEON FERNANDEZ. "*Colección*," &c., vol. iv, p. —.

Such was the original province of Costa Rica.

From 1560 to 1573 Phillip II gave her new limits, which, on the Atlantic side, were the same now claimed by this Republic.[1]

The province of Nicaragua was made a Government and entrusted to the command of Pedrarias Dávila by Royal Letters-Patent of June 1, 1527; but no limits were then assigned to it, nor were those suggested by Pedrarias approved of by the Court. According to Fernandez de Oviedo those limits extended from the port of La Herradura, 9° 38' north latitude, to the port of La Posesion (or Realejo), 12° 30' of the same latitude. But previous to 1540 it was generally thought that the limits of Nicaragua were from the Chiriqui plains to the Gulf of Fonseca. These boundaries gradually became reduced through the creation of the new provinces of Costa Rica (on the side of the Southern Sea) and of Nicoya, which, from the condition of a simple "encomienda" granted to Pedrarias Dávila and his successor and son-in-law, Rodrigo de Contreras, was raised to the station of an independent Mayoralty or "Corregimiento."

On the side of the Northern Sea, Nicaragua did not possess, before 1543, an inch of land.

The Province of Nicoya consisted of the peninsula of that name, and was situated between the Gulf of Nicoya and the Tempisque, or Del Salto river, and the Pacific Ocean, extending itself towards the north up to the shores of the Lake of Nicaragua.

Of the condition of Nicoya as an independent Mayoralty abundant testimony is given by different royal ordinances and by the chronicler Antonio de Herrera,[2] who says: "The following mayoralties are provided for by His Majesty, namely: El Cuzco, the La Plata city, and the mining seat of Potosi, * * * *the Province of Nicoya,*" &c.

---

[1] PERALTA. "*Costa Rica, Nicaragua y Panamá,*" &c., p. 500.
[2] *Descripción de las Indias Occidentales*, chap. 31.

Herrera wrote in 1599, or thereabouts.

The "Recopilacion" of laws for the Indies (Law 1, Title 2, Book 5) refers to the District of Nicoya as being an "Alcaldia Mayor" or district under the jurisdiction of a Judge of first instance, it being equal in this respect to Chiapas and San Salvador, ancient provinces of the Captaincy-General of Nicaragua, which, subsequent to their emancipation from Spain in 1821, freely disposed of their destinies, Chiapas annexing itself to Mexico, and San Salvador becoming one of the five States of the Federal Republic of Central America. Nicoya declared her will to be incorporated into the State of Costa Rica.

The final incorporation of Nicoya or Guanacaste into Costa Rica, which took place in 1824, has several historical antecedents.

Don Antonio Gonzalez, President of the "Audiencia" or Superior Court of Guatemala, appointed, in 1572, Perafan de Ribera, Governor of Costa Rica, to be the mayor or "correjidor" of Nicoya.[1]

Herrera, the chronicler, gives an account of this incorporation in Chapter XIII of his "*Descripcion de las Indias;*" and it also appears from the important document which Herrera consulted and which, under the title of "Demarcacion y Division de las Indias" (Demarcation and Division of the Indies), has recently been published. It reads as follows:

"And Nicoya, forty-eight leagues from the city of Granada, on the coast of the Southern Sea, a mayoralty (corregimiento), composed of Indians, which, together with the Island of Chira, within its jurisdiction, eight leagues from the coast, contains about 4,000 natives paying tribute to the Crown, who formerly, and up to the year 1573, were subject to the "Audiencia" of Panamá, for the reason that they had been pacified by captains appointed by that court. But in 1573, Nicoya WAS INCORPORATED INTO COSTA RICA, the Governor of

---

[1] PERALTA. "*Costa Rica, Nicaragua y Panamá,*" &c., pages 474 and 480.

which sends a lieutenant there. "The Bishop of Nicaragua has there a vicar. Nicoya has a tolerable good port."[1]

Philip II appointed in 1573 Diego de Artieda, and in 1593 Don Fernando de la Cueva, Governors of Costa Rica and "Alcaldes Mayores" of Nicoya. In this way Nicoya became in fact a part of Costa Rica.[2]

In 1665 Don Juan Lopez de la Flor, Governor of Costa Rica, asked the mother country for the final annexation of Nicoya to the Province of his command. The King referred his petition to the Bishop of Nicaragua and to the "Audiencia" of Guatemala. The Fiscal thereof (crown solicitor) reported in favor of the annexation.

Nicoya retained, however, some kind of autonomy, and was absolutely independent from Nicaragua in executive matters to such an extent that, according to a Royal ordinance of November 24, 1692, the appointment of its "Alcalde Mayor" was to be made directly by the King and not by the Audiencia, which could only provide for that position *ad interim* in case of vacancy.[3]

This constant separation of Nicoya from the Province of Nicaragua continued to exist in the middle of the XVIIIth century, as is shown by the "Relacion de la Visita Apostólica, topográfica, histórica y estadística del Ilmo. Señor Don Pedro Agustin Morel de Santa Cruz, Obispo de Nicaragua, Costa Rica y Nicoya." (Report of the Apostolic, topographic, historical, and statistical visitation made by the Most Illustrious Bishop of Nicaragua, Costa Rica y Nicoya, Don Pedro Augustin Morel de Santa Cruz).

---

[1] HERRERA. *Descripcion*, &c., chap. xiii.
TORRES DE MENDOZA. *Colección de Documentos*, &c., vol. xv, p. 409.
PERALTA. *Costa Rica y Colombia de 1573 á 1881*, pp. 50 and 56.

[2] PERALTA. *Costa Rica, Nicaragua y Panamá*, pp. 497, 512, 648.
TORRES DE MENDOZA. *Ubi supra.*
FERNANDEZ. *Colección*, vol. v, p. 55.
Biblioteca Nacional de Madrid. *Manuscritos*, Códice J., 15.

[3] Archivo de Indias de Sevilla. Registro de Reales Cédulas. Cartas y Expedientes del Presidente y Oidores de la Audiencia de Guatemala, file from 1694 to 1696.

Bishop Morel enumerates the towns included in each one of the three provinces of his diocese in the following way:

The Province of Costa Rica consists of the following towns: Cartago, Laborio, Quircot, Tobosi, Coó, el Pilar, Ujarras (Curredabat), Asserri, la Villeta, Pacaca, Currujuqui, Barba, Esparza, Cañas, Bagaces, Boruca, Térraba, Cabagra, Atirro, Pejivai, Jesus del Monte, Tucurrique, and Matina." "These are," he says, "the towns which I have seen and the roads which I have travelled.

The Province of Nicoya, although one of great territorial extent, scarcely has more than two towns, one of which is the town of Nicoya and the other Cangel.

The Province of Nicaragua, *which is the third one of this Diocese*, consists of the following towns: Villa de Nicaragua, Ometepe island, Granada, Aposonga, San Esteban, Popoyapa, Potosi, Ampompua, Obrage, Buena Vista, San Antonio, Nagualapa, Chiata, los Cerros, San Juan de Tolu, Apataco, España, Diria, Dinomo, Nandaimes, Jinotepe, Diriamba, Masatepe, Naudasmo, Jalata, Niquinohomo, Santa Catarina, San Juan, Masaya, Nisidiri, Managua, Namotiva, Mateare, Nagarote, Subtiada, Leon, y Pueblo Nuevo, &c., &c., &c.

"*The Diocese is as vast*, Bishop Morel further says, *as results from the aggregation of the three above-named Provinces.*"

The Episcopal See was Leon. In Cartago, the Capital of Costa Rica, there was a vicar. In the Province of Nicoya there was none; but at the time of the visitation, the priest, Don Tomás Gomez Tenorio, was appointed to fill that position.

Bishop Morel's report enjoys so much credit at Nicaragua that the Government of that Republic directed it to be sent to the historian, Hubert H. Bancroft, in order that he might use it for his "History of the Pacific States of North America."

Engineer Don Luis Diez Navarro, in his "Relacion del Reino de Guatemala" (Report on the Kingdom of Guatemala), addressed to his superior, the General of the Engineer Corps, Marquis of Pozo Blanco, says the following:

"On the 19th of January, 1744, I reached the mountain of Nicaragua, a very rough one, *which marks the end of the province of that name,* and I went up as far as I explained in the report of my former trip, and I ENTERED THE JURISDICTION OF NICOYA, which, although an "Alcaldia Mayor," separate from the Government of Costa Rica, *is reputed to belong to this province.*"[1]

The latter assertion seemed to be so unanswerable to the same Diez Navarro as to cause him to repeat it affirmatively in another of his papers, where he says that the coast of Costa Rica on the Southern Sea extends to the port of San Juan, two leagues far beyond the La Flor River, which is the boundary of Nicoya.

Upon these facts, the Spanish Cortes of 1812, then the legitimate and sovereign power in Spain, directed the district of Nicoya, afterwards called Province of Guanacaste, to be annexed to the Province of Costa Rica. United in this way, Costa Rica and Nicoya were called to perform together the most important function of the civilized nations, the exercise of their sovereign rights by means of suffrage; and the two, made one for political purposes, were caused to elect one representative to be sent to Spain, to the Cortes, and another to be sent to the local legislature, or provincial deputation, created at Leon. Subsequent to that time Nicoya ceased to appear as an individuality different from Costa Rica, and the local legislature was simply designated as "Provincial Deputation of Nicaragua and Costa Rica."

Such was the basis of the political union of Nicoya and Costa Rica, and such the situation of Nicoya was when the provinces of the Captaincy-General of Guatemala proclaimed their independence from Spain.

The declaration of independence was signed at Guatemala

---

[1] "*Descripcion del Reino de Guatemala,*" printed at Guatemala, 1850.
MOLINA. *Bosquejo de Costa Rica.* New York, 1850.
British Museum. Spanish Manuscripts, add. 17,566.
Depósito hidrográfico. Madrid.

on the 15th of September, 1821, without the distant provinces knowing anything about that happy event which rendered them free, without costing them a drop of blood or a single effort. The information of what had happened reached them from Guatemala, and they did not take long in making use of their freedom. Some of them proclaimed their annexation to Mexico, under the imperial sceptre of Iturbide, and elected deputies for the Cortes of the new Empire. Others chose to form a Federal Republic, and all of them except Chiapas, which remained attached to Mexico, even after Iturbide's fall, sent representatives to a constituent assembly, which met at Guatemala, and created the Federal Republic of Central America under the political constitution of November 22, 1824.

Nicoya, which found itself in an anomalous position between Nicaragua and Costa Rica, took advantage of the circumstances, followed the example of its neighbors, and, by an act of its free and spontaneous will, asked for its annexation to Costa Rica in 1824.

The Assembly of the new State of Costa Rica accepted the incorporation of Nicoya, subject, however, to what the Federal Congress should deem best to decide; and the Federal Congress, by decree of December 9, 1825, approved it and ordered it to be carried out; the grounds of this decision being that the authorities and the municipal bodies of the District of Nicoya had repeatedly requested the separation of Nicoya from Nicaragua and its annexation to Costa Rica, and also that the residents of Nicoya had actually effected the said incorporation during the political troubles of Nicaragua, and, furthermore, that so it seemed to be required by the topographic position of the district.[1]

Subsequently to this period, and in spite of the threats and pretensions of Nicaragua, the people of Nicoya have

---

[1] See Document No. 2.
PERALTA. *El canal interoceánico, Brussels,* 1887, p. 64.

maintained their firm decision to continue to be a part of Costa Rica. In 1836 they repelled by force a Nicaraguan invasion under the leadership of Manuel Quijano.

In 1838, when the Federal Republic was dissolved, in the midst of the confusion and agitation which caused the National Congress to take the desperate step of breaking the compact of 1824, the Province of Nicoya or Guanacaste felt once more the necessity of again emphatically expressing its desire to remain united to Costa Rica, and, by new acts, it renewed its annexation.

The Government of Costa Rica, on its part, has always performed the duties which the incorporation of Nicoya into its territory imposed on it. It has paid the portion of both the colonial domestic debt and the debt contracted by the Federal Republic, which belonged to Nicoya. It has given Nicoya peace, schools, and roads. It has sheltered it from the commotions which have afflicted Nicaragua. It has defended it. It has protected it against all aggressions and threats.

In 1842 the Congress of Nicaragua authorized the executive power to incorporate in fact the district of Guanacaste (Nicoya) into the territory of Nicaragua. The Government of Costa Rica looked at this decree as a declaration of war, proclaimed that Guanacaste was an integral part of its territory, and prepared itself for its defence. But Nicaragua did not stand by her provocation.

In 1848 representatives of Nicoya signed the constitution of the "Republic of Costa Rica," when Costa Rica deemed it advisable to take this name and cease to be called a "State" of a confederation which had ceased to exist ten years before. The citizens of Nicoya (Guanacaste) ratified, furthermore, their ancient annexation to Costa Rica. In 1856 Costa Rica maintained its rights and the integrity of its territory, invaded at Guanacaste, and repelled the invaders, and co-operated efficiently in expelling them from the Nicaraguan territory.

In 1857 Nicaragua attempted again, by means of a decree, to regain the eminent domain and sovereignty over Guanacaste; but, by another decree of October 27, 1857, she was pleased to declare that she would not oppose the inhabitants of Guanacaste to remain subject to the Government of Costa Rica, should they deem it advisable.

The validity of the last decree has been sanctioned by the accomplished facts; and the inhabitants of Guanacaste remain yet, because it is advisable for them to do so, under the sovereignty of Costa Rica.

Such were the facts and the law in 1858, before the celebration of the treaty of limits between Costa Rica and Nicaragua.

On April 15, 1858, the said treaty was signed, and by it Nicaragua finally re-acknowledged that the district of Nicoya was included within the territory of Costa Rica.

This is the treaty, the validity of which the Government of Nicaragua comes now to contest, after fourteen years of faithful execution on both sides.

Chapter II.

THE SAN JUAN RIVER DURING THE SPANISH RULE.

The San Juan river, also called Desaguadero (outlet), never belonged exclusively and in all its length to the Province of Nicaragua. Until 1539 it had not been explored or navigated as far as the sea, and then the Province of Nicaragua was understood to be the narrow strip running between the Southern Sea and the "fresh-water lake of the city of Granada," that is, the Lake of Nicaragua.

In the above-cited year of 1539 Alonso Calero and Diego Machuca de Zuazo, in compliance with the desires of the court, which had repeatedly invited the investigation of the secret of the outlet of the fresh-water sea, had the fortune and the glory of finding the mouth of the San Juan river, and pass through it into the Northern Sea.[1]

It was with abundant reason that Captain Calero, by letter addressed by him to the King,[2] reminds His Majesty that the undertaking to which he had given so successful a termination required some reward, and complains that, instead of receiving it, he had been wronged both by Rodrigo de Contreras, the Governor of Nicaragua, and by Doctor Robles, "Oidor" (Associate Justice of the Royal Court) at Panamá, each one of whom, he said, was trying to derive profit from what had cost them nothing.

Dr. Robles, on his own part, allotted to his son-in-law, Hernan Sanchez de Badajoz, all the lands adjoining the San Juan river, or "Desaguadero," and entered with him into an agreement for the pacification and submission of the natives, the limits described in the instrument having been from

---

[1] Peralta. *Costa Rica, Nicaragua, y Panamá*, p. 728 and the following.
[2] *Ibid.*, page 94.

the Dukedom of Veragua to the boundary of Honduras, or Guaymura.[1]

On the other hand, the "Council, Justices, and Board of Aldermen" (Concejo, Justicia y Regimiento) of the city of Leon, under date of May 25th, 1540,[2] in making opposition to the pretension of Doctor Robles, gave clear evidence that the "Desaguadero" and adjoining lands did not belong at that time to the Government of Nicaragua. Here are their own words:

"We request Your Majesty to take into consideration that the inhabitants of this province, since its discovery, and always, have been incurring expenses for finding out the secret of the outlet (Desaguadero), and of the lands adjoining it, and that they will continue to do the same until the secret is discovered; and not to allow either the Governor of Veragua, nor Doctor Robles, nor any other person whomsoever, except the Governor of this Province, or his Captains, and the residents or inhabitants of the same, to interfere with, or attempt to take away from this province, WHAT IS SO NEAR AND CLOSE TO IT, AND HAS COST IT SO MUCH," &c., &c.

But there was another party having an interest in the matter, and that was Diego Gutierrez, the Governor of the Province of Cartago (now Costa Rica), who asked for him, exclusively, the right to populate and reduce to submission the two banks of the "Desaguadero," because this and the lands adjoining it were found within the limits of his command. In support of his petition, Governor Gutierrez referred to the articles of agreement[3] he had entered into with the Crown on November 29, 1540, wherein the limits of his jurisdiction had been fixed by saying, "from the limits of the Dukedom

---

[1] See Letter of Dr. Robles to Cardinal Sigüenza, and the Council of the Indies.
PERALTA. *Costa Rica, Nicaragua*, &c., p. 741. Royal Letters-patent to Rodrigo de Contreras. *Ibid.*, p. 747.
[2] PERALTA. *Ibid., p.* 97, and the following.
[3] PERALTA. *Ibid.*, p. 89.

of Veraguas to the Rio Grande river, on the other side of Cape Camaron." The Desaguadero evidently remained included, under these circumstances, within the limits of his government.

The King set at rest all these differences by his celebrated Royal " Cédulas " or " ordinances," issued at Talavera on the 11th of January and 6th of May, 1541, and at Valladolid on the 14th of May of the same year.

In consequence of these decrees the river was divided into two parts. The upper part, 15 leagues long, from its outlet or origin from the lake down, was adjudicated to the Province of Nicaragua ; and the lower part, from the end of the above to the mouth of the river on the Northern Sea, was declared to belong to the Government of Costa Rica. And, as far as the use of the whole river and of the lake for the purposes of navigation and fishing was concerned, it was provided that both the river and the lake should be common for the two provinces, without any distinction.

And in order to prevent the Governor of Nicaragua from making opposition to this, the Council of the Indies and the King himself ratified and affirmed it, and declared that the penalty of removal from office and a fine of one hundred thousand " maravedis " should be incurred by any one attempting to go against it.[1]

Diego Gutierrez was succeeded in the government of Cartago, or of the " Desaguadero " as the Bishop of Nicaragua, Fray Antonio de Valdivieso, also calls it, by Juan Perez de Cabrera ; and the Royal Commission, signed at Valladolid on the 22d of February, 1549, contains the same provisions as to limits.

But the pacification of Cartago, or "El Desaguadero," was still to be accomplished. And, in order to accomplish it, the Crown decreed that Licenciate Ortiz, appointed "Alcalde Mayor" of Nicaragua, should take charge of the colonization of " A

---

[1] PERALTA. *Ibid.*, pp. 111, 113, and 128.

CERTAIN LAND WHICH IS FOUND BETWEEN THE PROVINCE OF NIC-
ARAGUA AND THAT OF HONDURAS AND THE DESAGUADERO OF THE
SAID PROVINCE, TOWARDS THE CITIES OF NOMBRE DE DIOS AND
PANAMA, BETWEEN THE SOUTHERN AND THE NORTHERN SEAS."
The instructions communicated to that effect to Licenciate
Ortiz were dated at Toledo on the 23d of February, 1560.[1]

Ortiz could not fulfil his mission, and the "Audiencia"
(Royal Court) of Guatemala, on May 17, 1541, by order of
the King, appointed Licenciate Don Juan Cavallon to be
"Alcalde Mayor" of the Province of New Cartago and Costa
Rica, and described the limits of his jurisdiction as follows:
"AS FAR AS THE BOUNDARY OF THE CITY OF NATÁ AND ITS JURIS-
DICTION, IN THE KINGDOM OF TIERRA FIRMA, OTHERWISE CALLED
CASTILLA DEL ORO, AND THEN ALONG THIS LINE TO THE LIMITS
OF THE DUKEDOM OF VERAGUA, AND FROM THE SOUTHERN SEA
TO THE NORTHERN SEA UP TO 'EL DESAGUADERO,' THIS BEING
INCLUDED."[2]

The same limits were marked down to Cavallon's successor, Juan Vazquez del Coronado; and the jurisdiction given
him over that territory was confirmed by the Crown in Royal
ordinances of April 8 and August 7, 1565.[3]

Vazquez de Coronado, who was "Alcalde Mayor" of Nicaragua and of Costa Rica about the year 1563, reduced to
submission and placed under the jurisdiction of the Province
of Costa Rica the Catapas Tices and Votos Indians who inhabited the shores of the Lake of Nicaragua and the banks
of the outlet.[4]

Upon the death of Vazquez, the King appointed Perafan
de Rivera Governor and Captain-General of Costa Rica, and

---

[1] PERALTA. *Ibid.*, p. 170.
[2] PERALTA. *Ibid.*, p. 194.
PERALTA. *The River of San Juan de Nicaragua*, in Ex Doc. Senate No.
50, 49th Congress, 2d Session, pp. 36–42.
[3] PERALTA. *Costa Rica*, &c., pp. 378 and 387.
[4] PERALTA. *Costa Rica*, &c. Letter or report of J. Vazquez de Coronado, pp. 230, 764, 766, 768.

the limits of his command were described by Royal ordinance of July 19, 1566, issued at Bosque de Segovia, exactly in identical terms as they had been marked down in Vazquez's commission.[1]

It appears, also, that among the distributions, "repartimientos," of Indians, made by Rivera, there was one which referred to the Botos, or Votos, Indians, who inhabited the banks of the "Desaguadero," and are mentioned in the " Relacion del descubrimiento " (account of the discovery) of the river, to which I have alluded. The act was done at Cartago on the 12th of January, 1569.

In 1573 articles of agreement were signed between the Crown and Diego de Artieda, who was appointed Governor and Captain-General of Costa Rica, wherein the limits of his government were described as follows: " FROM THE NORTHERN TO THE SOUTHERN SEA IN WIDTH, AND IN LENGTH FROM THE BOUNDARY OF NICARAGUA, ON THE SIDE OF NICOYA, RIGHT TO THE VALLEYS OF CHIRIQUI, DOWN TO THE PROVINCE OF VERAGUA ON THE SOUTHERN SIDE, AND ON THE NORTHERN SIDE, FROM THE MOUTH OF THE OUTLET WHICH IS TOWARDS NICARAGUA, THE WHOLE TRACT OF LAND AS FAR AS THE PROVINCE OF VERAGUA."[2]

In regard to the extent to be given to the mouth of the outlet, the Royal Letters-Patent and Ordinances above cited explain it sufficiently: " As far as El Desaguadero, *inclusive*," says the Royal Letter to Lic. Cavallon, the real conqueror of Costa Rica.

From 1573 to 1821, in which last date the power of Spain ceased, no alteration was made by the Crown in the limits of Costa Rica on the side of the outlet, although the Governors of Costa Rica exercised on different occasions acts of jurisdiction on the cost of Mosquitia.

The principal towns of the Province were founded in the

---

[1] PERALTA. *Ibid.*, p. 411.
[2] PERALTA. *Costa Rica*, &c., p. 497.
TORRES DE MENDOZA. *Colección de Documentos inéditos.*

interior of the country, but the Governors were careful to exercise jurisdiction over the whole territory intrusted to them. This is shown, among many other things, by the record of the possession taken of the Votos Indians, a ceremony which was performed on the right bank of the Desaguadero, at the place named "El Real de los Votos," on the 26th of February, 1640. It reads as follows :

"And on the 26th of February of the said year, the said Captain Jerónimo de Retes arrived with the said infantry to the house of the said Cacique, whom he found to have with him, called to that effect by him from different parts, eighty persons of all classes and ages, natives of the country, and among them thirty Indians ; and through the interpreter, Diego Latino, an Indian guide, who had been taken from this city, and speaks and understands the language of the said Votos Indians, the said Cacique said to the said Captain Jerónimo de Retes, that in obedience to his orders and trusting to his word, such as he had understood it through the said Indian Pisirara, he received him in peace, and by an act of his free will, without duress or coercion of any kind, he acknowledged for himself and for all the other people, native Votos Indians, both present and absent, the allegiance which he owes to the King, Our Lord, as was owed and acknowledged by their forefathers ; and he promised to be a faithful vassal, in order that the Holy Gospel should be preached to them, and to continue to be faithful. And this having been heard by the said Captain Jerónimo de Retes, who listened to the reasonings of the said Cacique Pocica, accepted in the name of the King, Our Lord, the said allegiance, which was offered and given, and took actual and bodily possession of the rights of sovereignty on these and all the other native Votos Indians of the province. This was said through the interpreter to the said Cacique, and he promised again and reiterated the said allegiance." (Colección de Documentos para la Historia de Costa Rica, by Licenciate Don Leon Fernandez. San José de Costa Rica, 1882, Vol. II, pp. 226–27).

Retes did this by commission of the Governor of Costa Rica, Gregorio de Sandoval.

By virtue of orders and decrees enacted by the King of Spain, subsequent to the instructions given by Licenciate Ortiz, a tract of land, fifteen leagues in extent, adjoining the left bank of the "Desaguadero," was segregated from the jurisdiction of Costa Rica; but the whole land which runs from sea to sea, from the southern bank of the river up to Nicoya, in latitude, and in longitude from the Southern Sea to the Escudo de Veragua and the Chiriqui plains, east of Punta Borica, was left to it.

In regard to the waters of the river and the lake, the use thereof was not exclusively given either to Nicaragua or Costa Rica, and in this respect, as was natural, all that had been previously decided about the community as to the rights of navigation and fishing in favor of the two bordering provinces, on both the river and the lake, was left in force.

In the above-cited "Descripción de las Indias Occidentales" (Edition of 1730, p. 25), a map of Costa Rica, Nicoya, and Nicaragua is found; and there it appears that the Desaguadero river is the border line between Costa Rica and Nicaragua on the side of the Northern Sea. A copy of this map has been appended to this argument.

Numerous ancient documents confirm the right of Costa Rica over the right bank of the San Juan river and its waters, the principal among them being the commission given by Velasquez Ramiro, "Visitador" and Juez de Residencia" (judge appointed to investigate the action of the superior colonial authorities for the Provinces of Costa Rica and Nicaragua), to Antonio Perera and to Francisco Pavon to explore the communication of the two seas (1591); the report of Diego de Mercado to the King upon the same subject (1620); the report made by Don Rodrigo Arias Maldonado, Governor of Costa Rica, to the King, on the towns of his Province (1662); the letter of Don Juan Lopez de la Flor to His Majesty upon the subject of the occupation of the castle by the English enemy (1670); the reports of Don Juan Francisco Laens to the King, making a geographical description of Costa Rica and suggesting the means of defending it (1675), &c., &c.[1]

In accordance with these documents, Juarros, the historian of the Kingdom of Guatemala, described the limits of Costa Rica on the side of the Northern Sea by saying "from the mouth of the San Juan river to the Escudo de Veraguas."[2]

In this description all the geographers as well as all the cyclopædias, especially the British, fully agree.

Both the sixth edition of the British Cyclopædia (the first one published after the Independence, some time between 1826 and 1830) and the last one, recently published, of this conscientious repository of human knowledge, prove this fact.

It will be seen, therefore, that, during the Spanish rule, Costa Rica was first the exclusive owner of the lower half of the river and of the neighboring lands on both sides all along the whole extent of the said half; and, subsequently, it was exclusive owner of the river and of its southern bank, without prejudice to the right that Nicaragua had to navigate and fish in the river, and which Costa Rica had, also, in the same river and in the lake, all of which has been shown by irrefutable documents.[3]

---

[1] All these documents can be found in the above cited work of Señor Peralta.

See also the work of the same author, The River of San Juan de Nicaragua, &c., previously cited and translated in Executive Doc. No. 50, Senate, 49th Congress, 2d Session, January, 1887.

[2] Vol. 1, part 1, chap. iii.

[3] The right of navigation was confirmed in favor of Costa Rica by Royal ordinance, dated at Aranjuez February 6, 1796.

Chapter III.

THE SAN JUAN RIVER FROM 1821 TO THE DATE OF THE TREATY OF 1858.

If, during the colonial regime, the San Juan river, otherwise called "Desaguadero," did not belong exclusively to Nicaragua, it was less hers afterwards.

The Constitution of Costa Rica of January 21, 1825 (Art. XV), explicitly declared that the limit of the national territory on that side was the mouth of the San Juan river;[1] and such was the territory which was acknowledged to belong to that State by the Republic of Central America, without a voice of dissent or contradiction having been raised against it either at the Federal Congress or at the bordering State.

This declaration was afterwards repeated and ratified in all subsequent constitutions of Costa Rica.[2]

Nicaragua enacted her Constitution one year after Costa Rica, in 1826, and marked as her frontier, on the Costa Rican side, the same which had existed during the Spanish rule, when the two countries were provinces of Spain. There was, therefore, between the two Constitutions, in regard to this point, the most perfect accord.

The pretension of Nicaragua to extend her frontier beyond the San Juan river was an afterthought which came to her mind long afterwards, and which originated in the idea of getting some compensation for the alleged loss she had sustained by the annexation of Nicoya to Costa Rica. Had the latter event never happened, surely Nicaragua would never have thought of denying Costa Rica its rights on the San Juan river.

The fact that an ancient fortress named "Castillo Viejo"

---

[1] See Document No. 63.
[2] Doc. No. 63.

(old castle), now possessed by Nicaragua, stood on the southern bank of the river, has been alleged as a ground for the claim of that country to exclusive jurisdiction on the said bank and on the river itself.

But to do so, it is indispensable either to forget history or to ignore the facts recorded by it.

What power, what authority, what jurisdiction could the Nicaraguan authorities exercise over that fortress when it was under the control of the Captain-General of Guatemala, who built it by order of the King and at the expense of the public treasury of the Kingdom of Guatemala, who repaired it when necessary, and who always kept it under his authority, putting it in charge of wardens and Alcaldes directly appointed by the King?

What power, what authority, what jurisdiction did the Governor of Nicaragua ever exercise over that fortress, when by express decision of the Council of the Indies it was declared that the fortress and its warden should be subordinate, not to the Governor of Nicaragua, but to the Captain-General of Guatemala?[1] The Governor of Nicaragua did not even supply it with provisions, which duty was incumbent upon the Governor of Cartago, as stated by Bishop Morel.[2]

When that Reverend Prelate visited the castle, and wanted to introduce in it certain reforms, he addressed the Governor of Nicaragua; but the latter answered at once that he had nothing to do with that fortress. Then the Bishop turned his eyes to Guatemala, and there his representations were listened to and decided favorably.

The agreement entered into between the Crown and Diego de Artieda is a document of such a strength as to have prevented Nicaragua from denying that the outlet, or "Desagua-

---

[1] Archives of Indies, of Seville. "Secretaria de Nueva España." Guatemala. Letters and records of secular persons. Years 1726–1736.
PERALTA. *El rio San Juan*, &c., p. 20.
Ex. Doc. Senate, No. 50, above cited.
[2] This is shown by the "Gaceta de Nicaragua" files of 1374.

dero," is the limit between the two Republics. But Nicaragua tries to escape from the difficulty by claiming, without foundation, that the outlet, or "Desaguadero," and the "San Juan river" are not one and the same.

In connection with this aspect of the question the Nicaraguan Foreign Office, presided over by Don Anselmo H. Rivas, expressed itself on June 30, 1872, in the following language:

"Your Excellency says that the Colorado river belongs to Costa Rica, not only under Art. II of the treaty of limits, but under the colonial charter issued by King Philip II at Aranjuez, on the 18th of February, 1574, which established the boundary of the Government and Captaincy-General of the Province of Costa Rica, as running from the mouths of the outlet 'Desaguadero' on the Atlantic (Rio de San Juan) to the Province of Veragua." * * *

"As to the Royal charter of Philip II, to which Your Excellency refers, it is a proven fact that Costa Rica cannot claim that its boundary goes as far as 'the mouth of the San Juan river,' which Your Excellency wishes to confuse with 'the mouths of the outlet, "Desaguadero,"' things which some other Royal orders, several historians and geographers, and even the tradition of the country, have proved to be different. Never has the San Juan river or its mouth been designated by names different from those which they have at present." * * *

"Let this be said solely to prove that the claims of Costa Rica to the waters of the Colorado river and the adjoining territory cannot be traced back to the antiquity which Your Excellency wishes to attribute to them, but that they are founded only on the treaty of limits of 1858."

The predecessor of Señor Rivas in the Nicaraguan State Department, Licenciate Don Tomas Ayon, author of a "History of Nicaragua *from the times of the Conquest*," said, also, in a pamphlet published a few days before the foregoing despatch of Señor Rivas, what I now transcribe, namely: "Which are the mouths of the 'Desaguadero?' Laws, historians, geographers, all, in one word, have, since the days of the discovery, given the name of 'San Juan de Nicaragua river' to the stream which we know now by the same name. NO ONE CALLED IT 'THE DESAGUADERO,' NOR HAS THE STREAM EVER HAD MORE THAN ONE MOUTH. It is, therefore, evident that the point called by the Royal charter 'the mouths of the "Desaguadero"' cannot be the mouth of the San Juan river, and certainly that point has to be found far beyond the Colorado river." * * *

It is truly astonishing that persons so enlightened and upright as Señores Rivas and Ayon should have used, in a discussion like this, an argument so much at variance with historical truth, and the most elementary notions of ancient and modern geography.

Señores Don Anselmo Hilario Rivas and Don Tomas Ayon affirmatively state that the San Juan river and the "Desaguadero" are two different things; but the fact that they are the same thing is witnessed by the Royal ordinance of Valladolid of September 9, 1536,[1] which ordered the exploration of the outlet, *Desaguadero*, of the Lake of Granada, by the writings of Calero and Machuca, who made that exploration; by the Council, justices, and aldermen (Concejo, justicia y regimiento) of the city of Leon; by all the Governors of Nicaragua, and by all historians and geographers from Pedrarias Dávila to Señor Ayon.[2]

Engineer Don Luis Diez Navarro says: "The three

---

[1] Archives of Indies of Seville. Audiencia of Guatemala, Nicaragua. Register of Royal Ordinances.
PERALTA. *Costa Rica, Nicaragua,* &c., p. 116.
[2] TORRES DE MENDOZA. *Colección,* &c.
TORQUEMADA. *Monarquía Indiana.*
PERALTA. *Costa Rica, Nicaragua,* &c., pp. 58, 94, 97, 113, 147, 189, 191, 559, 566, 641, 728, 752, and 754.
PERALTA. *Costa Rica y Colombia.*
See in Alphabetical Index of Geographical Names: Desaguadero, San Juan de Nicaragua.
Johnson's American Cyclopædia; word, San Juan River, &c.

mouths of the San Juan river are the outlet of the famous lakes of Managua and Nicaragua. They are called San Juan, Taura, and Colorado. Said lakes empty through the same three mouths which connect at six or seven leagues, and form but one river."

"From the first mouth, which is called *San Juan*, from west to east up to the second one, named *Taura*, there are two leagues; from Taura to the third mouth, named Colorado river, there are six leagues; from here to Matina, twenty. The rivers named *Reventazon*, or *Ximenez*, and *Suerre*, or *Pacuare*, which are large streams, are found between the three above rivers, and can be navigated towards the interior for more than ten leagues.[1]

Col. Don Josef Lacayo, formerly Governor of Nicaragua, entirely agrees with Diez Navarro, as shown by his report on the Lake of Nicaragua, and the San Juan river (Relación de la Laguna de Nicaragua y rio de San Juan), written in 1745. Lacayo affirms, furthermore, that, of the three branches of the San Juan river, the Colorado river is the most abundant in water, and is the most accessible, so that schooners and large vessels can easily enter it.

Finally, Señor Ayon, in his "History of Nicaragua," refutes both Señor Rivas and himself in four chapters of Vol. I of his work, wherein he gives the name of Desaguadero to the San Juan de Nicaragua river.[3]

The voluntary errors of such learned statesmen as Señores Rivas and Ayon, who, without taking the trouble even of consulting a geographical dictionary, locate the mouth of the

---

[1] Archives of Indies of Seville. Package, "Guatemala," correspondence of the Governors President, years 1758 to 1771.

Description of the whole coast of the Northern Sea and part of that of the Southern Sea of the Captaincy-General of this Kingdom of Guatemala, made by Engineer Don Luis Diez Navarro in 1743 and 1744.

PERALTA. *Costa Rica y Colombia*, p. 178 (edition de luxe) and p. 162 (ordinary edition).

[2] Manuscripts in the Depósito Hidrográfico of Madrid.

[3] See Document No. 62.

San Juan river, or Desaguadero, far to the south of the Colorado, in the valley of Matina, at more than twenty leagues southeast of its proper place, have constituted the ground upon which the supposed rights of Nicaragua rest, and have given color to their pretension of exclusive sovereignty over the San Juan river and its southern bank.

Long and troublesome was the discussion which took place between the two Republics, on account of this pretension, from 1838 to 1858, in which the signing of the treaty of limits seemed to have settled the question.

According to that treaty the right bank of the river, from its origin in the lake up to a point three miles from Castillo Viejo, belongs to Nicaragua. From that point to the sea, down to Punta de Castilla, the whole right bank, as well as the delta of the river, belongs to Costa Rica; but Nicaragua was given the sovereignty over the waters.

As it is seen, Costa Rica made a very important cession in favor of Nicaragua, and sacrificed for the sake of conciliation and fraternity a strip of territory two miles wide and more than one hundred miles long, from the neighborhood of Castillo Viejo up to near the mouth of the Sapoá river, deviating thereby its boundary, to the grave detriment of its interests and territorial rights, from the shores of the lake and the banks of the river.[1]

This treaty, in which Costa Rica is really the party who gives, because it has been proved that the alleged rights of Nicaragua lack foundation both in written history and international law, was concluded, consummated, and complied with by both parties during fourteen years, and it still continues to be the rule or basis of the present territorial *status quo ;* but Nicaragua, not contenting herself with the advantages secured by her, fifteen years ago, and moved by the desire to enter into

---

[1] See Executive Doc. No. 57, House of Reps., 49th Congress, 2d session. Mr. Reynolds to the President, p. 12.

contracts of interoceanic canals, right and left,[1] without any restraint, decided to argue that the treaty was imperfect.

---

[1] In 1876, or early in 1877, the Government of Nicaragua was negotiating at the same time for the construction of an interoceanic canal with Hon. Hamilton Fish, Secretary of State, in Washington, with Mr. Henry Meiggs, in Lima, and with Mons. Aristide P. Blanchet, a notary in France. The Government of Costa Rica contented itself with informing the Government of the United States, represented by the illustrious Gen. Grant and by Mr. Hamilton Fish, of its acceptance of the basis proposed by Mr. Fish.

Chapter IV.

NEGOTIATIONS FOR THE SETTLEMENT OF THE QUESTION OF LIMITS, FROM THE DISSOLUTION OF THE REPUBLIC OF CENTRAL AMERICA TO THE YEAR 1858.

During the whole Federal system (1825–1839) the question of Nicoya, which was the only one existing between Costa Rica and Nicaragua, remained in suspension. The circumstances, indeed, were not favorable for the latter nation to invite discussion upon it. It was known that the unanimous opinion, as well as the resolute determination, of the inhabitants of Nicoya was to remain united to Costa Rica; and, if the question would have been urged, the National Congress would have finally ratified the annexation. Such a result was so much the more to be apprehended as the credit which Costa Rica had won through its ability, prudence, and moderation in the discharge of its Federal duties, stood much higher than that of Nicaragua, which always, and at all times, had been the prey of all kinds of civil disturbances.

As Nicaragua could expect nothing from the Federal power in reference to the separation of Nicoya, it was better for her to keep silent. And owing to this, as well as to her ancient rivalry with Guatemala, and for other reasons, her aim was then to destroy the Federation. All historians agree to the fact that Nicaragua distinguished herself in that respect.

The Federation was dissolved in 1838 and 1839. The Nicoyans taking an advanced step in opposition to the pretensions of Nicaragua, and at the end of fourteen years of incorporation of its territory into Costa Rica, ratified by new acts their adhesion to Costa Rica. Upon the knowledge of this fact, and foreseeing that Nicaragua, which was then engaged in the revision of her Constitution, might perhaps insert in it some provision to the effect that Nicoya formed part of her territory, and thus give occasion to some conflict between the two countries, Costa Rica decided to establish a Legation at Nicaragua, and sent there as its Minister one of its very first public men, Señor Don Francisco Maria Oreamuno. It was hoped in Costa Rica that Nicaragua should recede from her attempt to ignore the accomplished facts, especially when seeing the manifest decision of the inhabitants of Nicoya not to submit to her rule. Señor Oreamuno expressed the desire that the perpetual annexation of Guanacaste should be recognized by Nicaragua, and declared that his country was ready to defend the frontiers of the San Juan river, the great Lake, and the La Flor river.

The Nicaraguan Government could not allow such representations to pass unnoticed, and resorted to the expedient of letting the matter remain in suspense. No conclusion was, therefore, reached, but the Revised Constitution expressed that THE LIMITS OF THE COUNTRY SHOULD BE FIXED BY AN ORGANIC LAW, WHICH WOULD BE A PART OF THE CONSTITUTION. It was avoided in this way, that the organic law of Nicaragua would contain a provision declaring that the district of Nicoya belonged to her. According to its own provisions, the fixing of the limits was left to an organic law, of secondary character, to be enacted afterwards. The idea entertained by Nicaragua of the firmness and energy of the administration of General Carillo in Costa Rica helped, no doubt, that result.

It must be noticed particularly that the Constitution of Nicaragua of 1838 provided nothing permanently in regard to limits with Costa Rica. This is a fact of extreme importance, as will be seen hereafter.

In 1843 Nicaragua sent to Costa Rica a legation, in charge of Licenciate Don Toribio Tijerino, and this officer presented a claim for the restoration of the district, together with its products and accessions, as might have been the case if the claim would have referred to a simple pledge. But he had not been given any authority to make or to entertain any proposition of arrangement, and, as it is easy to conceive, his mission did not bring forth any fruit.

In 1846 Costa Rica had to pass through an exceptional crisis. Coffee, its principal export product, had experienced remarkable depreciation in the foreign markets, and could not stand competition, owing to the high freight that it had to pay when carried by the way of Cape Horn. It was of vital importance, and worthy of any sacrifice whatever, to have a passage open to the Northern Sea, that is, the Atlantic Ocean. The old port of Matina could not answer the purpose, owing to insuperable obstacles, and no recourse was left except making the exports through San Juan del Norte.

As shown before, Costa Rica had always had a perfect and indisputable right of joint ownership in the San Juan river; but, as the harbor and bay were then occupied by Nicaragua, Costa Rica decided to make an effort, and seek for a settlement, which, setting aside interminable discussions, would enable its Government to carry into effect the purpose above referred to. To this end it sent to Nicaragua Señores Madriz and Escalante, with such instructions as proper, to treat with her Government.

The pretensions of Nicaragua were so exorbitant that neither the Government nor the Congress of Costa Rica, in spite of their determination to yield all that was practicable for the sake of obtaining an immediate adjustment, could approve of the arrangements made. Then it was when Nicaragua, for the first time, carried her territorial pretensions on the side of the San Juan river as far as the neighborhood of Matina, and when she suggested, as a compromise, that the territory between Matina and the San Juan river should be divided equally between both countries. She demanded besides a tribute to be paid to her for the transit of Costa Rican merchandise through the San Juan river!

In 1848, the Government of Costa Rica made another attempt to obtain from Nicaragua an equitable settlement, and accredited to her a Legation which it entrusted to Licenciate

Don Felipe Molina. Nicaragua appointed on her side, to represent her in the negotiations, Señor Don Gregorio Juarez. Señor Molina submitted several projects which he himself considered afterwards to have been of unreasonable condescension; but nothing was obtained. "Señor Juarez says Molina (Memoria, page 37) agreed to, and signed, one day, a convention, and on the following day he came and withdrew his signature, and explained that his Government had disapproved of his action."

Subsequently, while in London, Señor Molina received instructions' of his Government to enter into negotiations with Señor Castellon, the Minister of Nicaragua, and the latter Government was urged to instruct him accordingly. But no instructions were received by Señor Castellon.

In 1852 the Washington Cabinet, through its Ministers, Mr. Bancroft and Mr. Lawrence, kindly offered its mediation, but its good offices did not prove to be more successful than all the former efforts. The negotiations initiated in this respect were afterwards continued with Señor Marcoleta, the Nicaraguan Chargé d'Affaires at Washington; but this officer demanded that Costa Rica should sacrifice either the district of Nicoya, which by no means could be given up, or the right bank of the San Juan river, and the river itself, which since the foundation of the colony had been, and is, one of its principal exits to the Atlantic, and which will afford to it a proper communication with both seas when the work of the Interoceanic Canal shall be accomplished.

Under this condition of affairs, and owing to a great extent to the stubbornness of Nicaragua in attempting to exclude Costa Rica from the San Juan river, Nicaragua fell into the hands of the adventurers who had gone there under the leadership of William Walker, whom the people of Leon had received, strewing flowers before him in his passage.

The dignity and sovereignty of Central America having been trampled down in this way, Costa Rica was first in getting ready to defend the soil of the common country. What

Costa Rica did, and what enormous sacrifices it had to suffer for the expulsion of Walker, history has recorded. The single fact that the struggle, together with the cholera which it brought to the country, carried away from Costa Rica, according to the best calculations, fifteen thousand precious lives, will be sufficient to give an idea of the magnitude of those sacrifices.[1]

If Nicaragua suffered in like proportion, or more, perhaps, than Costa Rica, the undeniable fact remains, however, that Costa Rica had taken no part in calling the foreigners.

The Walker war had not yet terminated when the Nicaraguan people began to show their distrust of Costa Rica, and demanded her to abandon the positions which she, with the blood of her children, had conquered on both banks of the San Juan river, up to that time an open road for the invaders. It was not easy for Costa Rica to carry her sacrifices to such an extreme, much less when each mail brought news of a fresh invasion, and when the efforts of Costa Rica in opposing Walker and his followers had naturally caused her to incur their profound hatred and exposed her to their vengeance.

Things having come in this way to such a condition as to render a rupture between the two countries almost inevitable, Costa Rica, although at that time stronger than Nicaragua, decided to resort to conciliatory measures, and by decree of November 9, 1857, invited all the governments of Central America to put an end to the dispute, by the decision of a body of representatives appointed by them to that effect, who should agree by unanimous vote to all matters of common interest. Costa Rica could, but did not want to, dictate to Nicaragua. And as it was impossible for her to sacrifice her own cause, and for the common safety of Central America it was necessary that peace, union, and harmony should be preserved,

---

[1] STREBER. Census of Costa Rica, year 1864.
WALKER. War of Nicaragua, &c.

she preferred that all pending questions should be treated before a Central American Diet.

Subsequently to this step, which was fruitless, and when no possibility appeared to exist of preventing the question from being settled by force of arms, when further negotiations entrusted to Don Emiliano Quadra and General Don José Maria Cañas had also failed, the Government of the Republic of Salvador had the generosity to offer its mediation, and this was gladly and gratefully accepted by both parties. The interposition of Salvador brought things once more upon the ground of conciliation.

Chapter V.

CONTINUATION OF THE SUBJECT OF THE FOREGOING CHAPTER.

The Minister appointed by Salvador, who was Colonel Don Pedro Rómulo Negrete, made first his appearance before the Cabinet of Managua, then he came to Costa Rica, then he returned to Nicaragua, and always and in every respect he did all that could be desired to make his mission a success.

On the part of Costa Rica, General Don José Maria Cañas was appointed to treat the question. A similar appointment was made by Nicaragua in the person of Doctor Don Máximo Jerez. And both Ministers, in union with Colonel Don Pedro R. Negrete, met at San José of Costa Rica. That was, no doubt, the last and supreme effort of both countries, with the efficient assistance of a friendly government, to put an end to a question which was both ancient and apt to give occasion to a fratricidal war.

Then a settlement was reached. True it is that it abridged the rights of Costa Rica by throwing its limits back far away from the Great Lake, the La Flor river, and in part from the banks of the San Juan river itself—limits all of them which, as shown in the preceding chapters, indubitably belonged to it; but it is true also that the rights of Costa Rica as to the rest were recognized, and that by the settlement, peace, harmony, and good order between Costa Rica, Nicaragua, and the whole of Central America, were to be secured.

The line drawn by the Cañas-Jerez treaty was marked as follows:

"The dividing line between the two Republics, starting from the Northern Sea, shall begin at the extreme end of Point Castilla, at the mouth of the San Juan de Nicaragua river, and it shall run along the right bank thereof up to a certain point, three English miles distant from Castillo Viejo (the old castle), said distance to be measured from the exterior works of that fortress to the point above named. From here, and taking the said exterior works as centre, a curve shall be drawn which shall run all along the said works parallel to them, always at a distance of three English miles, until reaching another point beyond the castle and two miles distant from the right bank of the river. Hence, and always keeping at the distance of two miles from the right bank of the river, and following all its windings, it shall continue westwards as if to meet the Sapoá river until reaching the source or origin of the said San Juan river at the lake. From here it shall continue parallel to the right shore of the lake, always at the distance aforesaid, until reaching the Sapoá river, where the parallelism shall cease and the line shall coincide with the stream. From the point of contact, which shall be as aforesaid, two miles distant from the lake, an astronomical straight line shall be drawn up to the centric point of the Salinas Bay, on the Southern Sea, where the frontier between the two contracting Republics shall terminate."

As it is seen, the above line caused Costa Rica to recede from her natural and legitimate frontiers.

The extent of territory which Costa Rica gave up in this way is shown, therefore, to be considerable; but its importance certainly would be undervalued if it were to be appreciated solely by its superficial measurement. The sacrifice will not be estimated rightly except by taking into account the topographical situation of these tracts of lands and the fact that they lay on the banks of a river which is destined to be the principal interoceanic canal in the world, and on the shores of a first-class mediterranean sea, as the Lake of Nicaragua is, and on the isthmus between that lake and the Pacific Ocean, through which the above said canal will run.

It was provided in the treaty that Costa Rica should have the right to navigate the San Juan river from its mouth on the ocean up to three miles this side of Castillo Viejo and the community of sovereignty on the bays of San Juan and of Salinas.

General Don Tomas Martinez, Provisory President of Nicaragua, had been invested by the Constituent Assembly of that Republic, at that time in session, to which he had reported in full the situation, ample and unlimited faculties to get over its difficulties as he might deem best, by means of treaties, which would not need ratification by the same Assembly, except only in case that the agreements made and entered into by him should prove to be at variance with the secret instructions simultaneously communicated to him. Then, and only then, the ratification by the Assembly was necessary.

In compliance with this decree, President Martinez approved of and ratified the treaty of April 15, 1858.[1]

No one has ever said that he exceeded his instructions.

The decree by which he approved of and ratified the treaty reads as follows:

"Tomas Martinez, the President of the Republic of Nicaragua:

"Whereas, General Máximo Jerez, Envoy Extraordinary and Minister Plenipotentiary of Nicaragua to the Republic of Costa Rica, has adjusted, agreed upon, and signed, on the fifteenth instant, a treaty of limits, *fully in accordance with the bases which, for that purpose, were transmitted to him by way of instructions;* finding that said treaty is conducive to the peace and prosperity of the two countries, and reciprocally useful to both of them, and that it facilitates, by removing all obstacles that might prevent it, the mutual alliance of both countries, and their unity of action against all attempts of foreign conquest; considering that the Executive has been duly and competently authorized, by legislative decree of February 26th ultimo, to do everything conducive to secure the

---

[1] See Doc. No. 16.

safety and independence of the Republic; and by virtue, furthermore, of the reservation of faculties spoken of in the executive decree of the 17th instant:

"Does hereby ratify each and all of the articles of the treaty of limits made and concluded by Don José Maria Cañas, Minister Plenipotentiary of the Government of Costa Rica, and Don Máximo Jerez, Minister Plenipotentiary of the Supreme Government of Nicaragua, signed by them on the 15th instant, and ratified by the Costa Rican Government on the 16th. And the additional act of the same date is likewise ratified.

"Given at Rivas on the 26th day of April, 1858.
"TOMAS MARTINEZ.
"GREGORIO JUAREZ,
"Secretary."

On the side of Costa Rica the treaty was ratified without difficulty; and as its conclusion was deemed to be a happy event for Central America, and more especially for the Republics immediately concerned in it, the exchange of the ratifications was made with unusual solemnity by the Presidents of the two Republics personally, attended by their respective Secretaries of State, and with the intervention of the Mediator Minister, Colonel Negrete.

With the act of exchange of these ratifications, the old question, which so often had caused both countries to come to the very verge of unpleasant situations, was settled and set at rest.

The Nicaraguan Executive took, however, a step further, and submitted the treaty to the Assembly. This was done, not because necessary, for the treaty, according to the terms of the decree of the Assembly, was valid without such a requisite; nor because such a submission was required as a matter of form, since the ratifications had been exchanged, and this exchange is a formality which never follows, but precedes legislative sanction; but because of the importance of the matters involved in it. And the Assembly came then and added its supreme sanction to the treaty by decree, which reads as follows:

"NUMBER 62.

"The Constituent Assembly of the Republic of Nicaragua, in use of the legislative powers vested in it, decrees:

"Article only. *The treaty of limits concluded at San José on the 15th of April, instant, between General Don Máximo Jerez, Minister Plenipotentiary from this Republic, and General Don José Maria Cañas, Minister Plenipotentiary from the Republic of Costa Rica*, with the intervention of Colonel Don Pedro Rómulo Negrete, Minister Plenipotentiary from Salvador, IS HEREBY APPROVED.

"TO THE EXECUTIVE POWER.

"Given at the Hall of Sessions of the Constituent Assembly in Managua, on the 28th of May, 1858—Hermenegildo Zepeda, *Vice-President;* José A. Mejiá, *Secretary;* J. Miguel Cárdenas, *Secretary.*

"Thereupon: Let it be executed. National Palace, Managua, June 4th, 1858—Tomas Martinez."

In consequence thereof the treaty was published in the Official Journal,[1] and the text thereof was communicated as a law of the Republic to the diplomatic body, both foreign and national.

The same thing was done at Costa Rica.

The Constituent Assembly framed and enacted subsequently the Constitution of the Republic, and, by its Article I, declared that all special laws on limits formed part of the Constitution. By virtue of this provision the treaty of April 15, 1858, was clearly and indisputably embodied in the fundamental charter of that country.

The Costa Rican Constitution, which, in the following

---

[1] Gaceta de Nicaragua, No. 15, May 28, 1851.

year, December 26, 1859, was promulgated, in describing the limits of the Republic on the side of Nicaragua, set forth the same line as established by the treaty of April 18, 1858;[1] and this solemn enactment did not give rise to any protest on the part of Nicaragua.

The treaty continued to be in force and observed by both parties for fourteen years, during which it served as a basis for the Constitutions, laws, and mutual relations of the two countries.

In 1869, when the men and the circumstances of 1858 had long passed away, Costa Rica enacted a new Constitution,[2] and defined by it its frontier on the side of Nicaragua, as had been done before, in accordance with the treaty of 1858; and no protest was heard, either from the political powers of Nicaragua, nor even from the private press of that country. On the contrary, some documents of utmost importance, corroborative of the strength and vigor of the treaty of limits, emanating from the Nicaraguan Congress and Executive, were published in that year.

The germ of the dispute sprung up out of the displeasure which Nicaragua experienced with the measures taken by the administration of Don Jesus Jimenez, some time afterwards, to stop the destruction, by inhabitants of Nicaragua, of certain forests in the Costa Rican territory, between the regions of the Rio Frio river and the plains of Tortuguero, which the former used to invade in search of rubber. That circumstance prepared or opened the way to the ignoring of the treaty; but the withdrawal by Costa Rica, in 1870, of her adherence to the agreement Ayon-Chevalier, decided it.

Don Tomas Ayon, as Minister of Nicaragua in Paris, had entered into an agreement with Mr. Michel Chevalier for the building of a canal in the valley of the San Juan river, until reaching the Pacific Ocean. Chevalier and Ayon, well knowing the rights of Costa Rica, and the terms of the treaty of 1858, had set forth by one of the clauses of their agreement

---

[1] See Document No. 63.   [2] See Document No. 63.

that the consent of Costa Rica was essential for its validity. Costa Rica consented to it, but Nicaragua delayed for a while, and soon it was discovered, also, that Mr. Chevalier had no means to comply with the obligations he had contracted. Thereupon Costa Rica withdrew its consent.

This step irritated Nicaragua, or rather Señor Ayon, who was then the Nicaraguan Secretary for Foreign Relations, and had been the author of the agreement; and considering that it would be better for Nicaragua to act by herself, independently of Costa Rica, in all matters concerning interoceanic canals, the Nicaraguan Executive reported to Congress and set forth that it entertained some doubts about the validity of the treaty of limits, which, in its opinion, ought to have been ratified by two subsequent legislatures, and had been only by one.

The Nicaraguan Congress heard, not without profound surprise, these new and strange views about the treaty, but decided nothing whatever in the sense of its validity, or nullity. It followed that course which seemed to it to be most prudent and uncommital, which was to keep silent. Sixteen years have passed since, and the Nicaraguan Congress has never dared to pronounce itself in favor of the alleged nullity, although the relations between the two countries have been sometimes strained to the extreme that in 1876 a rupture seemed to be imminent, and that for a long time all official and commercial intercourse between them remained suspended.

Congress by this action, besides postponing a disagreeable solution of the problem, indirectly, but plainly, acknowledged that such alleged doubts were groundless.

Subsequent to the denunciation of the treaty there were still two attempts of arrangement. One took place in 1872, when the Presidents of Costa Rica and Nicaragua, General Don Tomas Guardia and Don Vicente Quadra, held, at the request of the former, an interview at the City of Rivas. And the second was the treaty Castro-Navas of January 19, 1884. Both projects failed.

Different questions, arising out of the anomalous condition in which the rights of both parties found themselves under these circumstances, such as trespasses on the frontiers on one and the other side, questions on navigation of the Colorado river, and also of the San Juan, &c., &c., have been discussed during these sixteen years. They all depended upon the principal question, which is the treaty; but they all have been decided by common agreement, and given origin to the *status quo* of 1858. So it is that, even under these circumstances, if it is true that there has been a protracted discussion between both countries on the theoretical validity of the treaty of limits, it is also true that, practically, the treaty of limits has never ceased to regulate, or govern, the relations between Costa Rica and Nicaragua.

PART SECOND.

PART SECOND.

ELUCIDATION OF THE PRINCIPAL POINT.

Chapter I.

EXPOSITION OF THE ARGUMENTS MADE BY NICARAGUA IN SUPPORT OF THE IDEA THAT THE TREATY OF 1858 IS NOT VALID.

WHAT reasons has the Government of Nicaragua alleged, in support of its pretension, that the stipulations of the treaty of 1858 are not binding upon it?

That the said treaty, although ratified by the Assembly of 1858, was not ratified as it ought to have been, to be valid, by the subsequent Legislature;

That the Government of Salvador, an essential party to the treaty because of having interposed its guarantee, did not ratify it;

And that the said treaty deeply wounds the sovereignty of Nicaragua, and is, to a great degree, injurious to her interests, and depressive of her dignity and autonomy.

No systematic and complete exposition of the reasonings of Nicaragua against the treaty can be found anywhere in the diplomatic correspondence of the Nicaragua foreign office; and for this reason I have been myself compelled, in order to speak intelligently, to peruse all that has been written on the subject, whether officially or unofficially, in the Republic of Nicaragua.

I shall try to set forth, as faithfully as possible, all the arguments that have been made.

It is said that the treaty of 1858 was signed under the sway of the Constitution of 1838; and that, therefore, in order to make the treaty binding upon Nicaragua, each and all of the formalities and requisites provided for by the Constitution ought to have been complied with. Every irregular proceeding not established and sanctioned by that Constitution was illegal, unauthorized, and productive of no effect.

By the treaty, Nicaragua ceded to Costa Rica a great portion of the national territory, as defined by her Constitution, namely, the whole district of Nicoya, and a portion of the right bank of the San Juan river. And that cession involved an amendment to the Constitution, for which, according to the express provisions of the same, the national consent was required to be given not only by one Assembly but by two subsequent Legislatures. The Assembly of 1858 which approved the treaty did not act as a constituent assembly, but as a legislative power; and so it itself declared in the preamble of its decree of ratification, therefore establishing in an implicit way the necessity of a second approval. In compliance with Article 149 of the Constitution, the treaty ought to have been ratified by two Legislatures; but it was ratified only by one. It was not sufficient that some of the formalities required should have been complied with; but it was necessary that all of them, without any exception, should have been fulfilled. The treaty of limits never reached perfection; it never had any effect between the contracting parties; it always remained in the condition of a project or a proposition; it has never been taken as a basis for legislation, or for regulating the relations between Nicaragua and Costa Rica; and if Nicaragua has given notice to Costa Rica of certain conventions, entered into by her, in regard to interoceanic canals, she has done so, not by virtue of the treaty, but because of the desire that the enterprise of the canal would not find any obstacle in a dispute about limits which ought to be smothered beneath the great interests to be created by that colossal work. And the proof that the treaty never reached perfection is that Costa Rica in 1869 asked Nicaragua to ratify it.

This is the argument of the Government of Nicaragua, set forth in all its force, in regard to the first point. As to the second, which is the alleged nullity of the treaty of limits for want of ratification by the Government of Salvador; and as to the third, which is the alleged injury to the interest, autonomy, and dignity of the Republic, the Nicaraguan Foreign Office has limited itself to make only assertions, without stating a fact, or giving a single proof, or showing any reason upon which they may be founded.

But as the Nicaraguan ex-Secretary of State, Don Tomas Ayon, the father and creator of the present controversy, published a pamphlet entitled, "Considerations on the question of territorial limits between the Republics of Nicaragua and Costa Rica," in which he extensively occupied himself in the discussion of this point, I have thought it pertinent to refer to it in this place, and show the manner of his reasoning.

"Nicaragua found herself," he says, "absolutely prostrated by both the severe civil war of 1854 and the national war against the filibusters; the treasury was empty; there was no armament; discouragement had taken possession of all minds; the heart of the Nicaraguans palpitated still with gratitude for the co-operation of Costa Rica in the national war; and under these circumstances the President of Costa Rica, Don Juan Rafael Mora, made his appearance, and with arms in his hands demanded a treaty of limits, in which Nicaragua should cede to Costa Rica as much as he was willing to ask. So it was done, and the treaty of April 15, 1858, was the painful miscarriage brought about by that act of violence."

But Nicaragua wanted to be protected against new surprises on the unpopulated parts of the banks of the river and on the lake, and required that the two nations should bind themselves not to wage at any time, under any circumstances, even in a state of war, hostilities of any kind against each other, either on the port of San Juan del Norte, nor on the San Juan river, or the lake of Nicaragua; and the Government of Salvador, through Minister Señor Negrete, guaranteed the faithful and exact compliance with that provision.

That special guarantee caused the Government of Salvador to become one of the contracting parties; but the treaty was not ratified either by the Executive nor by the Congress of Salvador.

It is known that all the clauses of a treaty are considered as conditions of each other, and that if one of them fails the whole treaty fails. The guarantee was a condition upon which Nicaragua contracted an obligation, and as it failed Nicaragua cannot be considered as bound to respect the treaty.

Every clause in a treaty has the same force as a condition, the failure in the performance of which invalidates the whole.

It is a truth beyond discussion that a treaty has no effect until the suspensive condition therein contained is complied with. Therefore, as long as the ratification of the treaty of limits by the Government of Salvador is not proved, no one of the contracting States must consider itself bound by it.

It is indubitable that, even if the treaty of limits had been ratified by Nicaragua, such ratification would not have been sufficient to carry it into execution, since it was, besides, necessary that the Government of Salvador, which intervened as guarantor or surety for the fulfilment of Article IX, should ratify the treaty. Therefore the treaty of limits has no effect.

Such is the conclusion reached in the statement made by the Nicaraguan ex-Secretary of State, Don Tomas Ayon.

As to the last point, neither the Government nor anything printed have gone beyond the mere assertion of the facts without proof or explanations, as above stated.

The arguments of the Government of Nicaragua to consider itself released from the obligations of the treaty of 1858 being, therefore, known in a general way, it is time to enter into its analysis and refutation; and this I shall do, dividing the matter in as many chapters as are required to convey a clear idea of the subject.

CHAPTER II.

THE TREATY OF LIMITS WAS NOT MADE UNDER THE SWAY OF ANY CONSTITUTION, BUT UNDER A GOVERNMENT TEMPORARILY ENDOWED WITH UNLIMITED POWERS.

THE treaty of April 15, 1858, was not concluded, approved, ratified, promulgated and carried into execution under the sway of the Constitution of 1838, but under the extraordinary and transitory circumstances of a regime in which the Constituent Assembly of that year exercised, in an unlimited manner, the whole power of the National Government—a regime which was created, subsequent to the civil struggles of 1854 to 1857, by the fusion and harmonization of the two parties, which under the names of Conservatives and Democrats, or Granadine and Leonese, had made on each other until then uncompromising war.

The Nicaraguan Government of 1858 was not born out of the Constitution of 1838, nor out of that of 1853, but out of a revolution; and it was simply what in the public law is called a *de facto* government. So it is easy to prove, by simply remembering the political vicissitudes of Nicaragua during the three years of her noisy civil war.[1]

On the 5th of May, 1854, the legitimate government of Nicaragua had been intrusted to General Don Fruto Chamorro, who had been elected in full accordance with the provisions of the organic law of 1853, and who had been recognized, inside and outside the country, as a constitutional Governor.

But Señor Chamorro belonged to the Conservative party,

---

[1] This statement is based upon the facts reported by the official press of Nicaragua, the "Anuario de Ambos Mundos," and the History of the Nicaraguan war by Walker.

and the hatred between this party and the one called Democratic had to lead the country into grave disasters.

It was on that memorable date that Gen. Don Máximo Jerez, and many others among his followers exiled from Nicaragua by Chamorro, succeeded in surprising the garrison of the port of Realejo, and in carrying their victorious arms as far as Leon.

There they organized a provisional government, at the head of which they placed Don Francisco Castellon, formerly a minister of Chamorro and his rival in the last election; and this Government was accepted and recognized by a considerable part of the country.

In the meantime Chamorro concentrated his forces in Granada, the stronghold of his principal followers, and prepared himself for the struggle.

The State saw itself divided, therefore, into two great hostile bands, one presided over by the legitimate Government, Conservative or Granadine, which supported the Constitution of 1853, then in force, and the other by the Revolutionary Government, Democratic or Leonese, which supported, as it alleged, the principles of the former Constitution of 1838, then abolished.

The struggle was stubborn and cruel; and, when the Leonese party saw itself doomed to perish, called to its assistance the adventurer, William Walker, who arrived in Nicaragua in June, 1855.

The cholera, which, at that time, ravaged the country, caused both belligerents to pay it their tribute by carrying off their leaders; but the place of Chamorro was filled by Dr. José Maria Estrada, and that of Castellon by Don Nazario Escoto, and the struggle continued with still more fury.

Foreign assistance inclined things in favor of the Leonese party, and on the 23d of October, 1855, General Corral, in the service of the Conservative Army, and with powers which he said he had received from Estrada, on the one side, and

Walker, in the name of the Democratic Government, on the other, signed a treaty by which a new Government was organized, and the civil war was terminated.

This treaty was afterwards ratified by the Democratic Government.

The new mixed Government was constituted as follows:
President, Don Patricio Rivas, of moderate opinions.
Secretary of War, General Corral, Conservative.
Secretary of Foreign Relations, General Jerez, Democrat.

The rival Governments of Estrada and Escoto disappeared from the political arena.

The new Government was recognized at home and abroad; but behind it the sinister figure of Gen. Walker, Chief Commander of the Army, carefully watching for the moment of taking possession of the power, prominently showed itself.

The outrageous assassination of the Secretary of War, executed by Walker under color of military justice, with the knowledge of and without opposition from the Rivas Cabinet, which was powerless to prevent it, afforded that occasion.

Rivas and Jerez, tired of being mere instruments in the hands of the ambitious foreigner, pronounced themselves against him.

Then Walker proclaimed Don Fermin Ferrer Provisional President of Nicaragua; and subsequently, under a sham election said to have been made under the constitution of 1838, proclaimed himself President; and there were distinguished Nicaraguans, such as Vigil, Pineda, Valle, and hundreds of others, who accepted, recognized, and supported those administrations. Such was the blindness of the political passions and the confusion of things in Nicaragua.

In view of the new turn which the events had taken, Estrada, then in Honduras, repealed and repudiated the treaty of the 23d of October, which had transferred the power to Don Patricio Rivas; but Don Patricio Rivas himself continued to maintain, on his part, that the only legitimate power of Nicaragua was represented by him.

Walker counted, however, with great elements for resistance, both inside and outside the country; and it was necessary for Nicaragua that the forces of Costa Rica, Salvador, Honduras, and Guatemala should come to her assistance to expel Walker, as they did on the 1st of May, 1857, from the Central American soil.

The Government which then remained standing was the government of Don Patricio Rivas, born out of the treaty of the 23d of October; but it did not satisfy the aspirations of either the Leonese or the Granadine party, which prepared themselves to enter again into a new struggle, until securing absolute control for the conqueror.

The two commanders of the rival forces, Generals Don Máximo Jerez and Don Tomas Martinez, succeeded in reaching an agreement by which they divided the power among themselves, and formed a duumvirate, which put an end to the administration of Rivas, and initiated the reorganization of the country.

Blood had been shed in torrents for the Constitutions of 1838 and 1853; and Jerez and Martinez thought that it was advisable to promulgate a new organic law, and convoke for that purpose a Constituent Assembly. At the same time they ordered also a general election for the office of President of the Republic.

Popular vote decided in favor of Martinez; and the Assembly which met in November declared all that had been done in Nicaragua during the revolutionary period to be null and void, and ratified the Presidential election.

It was in this way that the Government of Castellon and his rival Estrada, the Government of Don Patricio Rivas, both before and after the expulsion of Walker, the administrations of Ferrer and Walker, and even the duumvirate of Martinez and Jerez, were ignored and repudiated as if they had never existed; and all their acts, laws, decrees, decisions, orders, grants of land, letters of citizenship, treaties, promissory notes, contracts, and obligations of all kinds, became null and void, and adjudged to be without value or effect of any kind. Everything was embraced in the repudiation decreed by the Assembly.

The constituent body ratified, nevertheless, such decrees of the duumvirate as had been issued for the reorganization of the country.

This Assembly, where all the parties were represented, constituted itself, with the general consent of the country, as the supreme ruler of the destinies of Nicaragua. The Martinez Government lent to it unconditional support, and everything pointed to one object, which was the consolidation of peace and the re-establishment of order.

The principle of legality represented by Estrada and by the Constitution of 1853 was left buried under the rubbish heaped up by anarchy; and the triumphant legality was the one represented by the Constituent Assembly, which was the last and crowning step of the revolution.

Chapter III.

THE CONSIDERATION OF THE EXCEPTIONAL REGIME EXISTING IN NICARAGUA IN 1858 CONTINUED.

The Assembly undertook the great work of the political organization of Nicaragua in November, 1857, and the new Constitution did not appear until the 19th of August, 1858.

During the time which intervened between the former and the latter date the Assembly exercised unlimited powers, both constituent and legislative, without restriction of any kind.

That body was not a mere constituent congress in the ordinary sense of the word. It was much more than that; it was a great national convention. Now it acted as a Legislature, then as a Constituent Congress; now as forming but one chamber, then as a Congress consisting of two co-ordinate Houses; now enacting organic laws, and then promulgating municipal statutes; creating tribunals, amending codes, approving treaties, and promulgating the Constitution. Its omnipotence was superior even to the principle that the laws have no retroactive effect, which is found at the very root of the legislation of all countries.

The Assembly which acted in that way certainly exercised an unlimited power, the greatest which can ever be exercised among men constituted in society, and did not find itself under the sway of any written law regulating its action or embarrassing its movements.

Instances of such assemblies are not frequent in the lives of the nations, but they always occur after great social revolutions. I need not cite examples which are perfectly well known.

These extraordinary constituent bodies are vested, owing to their own nature, with the plenitude of power which constitutes sovereignty. All that the Sovereign can do they also can accomplish.

The abolished Constitution of 1838, which was the flag harbored by the revolution of May, 1854, was the starting-point of the labors of the Constituent Assembly, as provided by the decree of Convocation; but the provisions of that organic law, thousands of times trampled upon by the belligerent parties, affected nothing, nor could they affect the action of the Assembly.

That Constitution forbade the Chief Executive Magistrate to command the army; but the Assembly decreed the contrary.

That Constitution forbade the members of the Legislative body to be, simultaneously, members of the Supreme Court of Justice, or officers and clerks in the Executive Department; but the Assembly enacted otherwise.

That Constitution provided that the Presidential term of office should be two years; but the Assembly decided that it should be four.

That Constitution established the principle that no retroactive effect should be given to laws; but the Assembly enacted laws to which it gave retroactive effect; something monstrous in theory, but claimed to be necessary, absolutely indispensable in practice, under those circumstances, as ground and foundation for a new legal order subsequent to revolution and anarchy.

Shortly after the meeting of the Constituent Assembly difficulties arose between Costa Rica and Nicaragua, as always happened, on account of the unfortunate question of limits. Nicaragua thought that Costa Rica had invaded her territory, and prepared herself for defence, and issued a decree, under date of the 25th of November, 1857, declaring war against Costa Rica.

In addition to that decree, and foreseeing that some arrangement could be made with Costa Rica, the Assembly enacted another decree, dated on the 10th of December following, by which it vested in the Executive, in full, all the powers which, in regard to foreign relations, had already been agreed to be given it by the Constitution which was then under discussion, and which some months afterwards, in August, was in fact promulgated.

Let us see now which were those faculties. I shall copy from the Journal itself of the Assembly of the 25th of November, 1857. I find there the following passage:

" It was resolved that Section 8, relative to foreign relations and negotiations of treaties, should be divided into two parts, and, upon consideration of each one, they were finally approved, as follows:

" 1st. To conduct the Foreign Relations; to appoint and accredit diplomatic ministers of all grades, agents and consuls of the Republic, near the Foreign Governments and courts; to receive or admit those sent here, when legally authorized.

" 2d. To negotiate treaties and all other contracts whatsoever interesting the Republic, whether with companies or private persons, both native or foreign ; to adjust treaties of peace; to celebrate concordats with the Apostolic See—all these acts being subject to ratification by the Legislative Power, and to exercise the patronage according to law."

And as in this section, section 17th of the project has been embodied, the Assembly went on to discuss the other two.[1]

In use of these faculties, agreed upon by the Assembly since the 26th of November, and sanctioned and put into operation on the 1st of December, owing to the urgency of the occasion, the Government of Gen. Martinez entered into negotiations with Costa Rica to rid the country of a war which was believed to be imminent.

Supposing that the Constitution of 1838 would have had any value at all up to that time, as rule of action for the supreme powers, the decree of December 1st, as far as for-

---

[1] These faculties are the same described in Secs. 14, 15, and 16 of the Nicaraguan Constitution of Aug. 19, 1858.

eign relations and international treaties were concerned, buried it finally in the grave of history.

But circumstances were most grave, and the Constituent Assembly did not content itself with the facilities it had given the Executive for the termination of the differences between Costa Rica and Nicaragua. And, for the sake of obtaining an immediate arrangement, it issued on the 5th of February, 1858, the decree which reads as follows:

"The Constituent Assembly of the Republic of Nicaragua, in use of the legislative faculties with which it is invested, decrees:

"Article 1. For the purpose that the Executive may comply with the Decree of January 18th instant,[1] the said Executive *is hereby amply authorized to act in the settlement of the difficulties with the Republic of Costa Rica in such manner as it may deem best for the interests of both countries, and for the independence of Central America*, WITHOUT THE NECESSITY OF RATIFICATION BY THE LEGISLATIVE POWER.

"Article 2. *Such treaties of limits as it may adjust* SHALL BE FINAL, *if adjusted in accordance with the bases which separately will be given to it; but, if not, they shall be subject to the ratification of the Assembly.*

"To the Executive power.

"Given at the Hall of Sessions in Managua, on the 5th of February, 1858.

"TIMOTEO LACAYO, *President.*
"ISIDORO LOPEZ, *Secretary.*
"PABLO CHAMORRO, *Secretary.*"

This decree was ordered to be executed by the President

---

[1] By this decree the Constituent Assembly had ordered new Commissioners to be appointed, who, under new instructions, should enter into the negotiation of treaties of peace, limits, friendship, and alliance between Nicaragua and Costa Rica, which would harmonize their respective interests, and affirm the independence of the two countries, said treaties being subject to the ratification of the Assembly.

on the same 5th day of February, and was duly published and promulgated.

By virtue of its provisions the Executive power became vested with the faculty of making a final treaty with Costa Rica, without needing legislative ratification, provided, however, that as far as limits were concerned it would conform itself to the bases or instructions separately communicated to it, the ratification being indispensable only in case that the stipulation made in regard to limits should deviate from those instructions.

The treaty of April 15, 1858, was made under the sway of this decree, and of the former one of December 1, 1857; not at all under the sway of the Constitution of 1838.

The separate instructions or bases framed by the Assembly were respected and complied with, and no legislative approval was, therefore, necessary. In proof thereof the fact can be mentioned that the treaty was published as a law of Nicaragua, and no objection was raised in the Assembly against its language. Had the Executive deviated from the instructions or bases given it by the Assembly, such an acquiescence would never have been witnessed.

The subsequent administrations of Nicaragua have made stupendous efforts of imagination to find out flaws in the treaty of limits; but it has never occurred to them that Gen. Martinez went beyond the instructions given him by the Assembly of 1858. This is a good indication that the treaty was made in compliance with them.

The treaty did not require, as I have said, legislative ratification; but for the greater approval thereof the said ratification was granted to it by the decree of May 28, 1858.[1]

The treaty of limits became, then, for Costa Rica, for Nicaragua, for the friendly nations, and for the whole world, an international compact, inviolable and sacred.

The Constituent Assembly went on with its work, and in the new organic law, Article I, it provided as follows :

---

[1] This decree has been embodied in First Part, Chapter V, p. 55.

"THE LAWS ON SPECIAL LIMITS FORM A PART OF THE CONSTITUTION."

The treaty of April 15, 1858, which was, as it is now, a law of Nicaragua, and was, as it is now, a law on special limits, became, therefore, a part of the Constitution, and acquired, in a still more firm and solemn manner, the character of Nicaraguan organic law.

It is therefore shown by proof of irresistible character:

1st. That the treaty of limits was not adjusted under the sway of the Constitution of 1838.

2d. That it was initiated, concluded, ratified, exchanged, promulgated, and carried into execution under a transitory regime where the Government was vested with unlimited and extraordinary constituent power.

3d. And that it was made a part of the Nicaraguan Constitution of 1858.

What now remains to be known is whether the action of a special and extraordinary regime, if a government of political reorganization, such as the one existing in Nicaragua in 1858, can bind the country.

The answer is very simple. It is given by the well known authority of Don Carlos Calvo.

"A *de facto* government, recognized by the other States and in intimate communion with the mass of the nation, possesses in regard to the national territory the same powers, the same faculties, as the legitimate government which it replaced. All that is done by it within the limits foreseen and determined by the domestic public law of the State, whether for acquiring or for alienating territory, is absolutely valid and irrevocable. This is a principle of high practical importance from an international point of view."[1]

Of the opinion of Calvo are also Vattel, Phillimore, Heffter, Kent, Ortolán, Bello, Riquelme, Pradier Foderé, Halleck, Garden, Desjardins, and Klüber, cited by him.

---

[1] Droit international théorique et pratique, vol. 1, § 711.

Which was the domestic public law of Nicaragua at the time of the conclusion of the treaty? Was it, perhaps, the Constitution of 1838? No; by no means. We have seen already, that, as far as foreign relations in general, and especially as far as negotiations with Costa Rica about limits were concerned, the said constitution had been abrogated by specific decrees enacted, *ad hoc*, by that Constituent Assembly.

The domestic public law of Nicaragua, at the time of the conclusion of the treaty of limits, consisted in the decrees of December 1, 1851, and February 5, 1858.

The treaty was adjusted in conformity with those decrees.

It was, besides, ratified by the Constituent Assembly.

It was subsequently made a part of the Constitution of 1858.

Its validity is therefore indisputable, and its firmness uncontrovertible.

Chapter IV.

THE TREATY OF LIMITS DOES NOT IMPLY ANY REFORM OR AMENDMENT OF THE NICARAGUAN CONSTITUTION OF 1838.

EVEN if taken for granted that, at the time of the approval of the treaty of limits, Nicaragua found herself under a regular constitutional regime, where the charter of 1838 ruled supremely, and not under the extraordinary circumstances above explained, still the efficiency and validity of the compact would not be less.

The Constitution of 1838 did not define the frontier of the Nicaraguan territory on the side of Costa Rica. And the reason of this omission was that Nicaragua had then a question pending with her neighbor about limits, and the Constituent Legislature did not want to prejudge it in any way whatever. Therefore it chose to preserve the *status quo*, and declared, in general terms, that the national territory reached on the southeast as far as the frontier of Costa Rica; and it added that the boundaries with the *bordering States should be marked by a law which would make a part of the Constitution.*

Here is the text of this provision:

"Article II. The territory of the State is the same as was formerly given to the Province of Nicaragua; its limits being, on the east and northeast, the sea of the Antilles; on the north and northwest, the State of Honduras; on the west and south, the Pacific Ocean; and on the southeast the State of Costa Rica. THE DIVIDING LINES WITH THE BORDERING STATES SHALL BE MARKED BY A LAW WHICH WILL MAKE A PART OF THE CONSTITUTION."

The Constitution, therefore, was left incomplete; but it provided for the means of completing it, which should be by a law.

To say that the Charter of 1838 carried the frontiers of the State as far as the Jimenez river on the Atlantic and the Salto river on the Pacific, as has been held during the last years, is to assert what the Charter itself does not say. It is to contradict openly the provision which it contains, and which postpones, until a law for that special purpose should be enacted, the determination of the bordering line.

It will be remembered that when, in 1838, Nicaragua was engaged in the reform of the Constitution of 1826, Don Francisco Maria Oreamuno, Envoy of Costa Rica, requested Nicaragua, finally, to recognize the annexation of Nicoya to Costa Rica, and that, as no treaty upon the subject could then be made, and there was some hope of an amicable settlement more or less speedy, but sincerely and ardently desired by both parties, it was decided, in order that the new Constitution should not offer any obstacle to the said settlement, that the language thereof would be that which has already been quoted.

In view of Article 2 of the Constitution of 1838, as framed under the circumstances aforesaid, it can be asserted without any hesitation that the said Constitution of 1838 did not mark out the boundary between Nicaragua and Costa Rica; nor could it do so reasonably, since there was an international controversy pending upon that very point, loyally conducted on diplomatic grounds, the solution of which, amicably and peacefully, was desired by both parties; and it was not proper that, by a declaration *ex abrupto*, made by one of them, by its own authority, the cause would be decided in its favor, and the question would be placed on the ground of accomplished facts.

A public treaty, clothed with all the force of a law, was destined to supplement and complete the Constitution in which it had to be embodied so as to become a part of the organic law of Nicaragua, and as long as the treaty was not concluded the Constitution ought to remain incomplete.

Such is the clear right and natural construction, as well as the only possible one, to be placed upon the constitutional text, and any other which may be attempted to be placed upon it will be violent and in open contradiction to its letter and spirit.

So that the treaty by which the unfortunate question of limits between Costa Rica and Nicaragua was set at rest, far from involving or implying a constitutional reform or amendment, was, as expressed by the text of the charter itself, the natural complement of it. It became a part of it since the very moment in which the character of a national statute was given to it.

It was not necessary, under these circumstances, for the treaty of limits to be approved either by a Constituent Assembly, convoked *ad hoc*, or by two subsequent Legislatures.

There was no amendment to make, and there was only one void to fill. This was to be done as the Constitution provided; that is, by means of a secondary law or statute, which was the treaty of limits.

Even supposing that this treaty was concluded under the sway of the Constitution of 1838, Article 194 of the same, which refers to constitutional amendments or reforms, an article on which the Government of Nicaragua grounds its argument, has nothing at all to do with the question, because Article 2, which created the void, provided at the same time for the manner of filling it. Article 2, therefore, and not Article 194, is the one at which it is necessary to look for the decision of the point.

This construction, which, as has been proved, is the only admissible one, was also the one which the supreme authorities of Nicaragua placed upon the domestic public law of that country when the treaty was made. Neither the Commissioners of the Nicaraguan Government, nor the Executive power of that Republic, nor her Constituent Assembly, nor her public press, nor any person whatever, said then, or even thought, that the treaty of limits would not be binding upon Nicaragua unless subject to special proceedings never before resorted to for the perfection of treaties among nations.

It cannot be thought, or admitted, that a whole generation of public men would be ignorant to such a degree of the constitutional law of their own country.

It cannot be thought, either, that the organic laws of Nicaragua were then constructed in bad faith, so as to leave the door open to future controversy and afford opportunities to violate pledged faith.

The only thing which can be said and thought is that the doubts which occurred to the mind of Secretary Ayon, after fourteen years of mutual and faithful execution of the treaty, on the part of both countries, has no rational foundation.

The Assembly which approved the treaty was not an ordinary Congress, subject to the provisions of a charter, but an extraordinary Constituent Assembly, which ruled with sovereign unlimited power. But even supposing that it was the former, and that the Constitution of 1838 was the rule which should have governed its acts, it is clear that it had perfect authority and power to finally approve that treaty. I have maintained that the arrangement of limits did not imply a constitutional amendment or reform, and I have proved it superabundantly. But in order that even the last vestige of doubt should be vanished in this respect, I beg to be allowed to refer to Article 42, chapter 13, of the Nicaraguan Constitution of 1858, which is the one now in force. It reads, as far as this special matter is concerned, in the following words:

"*Faculties of Congress in Separate Chambers.*"

"It belongs to Congress, * * * 24. To decide by a two-third vote on the following subjects: * * * 3d. ALL LAWS FIXING THE BOUNDARIES BETWEEN THIS AND THE OTHER REPUBLICS. * * * 5th. THE RATIFICATION OF ALL TREATIES, *agreements and contracts of canalization, highways and loans* ENTERED INTO BY THE EXECUTIVE."

Before 1858 the marking out of the boundaries of the country was, according to a provision *ad hoc* of the Constitution, a proper subject of a statutory law; after the Constitution of 1858 the exception became the general rule.

During half a century, therefore, both before and after the treaty of limits of 1858, it has been held in Nicaragua, as a constitutional principle, that the questions of limits are proper matter for secondary laws or statutes, to be enacted by ordinary legislatures, without the special requisites or proceedings which are necessary for the enactment of organic laws.

All the efforts of Dialectics which Señores Ayon and Rivas have made to convey the idea that the treaty in question involved, or implied, an amendment or a reform of the organic laws of Nicaragua, have fallen to the ground before the literal, plain, express, and unmistakable text of the Nicaraguan Constitutions themselves.

Chapter V.

THE TREATY OF LIMITS WAS RATIFIED, NOT ONCE OR TWICE, BUT ON SEVERAL REPEATED OCCASIONS, BY THE NICARAGUAN LEGISLATURES.

It has been shown in the preceding chapters that the treaty of limits was not concluded and approved under the sway of the Constitution of 1838; and, furthermore, that, even in case that such a thing should have happened, it would have been sufficient for the perfect validity of the said treaty that the ratification by one Legislature had been obtained because the treaty did not involve any amendment or reform of the organic law.

But in order to follow up and refute in every respect the arguments of the opponent, I will now take it for granted that the approval of the treaty did indeed involve a constitutional reform, and that, therefore, two legislative ratifications were required.

Under this aspect of the case I shall set forth and prove that not only those two ratifications, but many others subsequent, have been imparted to the treaty.

In 1858 Mr. Felix Belly asked the Government of Nicaragua for a grant for the opening of an interoceanic canal. In 1859 the petition was referred to the Chambers; and the Chambers, before taking any action, *having in view the provisions of the treaty of limits, decided that the Executive should first comply, in full, with Article VIII of the said treaty*,[1] and the Executive did as directed.

Lately, in the same year, 1859, the same Chambers which had respected and obeyed Article VIII of the treaty of limits, decreed by one of the articles of the law enacted by them in regard to the Belly canal, as follows:

---

[1] Documents, Nos. 19 and 20.

" Article 4th. In case that the line to be drawn, beginning on the Sapoá river on the Lake of Nicaragua, and ending in the Salinas Bay on the Pacific Ocean, should be considered practicable by the engineers, the company shall be bound to select that line with preference to all others, for the route from the Lake of Nicaragua to the Pacific Ocean, and the route so opened shall be, by the same fact, and all along its extent, the definite limit between the two States of Nicaragua and Costa Rica. *If not considered practicable this limit shall remain as it is now, subject to subsequent regulations.*[1]

As it is seen, the canal had to follow on the Pacific side, if possible, the same course as the line between the Sapoá river and the Salinas Bay, and become, whether built on one side or the other of the astronomic line marking the boundary, the definitive and permanent limit, forever dividing the two Republics: If the canal was built elsewhere, because the above said route proved to be impracticable, no change should be made on the frontier, which would remain as it was; that is, as marked by the treaty of 1858, subject to subsequent arrangements.

The Legislature and the Executive of Costa Rica adhered to the Belly contract; and this was promulgated as law both in Nicaragua and Costa Rica.[2]

Can any one desire a more explicit recognition that the treaty was a law of Nicaragua? Can any one desire a more authorized and authentic interpretation than the one given by the same Nicaraguan Legislature of 1859?

The treaty did not require, indeed, any ratification; but it was certainly given to it by the Nicaraguan Chambers of 1859.

In 1861 the Nicaraguan Government, with the approval of the Legislature, entered into a contract with an American

---

[1] Convención Internacional entre los Gobiernos de Nicaragua y Costa Rica y Don Felix Belly para la canalización del Istmo. Managua Imprenta del Progreso, frente al Palacio Nacional 1859.

[2] See Pamphlet named in the preceding note.

company for interoceanic transit. When the Government of Costa Rica was consulted about it, in obedience to Article VIII of the treaty of limits, the latter Government suggested, by despatch of the 2d of March, that a special clause should be inserted in the grant saving the rights acquired by Costa Rica under Article VI of the Cañas-Jerez treaty of April 15, 1858, which reads as follows:

"The Republic of Nicaragua shall have, exclusively, the dominion and sovereignty on the waters of the San Juan river from its origin in the Lake to its mouth in the Atlantic; but the Republic of Costa Rica shall have, in the same waters, the perpetual rights of navigation between the said mouth of the river to a point three English miles distant this side of Castillo Viejo, for purposes of commerce, either with Nicaragua or with the interior of Costa Rica, through the San Carlos or Sarapiquí rivers, or any other way, starting from the part of the bank of the San Juan river which is hereby established to belong to Costa Rica. The vessels of both countries shall have the power indiscriminately to land on both sides of the river, in the part thereof in which navigation is common, without charges or tax of any kind, unless levied by agreement between the two Governments."

And, by note of the 4th of March immediately following, the Nicaraguan Secretary of State replied as follows:

"NATIONAL PALACE,
"MANAGUA, *March* 4, 1861.

"SIR: The Chamber of Deputies, upon consideration of the remarks made by you under instructions of your Government, under date of the 2d instant, has been pleased to resolve as follows: * * *

"And the Chamber further resolved to communicate to the Department under my charge for the information of Señor Volio, THAT BEFORE RECEIVING THE COPY OF HIS RESPECTABLE OFFICIAL DESPATCH, AND WHEN THE CHAMBER WAS ENGAGED IN THE EXAMINATION OF ARTICLE VII OF THE ABOVE-NAMED CON-

TRACT, IT HAD ALREADY RESOLVED TO INSERT A CLAUSE BY WHICH THE RIGHTS OF COSTA RICA WERE SAVED, AS SUGGESTED IN THE FIRST POINT OF THE ABOVE-NAMED OFFICIAL DESPATCH, AND IN SO DOING THE CHAMBER HAS DONE NOTHING ELSE THAN COMPLYING WITH ONE OF ITS MOST STRICT DUTIES."

"And, by order of the President, I transmit it to you, subscribing myself at the same time your most attentive servant,
"J. MIGUEL CARDENAS.
" To the Licentiate DON JULIAN VOLIO,
 " *Envoy Extraordinary and Minister Plenipotentiary*
 " *of the Republic of Costa Rica.*"

The foregoing despatch is the answer given to the note addressed by Licentiate Don Julian Volio, Minister of Costa Rica in Nicaragua, under date of February 23, 1861, suggesting to the Government of Nicaragua to save by an especial clause in the contract of transit the rights acquired by Costa Rica under Article VI of the treaty of limits of 1858.

Article VII, of the law making the grant in favor of the Central American Company of Transit, enacted by the Nicaraguan Chambers, *confirmed and ratified*, solemnly, the treaty of April 15, 1858; and anticipated the wishes of the Government of Costa Rica, founded on the said treaty, by stating that, in doing so, they only complied with one of their most strict duties.

In 1863 John E. Russell and Don José Rosa Perez submitted to the Government certain propositions intended to be the bases for an enterprise of interoceanic transit through the Nicaraguan Isthmus; and, the subject having been referred to the consideration of the Legislature, the latter resolved *to refrain from taking any action on it until the Executive should have complied with the provisions of Article VIII of the treaty of limits concluded with Costa Rica in* 1858.[1]

This was a new authentic recognition by the Nicaraguan legislative power of the fact that the treaty was a law of the

---

[1] Documents, Nos. 30 and 31.

Republic. And if the second ratification spoken of would have been necessary, the recognition now made should be considered as such.

In 1864 arrangements were undertaken in Nicaragua for an enterprise of interoceanic canal, at the head of which appeared Mr. Bedford Clapperton Trevelyn Pim, a Captain in the English Navy. The Government celebrated with him a contract, which was submitted to the consideration of the Chambers. And one of the modifications which the Legislature made to the contract was to insert in it the express provision that *the contract would have no effect until the Executive should have heard the opinion of the Government of Costa Rica.*[1]

The territory of Costa Rica was not touched in this case; but the treaty of 1858 provided that Costa Rica should be heard in all grants of this kind, and the Chambers refused to consent to any omission on the part of the Executive in fulfiling an international engagement.

We see, therefore, that instead of that second ratification, which in 1871 Secretary Ayon failed to discover, I have shown that actually there have been four, and I should still be able to show a great many more by only slightly perusing the laws of Nicaragua, which seem to be so lamentably unknown or forgotten by some of her first statesmen of the present day.

If I open the volume published under the title of " Código de la Legislacion de la República de Nicaragua en Centro America" (Code of the Laws of the Republic of Nicaragua in Central America), compiled by Dr. and Master Lic. Don Jesus de la Rocha, by order of His Excellency the Senator President, Don Nicasio del Castillo, &c., &c., Managua, 1874, I find on its very first page a description of the territorial division of Nicaragua, made in pursuance of the laws of August 28, 1858, and March 2, 1859. And that description,

---

[1] Document No. 32.

which I do not copy here, owing to its considerable length, is based upon the treaty of limits with Costa Rica, and does not include, as it could not, in the Nicaraguan territory, the district of Nicoya, which before the treaty had been disputed between the two Republics, and which after the treaty had been finally recognized to belong to Costa Rica.

The law in which this territorial division appears, and which is the first one of Title 1, Book IV, of the Code of Nicaragua, is the basis of the administration of her Government in economical and political matters, as well as municipal, judicial, electoral, and in all that is relative to general police and public order. So the law itself declares.

I do not feel disposed to enter into a minute examination of the domestic law of Nicaragua, and thereby exhibit further eloquent proofs, certainly to be found abundantly, that the treaty was deeply incorporated and embodied—if so it can be said—into all the branches of law, beginning with the Constitution and ending with the most secondary statute. Such a labor is unnecessary; the proofs already given being sufficient to establish the truth of my assertion. One ratification was sufficient, and I have shown that four were given.

Many and repeated have been, therefore, the legislative confirmations and ratifications made in Nicaragua of the treaty of limits of 1858; but the truth is that the Government of the said Republic does not repudiate that treaty because it lacks the formality of ratification by one Legislature, but because it thinks that it is injurious to its interests.

I am not the one who has made this strange assertion. Its author is no less a person than Gen. Don Joaquin Zavala, the Commissioner appointed in 1872 by the Government of Nicaragua to treat with Dr. Don Vicente Herrera, Minister of Costa Rica.

General Zavala, in his despatch of April 8, 1872, expressed himself as follows :

" The public opinion of the country rejects the Cañas-Jerez treaty, NOT BECAUSE IT LACKS THE RATIFICATION OF ONE LEGIS-

LATURE, but because since the unlucky day in which that document was signed it has considered it as highly injurious to the interests of the country and depressive to its dignity and autonomy."[1]

These words, which the Costa Rican Minister, with profound surprise and deep sorrow, read in an official despatch addressed to him, were transmitted by him to the Cabinet of Managua; but this, far from taking them back, gave them, on the contrary, through Señor Don Anselmo H. Rivas, the Secretary of Foreign Relations, by despatch of April 18, 1872, the most complete confirmation.

And how could it be expected that those words would have been taken back if, as stated by Mr. C. A. Riotte, the United States Minister in Central America, in his note to Mr. Fish, Secretary of State of the United States, dated in Managua on the 20th of June, 1872, the editor of the official journal publicly maintained, in a paper named *El Porvenir*, that it was a maxim of international law that the stipulations of a treaty must be complied with only when advantageous, or as long as there is no power to break them? Did not this untenable and revolting opinion receive general support instead of condemnation in the Republic of Nicaragua?[2]

---

[1] This despatch is inserted in "Documentos relativos á las últimas negociaciones entre Nicaragua y Costa Rica sobre límites territoriales. Canal interocéanico, Managua, 1872.

[2] Foreign Relations of the United States in 1873, Vol. ii, p. 738.

Chapter VI.

THE PUBLIC LAW OF NICARAGUA RECOGNIZES THE PRINCIPLE THAT THE REPUBLIC IS BOUND BY AN INTERNATIONAL TREATY, WHATEVER THE IMPORTANCE THEREOF MAY BE.

It has been seen in the foregoing chapter that the determination and alteration of the national territory does not belong in Nicaragua to the organic laws, but to statutory legislation.

The Nicaraguan Public Law goes still farther, as I am going to show.

By the treaty, Zeledon-Wyke of January 28, 1860, Great Britain, up to that time protectress of what is called the King of Mosquitia, recognized the sovereignty of the Republic of Nicaragua over the whole territory under him; but, in 1867, the very same power deemed it advisable to notify Nicaragua that the said Nicaraguan sovereignty over Mosquitia could not be understood to be full and complete, but limited to only those rights which, according to feudal law, the Supreme Lord retained in the domains of his vassals, and consisted only in preventing the fief from being alienated in favor of a third party.

The Government of Nicaragua refused to accept such a construction which left to that Republic no more than a nominal sovereignty over a territory which really was an integral part of her dominion, and suggested to Her British Majesty that the question should be submitted to arbitration. The proposition was accepted, and by common consent His Majesty the Emperor of Austria was appointed to decide the question.

From the very moment in which that matter was referred to arbitration, it was recognized as possible that the decision might be unfavorable, as it was to a great extent, to Nicaragua, and that thereby the national sovereignty might suffer detriment. Therefore, in order that the treaty of arbitration celebrated with Great Britain should be firm and binding upon Nicaragua, it was necessary that it should be clothed with all and each one of the formalities which the Constitution prescribed.

It cannot be believed that a serious Government as the Nicaraguan is, in dealing with such a grave and transcendental matter and with such a Government as that of Her British Majesty, would have indulged in mental reservations and omitted formalities constitutionally required for the validity of the treaty. It must be taken for granted, on the contrary, as has been said, that every required formality was faithfully complied with.

But it appears that this treaty, which, no doubt, referred to a question much more important for Nicaragua than the one settled by the treaty of limits of 1858, since it did not involve a simple adjustment of disputed rights, but the affirmation or negation of her sovereignty over an important portion of her territory which had been formerly recognized by Great Britain, DID NOT OBTAIN, HOWEVER, DOUBLE LEGISLATIVE APPROVAL. And this being the fact, it seems that it proves by itself, without possible contradiction, that the public law of Nicaragua, in conformity in this respect with the laws of most civilized nations, recognized the principle that a nation binds itself by its public treaties, even in matters not purely commercial but concerning territorial integrity and the exercise of sovereignty.

On June 2, 1881, Emperor Francis Joseph I rendered his decision, which, among other things, declared that the sovereignty of Nicaragua over Mosquitia is not full, but limited; that the Mosquito King has the right to use his own flag; that Nicaragua has no right to control or take advantage of the natural productions of the Mosquitian territory, nor the power to regulate the commerce of the Mosquito Indians, &c., &c. And Nicaragua accepted with respect the decision of His Apostolic Majesty, and ordered it to be complied with and carried out faithfully, without thinking for a moment that by invoking the omission of a double legislative approval she might evade the consequences of a decision which indisputably affects her sovereignty and reduces the territory of the Republic.

Far from that, the official organ of the Government expressed itself at that time in the following words:

"Let us congratulate ourselves that questions as old (1865) and embarrassing as these have been settled in such a peaceful and harmonious way."

In view of this precedent it can be affirmed without hesitation that according to the Nicaraguan public law, in order to render international conventions firm and valid, no matter what their nature may be, and even when affecting the national territory and sovereignty, it is not necessary to amend the Constitution.

Let it not be said that one thing is a treaty of limits and another thing a treaty of arbitration. As public treaties, the one and the other, there is no difference between them; and, on the contrary, it plainly appears that the same effect, which is the dismemberment of the territory, or the abridgement of sovereignty, can be accomplished in the same way by each of them.

If any difference can be found, or suggested, it will be in favor of the direct treaty of limits; because if something is given up by it, something, or a great deal, is also obtained through it in compensation; while in the treaty of arbitration the whole thing is placed in danger. For this reason the effects of the treaty of arbitration are graver.

The legal principle that the only one who can compromise or submit to arbitration is the same one who has the right to alienate the thing in controversy, is perfectly well known and needs no demonstration. From the point of view of the capacity and of the form of the transaction, there is complete identity between alienation, compromise, and submission to arbitration.

When the dispute about Mosquitia was submitted to arbitration all the formalities and requisites which are now claimed to be wanting in the treaty with Costa Rica should have been also complied with, and, if they were not, their omission proves only that the public powers of Nicaragua did not consider them necessary, according to their constitutional law, for the validity of a treaty, whatever its importance might be.

Chapter VII.

THE WHOLE OF THE PRESENT CONTROVERSY RESTS SUBSTANTIALLY UPON THE USE OF A CERTAIN WORD — VALIDITY OF THE TREATY IN GOOD FAITH.

Now, I want to lay aside all that has been said in the foregoing chapters in support of the perfect validity of the treaty of limits, and place myself on a ground much more favorable to the cause of the opponent; that is, that the treaty really involved a reform of the Constitution of 1838.

Even on that ground, which I only accept for the sake of the argument, because it is false, I will show that the approval given to the treaty by the Assembly was clothed with the character of an amendment to the Constitution.

If the argument of the opponent is carefully examined it will be found, without any great effort, that the whole of the present discussion rests fundamentally on the use, whether proper or improper, of one word.

The preamble of the decree, by which the treaty of limits was approved, reads as follows:

"No. 62.

"The Constituent Assembly of the Republic of Nicaragua, in use of the *legislative faculties* with which it is invested, decrees," &c., &c.

Should the language just quoted have been changed into, and substituted by, the following:

"The Constituent Assembly of the Republic of Nicaragua, in use of *its faculties*, decrees," &c., &c.;

or simply by

"The Constituent Assembly of the Republic of Nicaragua decrees," &c., &c.—

the present controversy would have been avoided. No one

could have then said that a Legislature, and not a constituent body, had approved the treaty.

The gist of the reasoning of Señor Ayon lies in the word "legislative," which was used in the decree. Remove that foundation and the whole building raised upon it by Señores Ayon, Rivas, and Zavala will fall to the ground with a mighty crash.

The question is, therefore, reduced to only one word.

Now, it cannot be doubted that the Assembly acted seriously, and with the intention that its action should be efficient; and under this assumption, and following the same order of ideas of the opponent, it must be reasonably supposed that it was only by mistake, or through a *lapsus calami*, that the decree of approval misstated the kind of power which was necessary to give the act all the desired efficiency; otherwise, instead of an error, bad faith would be found, and this is inadmissible.

And now, I ask, could ever the substance or the subject-matter of a decree be sacrificed to a simple, unessential form? Could such a thing be possible when the Assembly held in its hands, in an indivisible manner, both the legislative and constituent powers, and could exercise, untrammelled, whichever of the two it might deem best?

Señor Ayon says that the Assembly intended to give a chance to a subsequent Legislature to examine such a grave and serious point as was the arrangement of limits with Nicaragua. But, following this line of argument, I cannot perceive how the Assembly did not leave, also, to the subsequent Legislature the framing of the Constitution and the reorganization of the country—points, both of them, which were indubitably of greater gravity than the fixing of limits.

At the present age, only the theological casuistry of certain sects admits of sacramental words; but the public law of nations admits of none, and truth and good faith, and not legal subtleties, are called to preside over the relations between countries.

A word badly used, if, indeed, so used, which I do not admit, in the text of the document witnessing the obligation contracted, never could destroy the efficiency of the substance or subject-matter of the obligation itself.

Calvo, a well-accepted authority in the modern law of nations, in handling this question, decides it as follows :

" When the expression, although intrinsically correct under the circumstances, does not convey the idea involved in it, but inexactly, it is evidently necessary, as the jurists say, to sacrifice the means to the end, set the word aside, and look at nothing else than the idea itself."[1]

" International treaties," he says elsewhere, "are before all *actus bonæ fidei*."

At the bottom of the more or less correct wording of the Nicaraguan approval of the treaty lays the consent of the Nicaraguan nation, expressed by an Assembly legally representing her, vested with unlimited powers to reform the Constitution and to organize and regulate the relations, both foreign and domestic, of the Republic.

If, for the validity of the obligation thereby contracted, it was necessary, according to the domestic law of the State, that the compact should be clothed with the character of a constitutional amendment, that character was given to it, virtually and implicitly, by the mere fact that the approval was made by a Constituent Assembly, with the full intent and purpose that it should be efficient in every respect. Whatever language was used in the preamble of the decree makes no difference. Put the badly-used word aside, and only consider the meaning which it was intended to convey.

It is a principle of legal hermeneutics that, in the interpretation of compacts, both between private parties and nations, that sense which produces some effect should be preferred to that which produces none. If the Assembly meant

---

[1] CALVO. Droit international, théorique practique.

to stipulate in favor of Nicaragua, and bind her, in her turn, an intention about which no reasonable doubt can exist, it must be thought that it rather acted as a constituent body exercising all its faculties, than as a simple ordinary Legislature with restricted powers whose deeds were subject to a subsequent ratification, of which no one dreamt at that time.

On the 19th of August, 1858, the date of the new Constitution, the Constituent Assembly, which had framed it, enacted a decree directing itself to continue to exercise the legislative power of the nation until the new Constitutional Congress should meet.

If, after that date, the treaty of limits should have been approved, then some shadow of reason would exist for claiming that it had been approved by a legislature and not by a constituent body; but as the ratification of the treaty was made some months before the 19th of August, 1858, at a time in which the Assembly was vested with all kinds of powers, it cannot be doubted that it acted in the capacity of a constituent body, and with the plenitude of faculties which was required to give perfect efficiency to its action. No other conclusion can be reached in good faith—the only possible criterion in international conventions.

Chapter VIII.

REPEATED ACKNOWLEDGMENTS OF THE VALIDITY OF THE TREATY BY DIFFERENT NICARAGUAN ADMINISTRATIONS.

It has been said in Nicaragua that the treaty of limits never reached perfection; that it never went beyond the category of a project; that it never served as a basis for laws or treaties, or for the relations between Costa Rica and Nicaragua; and that the Nicaraguan Government never recognized its validity. But there is such an abundance of documents which prove the contrary that it would be tiresome to cite them all. For this reason I shall confine myself to the principal ones.

In the "Official Gaceta" of Nicaragua, No. 15, of May 8, 1858, the treaty of limits was published, not as a project, not as a law in process of enactment, but as an international compact already entered into, accomplished, and perfected, and having the *Exequatur* required for its being carried into effect.

In the letter by which Gen. Don Juan Rafael Mora, President of Costa Rica, took leave of Gen. Don Tomás Martinez, President of Nicaragua, subsequent to the exchange of the ratifications solemnly made by the two Presidents, attended by their respective Secretaries of State, the following phrases occur: "The great purposes which caused us to meet in the city of Rivas having been fully accomplished with so much happiness, I return to my country," &c., &c. "I congratulate myself for having had the good fortune of signing, together with Your Excellency, the compact which puts an end to all our causes of misunderstanding and unpleasantness."

The official paper above referred to printed, also, the following: "Those hands which have just grasped each other have not done so in vain; the assurances of peace and eternal friendship which have been given spring from a deep conviction, and such a permanent one as scarcely has been seen to preside over the treaties among nations."

Col. Negrete was given by the Government of Nicaragua, in recognition of his good offices, the rank and title of General in the Nicaraguan army.

All these facts and documents prove that the treaty was final, perfect, and binding upon the nation, and that Nicaragua believed herself, with reason, to have been benefited by it. Shortly after the exchange of the ratification of the treaty, an enterprise of interoceanic canal was initiated in Nicaragua. Under Article VIII of the instrument, Costa Rica had the right to express its opinion upon the subject, and the Nicaraguan Government, in compliance with the said provision, informed the Government of Costa Rica of the nature and circumstances of the contract, and in the official despatch, in which the Nicaraguan Secretary of State transmitted that information, he took pains to state that he did it *for the purpose of complying with the engagement of this Republic* (Nicaragua) *with Costa Rica, set forth in Article VIII of the treaty of limits, and in order that when the opinion of the Government of Costa Rica is heard the proper final action may be taken by this Government.*

At all times, and without a single exception, the Government of Nicaragua did always comply faithfully with the provisions of Article VIII, as shown by the documents appended to this argument.

But laying aside this point, which may be considered of secondary importance, and looking for something graver and more transcendental than the right acknowledged to Costa Rica of passing an opinion upon questions about canal and transit, I shall now refer to the most delicate subject of the frontier.

By despatch of April 27, 1859, the Nicaraguan foreign office acknowledged that the national territory of Nicaragua ends at the Salinas Bay. According to Article II of the treaty of limits of 1858, the Salinas Bay is the western extremity of the border line. Therefore the declaration of the Nicaraguan Secretary of State presupposed the validity and efficiency of the treaty which marked that limit.

By official letter of August 3, of the same year, from the same Nicaraguan foreign office, Costa Rica was requested to withdraw its custom-houses and other revenue posts from the La Flor river, which was the ancient boundary between the two countries, and situate them on the new line marked by the treaty of 1858, and, in order to avoid difficulties, it suggested the idea that the astronomical line provided for by the treaty should be actually and materially drawn and located.

This shows evidently that the validity and efficiency of the treaty was recognized.

Several years afterwards, on January 12, 1867, Nicaragua complained that a sanitary cordon established by the Government of Costa Rica had trespassed upon her territory by crossing the frontier established by the treaty of 1858. This complaint implied the recognition of the validity of the treaty.

This is as far as the western extremity of the line is concerned. Let us see, now, what happened in regard to the other extremity.

On December 13, 1859, Nicaragua asked Costa Rica to assist her in improving the navigation of the San Juan river, and said that she did not doubt the co-operation of Costa Rica, because, *under the treaty of limits,* Costa Rica had as much interest as Nicaragua in the navigation of the river.

On September 5, 1860, Nicaragua reminded Costa Rica of the duty which devolved upon it, under Article IV of the treaty, to contribute to the defence of the San Juan river and of the Bay of San Juan, and to the custody of the other extremity on the border line, the Salinas Bay.

In 1863 a grave diplomatic difficulty between the United States and Nicaragua grew out of certain claims made by American citizens before the Cabinet at Washington, wherein it was supposed that Nicaragua had publicly insulted the flag of the United States.

The Nicaraguan Minister, Don Luis Molina, handled the case successfully, and a settlement satisfactory to both parties was reached, wherein the principle was established, that on the Nicaraguan soil and waters no other flag could rightfully be carried than the one of Nicaragua.

In the letter addressed to Mr. William H. Seward, Secretary of State of the United States, on October 7, 1863, the Nicaraguan diplomatist expressed himself as follows:

" On the other hand I can assure Your Excellency that the present administration of Nicaragua does not feel disposed to consent that any other flag, except her own AND THE ONE OF COSTA RICA, AS BORDERING STATE, should float in the navigation of her interior waters; that it considered as unauthorized the use of the United States flag made by the Central American Transit Company, and even by the least of its laborers, for the purpose of evading the orders of the Government and escaping the authority of Nicaragua; and that it being persuaded that such an abuse can lead only to complications, it will maintain its right and demand that the aforesaid Company, or any other owing its existence to it, be rooted and nationalized in the country in accordance with the Law of Nations, and that the national flag be used preeminently whenever a flag be required within her jurisdiction, without admitting any other, except under exceptional circumstances and through courtesy."

There cannot be found a more striking acknowledgment of the rights of Costa Rica under the treaty of 1858.

Neither the United States of America nor any other power has the right to carry its flag into the interior Nicaraguan waters, this right belonging only to Nicaragua herself by virtue of her sovereignty *and to Costa Rica as a bordering nation*.

The action of the Nicaraguan Minister in Washington was not only approved and commended, but especially rewarded by the Government of that country.

The fact was made known to the Chambers, and they also approved what had been done.

In 1864 the project was made in Costa Rica of opening a road from the interior of the country to the San Juan river, and notice of this enterprise was given to the Government of Nicaragua, and in the answer made by the said Government on the 23d of August of the same year the following was said: "*This road may be built up to the San Juan river, always within the territory of your Republic, according to the treaty limits made with Nicaragua;* but it may also be built, for the sake of shortening the distance, in the territory which Nicaragua reserved for herself for the safety and protection of Castillo Viejo and the communication between that castle and San Carlos; and in that case a previous arrangement between the two Governments should be required."

By the treaty of 1858 the Colorado river was declared to belong to Costa Rica. The Transit Company attempted to close the mouth of that river, and Costa Rica protested before the Government of Nicaragua against that outrage.

The Nicaraguan Government, under date of July 21, 1863, wrote to the United States Minister, and told him, for the information of the Company, that Nicaragua *could not allow* the mouth of the Colorado river, *which was situated in Costa Rican territory*, to be closed, and that it would resist it as Costa Rica did. In transcribing this communication to the Minister of Costa Rica, he added: "I assure you that my Government will always prevent any new work, which may be attempted *in the territory of your Republic*, from being executed."

In 1866 another attempt was made to obstruct the mouth of the Colorado river, and Costa Rica again protested against it. The Nicaraguan Government, in despatch of June 26, stated that the Government of Costa Rica could rest assured that, on the part of Nicaragua, the rights claimed by it should always be respected, and that the proper care would be taken to prevent its interests from sustaining detriment.

Can any one desire a more explicit confession of the validity of the treaty of 1858, and of the intention to faithfully comply with it?

In 1869, shortly before the denunciation of the treaty, the "Gaceta de Nicaragua" expressed itself as follows:

"It is indubitable for the foregoing reasons that our contract of canal has been made under the most favorable auspices. What now remains is only that the Republic of Costa Rica co-operates on its part in its realization, and in fact the topographic situation of the San Juan river and of the Lake of Nicaragua, WHICH SERVE FOR SOME DISTANCE AS DIVIDING LINE BETWEEN THE TERRITORY OF BOTH REPUBLICS, demands that co-operation."

The "Gaceta de Nicaragua" is the official organ of its Government.

It is to be noticed that, a few months before, Costa Rica had closed the mouths of the San Carlos and Sarapiquí rivers to the abusive traffic which was carried on in Nicaragua of the natural products of the Costa Rican forests on the right bank of the San Juan river.

Shortly afterwards, Don Mariano Montealegre, Minister Plenipotentiary and Envoy Extraordinary of Nicaragua, presented himself at San José, the capital of Costa Rica, entrusted with the special mission to negotiate for the use of the waters of the Colorado river, to improve the San Juan, and for obtaining the consent of Costa Rica to the canal contract known as the Ayon-Chevalier. Both negotiations were founded upon the basis of the existence and validity of the treaty of limits.

Now, in the presence of all this, let it be said, what is the faith with which it is asserted emphatically that the treaty of limits never reached perfection, nor did it serve as basis for laws and for the relations between Costa Rica and Nicaragua; let it be said whether it is true that "there is not a single law, nor a single act having for basis that treaty."

The convention of limits was punctually observed by both parties during 14 years in succession, but Señor Ayon had centred the ambition of his whole life in the success of the contract which he had celebrated with the French Senator,

Monsieur Chevalier, and this contract was frustrated, as Señor Ayon believed, by the will of Costa Rica.

Señor Ayon, resenting this failure, considered that for the happiness of his country it was required that the treaty of limits should be made to disappear, and his fertile mind did not take long to find reasons for attacking it.

The simple reading of the words with which the same Señor Ayon prefaces his pamphlet, entitled "The Question of Territorial Limits between the Republics of Nicaragua and Costa Rica, Managua, 1872," will be sufficient to prove how little favor his opinion met with, in the beginning, in his country. Here are his words:

"I EXPECT THAT MY INSISTANCE IN SAVING SUCH GREAT OBJECTS (THE HONOR OF THE NATION, HER WELFARE AND PROSPERITY ! * * *) WILL NOT BE ATTRIBUTED BY MY COUNTRYMEN EITHER TO STUBBORNNESS, OR TO A DESIRE OF MAKING MYSELF CONSPICUOUS ; AND THAT EVEN IN CASE THAT MY IDEAS ARE CONSIDERED AS ERRORS OF THE UNDERSTANDING, THEY WILL BE OVERLOOKED AND EXCUSED ON THE GROUND THAT THEY PROCEED FROM MY ZEAL FOR THE PUBLIC GOOD. OF THOSE ERRORS I DO NOT CONSIDER THAT EVEN THOSE HAVING THAT ZEAL MORE DEEPLY ROOTED IN THEIR HEARTS ARE EXEMPT."

Interest is a bad adviser, and the opinion of Señor Ayon soon found followers ; but it is worthy of remembrance what President Quadra, in his correspondence, above cited, with the Minister of the United States, plainly set forth. He said that "his honesty and good sense told him that Nicaragua should abide by the stipulations of the treaty, and not touch the old wound of Guanacaste" (Nicoya).

But the sense of justice of Señor Quadra, and his upright spirit, could not prevail against the futile reasoning of Señor Ayon.

The United States Minister in Central America, at that time, expressed himself as follows:

"It is most unfortunate that Nicaragua herself, led on by that fatal man, Mr. Ayon, when Minister of Foreign Relations, took the first false step."

Chapter IX.

COSTA RICA HAS NEVER ADMITTED THAT THE TREATY OF LIMITS REQUIRED FOR ITS VALIDITY FURTHER RATIFICATION.

It has been argued that Costa Rica acknowledged the invalidity of the treaty of 1858 by the fact that the Secretary of Foreign Relations of Costa Rica, Don Agapito Jimenez, in drawing up the convention concluded by him with the Plenipotentiary of Nicaragua, Don Mariano Montealegre, on July 21, 1869, allowed a phrase to be inserted in Article VI of the instrument stating that Nicaragua did thereby ratify that treaty.

This action of Señor Jimenez, it is said, shows conclusively that, in 1869, the Government of Costa Rica recognized that the treaty of 1858 was not perfect; since otherwise it would have been entirely unnecessary to ask for its ratification. This was precisely, they say, that second approval which, according to the Nicaraguan Constitution, could really have impressed upon the treaty the rank or character of constitutional amendment in the matter of limits with Costa Rica.

It is utterly incorrect that the Government of Costa Rica, through the instrumentality of its Secretary of State, Don Agapito Jimenez, did ever at any time ask the Nicaraguan Government for the ratification of the treaty of limits of 1858. The Costa Rican Government never doubted the validity of the treaty, and from the date in which it was signed until the present day, not a single act on the part of Costa Rica can be found which may show the slightest doubt, or the most insignificant hesitation, in that respect. Much to the contrary, all its acts reveal the assurance that it has now, and has had at all times, of the firmness and validity of that compact.

Let us see what happened in 1869, and why the treaty of

1858 was mentioned in the Jimenez-Montealegre project of convention. For a long time some residents of San Juan del Norte, both foreigners and Nicaraguans, had been engaged on a large scale in the rubber trade, an article which is found in great abundance in the Costa Rican forests adjoining the San Carlos, Sarapiquí, and San Juan rivers.

This commerce, which was carried on without permission of the Government of Costa Rica, caused the colony of San Juan for several years to be flourishing. Almost the whole of it was engaged in this trade. And there were some years in which, as acknowledged by the official organ in reference to a report of Don L. Urtecho, the Governor of San Juan del Norte, the exportation of rubber amounted to the sixth part of the whole exports of the nation.

Nicaragua has 400,000 inhabitants; the colony of San Juan, according to that paper, had only 736; the result could not but be astonishing.

How was such an extraordinary production obtained? The answer is very simple: by stripping the forests of the neighbor and exhausting at once the sources of the coveted juice.

The Government of Costa Rica, then presided over by Lic. Don Jesus Jimenez, could not consent to such an abuse, and issued the decree of April 28, 1869, forbidding the exportation, without permission of the Costa Rican authorities, of the natural products of the public lands of Costa Rica situated on the banks of the San Juan river, imposing severe penalties upon the violators of this prohibition and establishing watch-houses and revenue posts at the place of the confluence of the San Carlos and Sarapiquí rivers with the San Juan.

This step, which was perfectly legitimate on the part of Costa Rica, because it legislated only upon its own territory, did not excite any protest on the part of Nicaragua. Costa Rica made use of its right, and injured no one by doing so, although it affected thereby the principal industry of San Juan del Norte. Nicaragua was silent; she had before her eyes the treaty of 1858, and that treaty forbade her to speak.

To protest against the acts of the Government of Costa Rica and infuse new life into the extinguished industry, one thing was necessary, and that was the disappearance of the treaty. It was then, when for the first time, the thought presented itself of ignoring it; and the deliberations on the subject were not conducted so secretly as not to reach the ears of the Costa Rican Government. It was then when Don Mariano Montealegre came to San José as Envoy Extraordinary of Nicaragua, with the mission of securing the adherence of Costa Rica to the Ayon-Chevalier contract of interoceanic canal, and also the use of the waters of the Colorado river.

These negotiations, entrusted to the Nicaraguan diplomatist, necessarily presupposed the firmness of the treaty of 1858; and upon that basis, and no other, the convention to be made ought to be as it was framed; so it is clearly shown by its language from the first to the last word. Señores Jimenez and Montealegre proceeded with frankness, loyalty, and good faith, and agreed with each other to smother the germ of a quarrel, remote, but possible, between countries called for many reasons to become united, which might lead them to disastrous consequences. On the part of Secretary Jimenez there was no doubt or hesitation in regard to the validity of the treaty; but as the possibility of a contention in this regard had become known, it was sound policy to cause the Nicaraguan Government to put itself on record with an express declaration in this regard. That is what was done in the Jimenez-Montealegre project of convention. Señor Montealegre, on his part, abounded in the same feelings; and the clause was drawn up in the way it reads. Now, forgetting the facts, it is attempted to be turned against Costa Rica.

In 1869 Señor Jimenez might have been thought to be too suspicious; but the facts have subsequently come to prove that his lack of faith, not in the treaty and its validity, but in the will of the public men who were called to execute it, was unfortunately well founded.

These are the facts such as they happened; and it is therefore untrue that Costa Rica did ever ask Nicaragua for the ratification of the treaty of limits, as if it were an imperfect and unconcluded convention.

Chapter X.

THE SECOND ALLEGED CAUSE OF NULLITY OF THE TREATY OF LIMITS, WHICH IS THE WANT OF RATIFICATION BY SALVADOR, EXAMINED IN GENERAL.

The first alleged cause of nullity of the treaty having been examined and refuted under all its aspects, I shall now pass to the consideration of the second.

It is said that Article IX of the treaty of 1858 stipulated that, "under no circumstances, even in case that the Republics of Costa Rica and Nicaragua should unfortunately find themselves in a state of war, it shall be permitted to them to wage hostilities against each other either at the port of San Juan del Norte, or the San Juan river, or on the Lake of Nicaragua." It has been said, further, that Article X of the said treaty stated : " That the stipulation of the foregoing article, being of essential importance to the proper protection of the port and river against a foreign aggression, which would affect the general interests of the country, the strict compliance with it remains under the special guarantee, which, in the name of the Government Mediator, its Minister Plenipotentiary is disposed to give, and does hereby give, by virtue of the faculties which he declares to have been conferred upon him for that purpose."

Upon these two clauses, foreign by their nature to the question of limits, which was the primordial object of the treaty, as shown by its own title, and which were no more than an appendix, not affecting at all, nor being able to affect, the subject-matter of the principal obligation, the Government of Nicaragua has raised the following argument:

The Government of Salvador was an essential contracting party to the treaty, and the lack of its signature destroys the force and effect of the compact.

The guarantee of Salvador was not only a condition for the validity of the treaty, but a condition *sine qua non*.

That condition being clothed with the character of *suspensive*, the treaty could not begin to be operative, even after its ratification by Nicaragua and Costa Rica, until Salvador should have ratified it.

The guarantee and the ratification having failed, the whole structure of the treaty falls to the ground and becomes invalidated and useless in every respect.

These are the grounds of law upon which the second cause of nullity has been founded. To them there has been added another one, moral and historical; that is, that the treaty was obtained by violence by the President of Costa Rica, Don Juan Rafael Mora, who compelled Nicaragua to give away all that he was pleased to demand; and in speaking of the treaty it is referred to as being a " disastrous miscarriage brought about by that violence."

It is sufficient to enunciate these reasonings of the Nicaraguan statesman and historian, Señor Ayon, to perceive, at once, that they were due exclusively to an almost inconceivable dialectic effort, so artificial and strained as to fall of its own weakness.

If there is any difficulty in answering them, it is not certainly on account of their incorrectness, or because their faults are not transparent; but on account of their own subtlety and rather incoercible nature. It is always difficult to handle what lacks substance.

The arguments of Señor Ayon rest upon a lamentable confusion of facts and doctrines.

The statement is incorrect that the Government of Salvador is an essential contracting party to the treaty of limits, which was concluded only between Costa Rica and Nicaragua, and in which the Government of Salvador was primarily a fraternal mediator, and secondarily, and only for an especial clause, accessory to the treaty, which was Article IX, a secondary party to the same, as guaranteeing the compliance with the special stipulation contained in that article.

The statement is incorrect that the guarantee, the suretyship, the accessory contract, became, by a strange legal evolution, the subject-matter of the compact, and converted itself into a condition suspensive of its effects, and not only a simple condition, but one of those most special and important ones which, in law, are called *sine qua non* conditions.

The statement is incorrect that the said condition, even taking it for granted that it was stipulated, can ever be considered to be *suspensive*.

The statement is incorrect, in fine, that the want of ratification or signature by the Government of Salvador, and the consequent want of the guarantee, may legally produce the effect of annulling, as far as the principal contracting parties are concerned, either the special stipulation, in regard to which the guarantee was offered, or the agreement about limits.

Method requires that each one of these points should be treated separately. But as the charge made against Costa Rica, with marked injustice, that the treaty was obtained by violence, is very grave, I must be permitted to begin this portion of my work by its refutation.

CHAPTER XI.

WHETHER THE TREATY OF 1858 WAS OR WAS NOT THE RESULT OF VIOLENCE USED AGAINST NICARAGUA BY THE ADMINISTRATION OF DON JUAN RAFAEL MORA, PRESIDENT OF COSTA RICA.

THIS is not the opportunity to recall to mind the action of Costa Rica when Nicaragua saw herself conquered by the very same foreign element which she had called to her country to mingle in their domestic troubles. Costa Rica was the first to raise the cry of war against the usurper of the public power of Nicaragua, and the last to retire from the field of battle. I shall not enter into any explanations of this kind, even in face of the provocation of the opponent, and of the recriminations untenable in point of justice, made by Secretary Ayon, as already remarked; and I shall confine myself to showing that the treaty of limits of April 15, 1858, was not *a disastrous miscarriage* brought about by any violence exercised by Costa Rica against Nicaragua, her sister, but the result of peaceful negotiations, initiated by Nicaragua with the generous mediation of Salvador, conducted in the capital of Costa Rica, in a state of full and perfect peace, and sealed in Nicaragua under the auspices of the most cordial friendship and good understanding. Only by remembering what has been said about the outlet of the Lake of Nicaragua, or Desaguadero, it can be conceived how the historian of that country, Señor Ayon, blinded by the most vehement passion, has been able to state under his signature a fact so positively at variance with truth.

To prove that the treaty of 1858 was the result of violence, it would be necessary to bring evidence that the Government of Costa Rica at the time of the negotiation of the said treaty, from the beginning thereof to the moment of the exchange of ratifications, or at least during some part of that time, whether a day or an hour, had caused its naval or land forces to go to Nicaragua, or stationed them on the frontiers, or prepared to take there said forces, or threatened in some way the ports of Nicaragua, or at least given orders to raise said forces for the purpose of making hostilities against that Republic.

For the sake of clearness, and to avoid confusion of facts, dates, places, and persons, I deem it necessary to fix here the date which was the starting-point of the negotiations, and the date in which the negotiations were ended by the signing of the act of exchange.

The first date was the 15th of February, 1858, a date on which Col. Negrete presented himself to the Cabinet of San José to open the negotiation, and the second was the 16th of May, 1858, the day on which the exchange of the ratifications of the treaty took place.

Long before the former of these dates, the peace between Costa Rica and Nicaragua had been fully re-established, although the question of limits was still pending.

The proof of this assertion is found in the editorial of the *Gaceta de Nicaragua*, No. 5, of January 30, 1858.

Another proof, more conclusive still, of this fact will be found in the following passage of the speech which Mr. Mirabeau B. Lamar, Minister Plenipotentiary and Envoy Extraordinary of the United States in Nicaragua, delivered on the day of his official reception there, on February 8, 1858. It reads as follows:

"Allow me to conclude my remarks by setting forth how gratifying it is to me to see that the threatening storm of war, which a short time ago was impending between this nation and one of her neighboring sisters (Costa Rica), has vanished before the serene brilliancy of a most acceptable policy; that Nicaragua and Costa Rica have put an end to their contentions, and that everything announces the prompt re-establishment, founded upon substantial basis, of their ancient relations of fraternal concord. Who knows what may come out of such a happy event? It may, perhaps, bring with it the union of the two countries. And, indeed, I have sometimes thought that such a policy would necessarily be conducive to the happiness of the two Republics. In my opinion this union would be an example worthy to be followed by all the other States of Central America, the reunion of which under the ancient Federal constitution would give them not only peace, strength, and dignity, but would place them on the same level with other important nations, enabling them to compete with the most enlightened in the career of prosperity and glory. If Nicaragua, inspired by such sentiments, should take the first step for the realization of such a great enterprise she will crown herself with immortal glory and would deserve the gratitude of every heart which throbs for the welfare of this country and for the future progress of its people."

The conferences between the plenipotentiaries, Gen. Don José Maria Cañas and Don Maximo Jerez, took place in San José in Costa Rica. On April 15, 1858, the treaty was signed. For the sake of solemnity, and for the purpose of entering into another treaty of friendship, union, and alliance, which was happily concluded, President Don Juan Rafael Mora went over to Rivas, where he was received with the most perfect cordiality by General Martinez, the President of Nicaragua. There the exchange of the ratification took place. Subsequently to all this President Mora took leave of President Martinez in the friendly terms which I have reported elsewhere. And then it was said by the official Nicaraguan organ that the hands of the illustrious Presidents had not been grasped in vain; that the promises made and the faith pledged were due to a deep conviction, and to such a feeling as has seldom been seen to preside over treaties among nations, &c., &c.

Where is, therefore, the violence which the President Don Juan Rafael Mora, according to Señor Ayon, made against the Republic of Nicaragua, to take from her by force all that he deemed advisable to demand?

8

The phrase of Señor Ayon, "So it was done, and the treaty of April 15, 1858, was the disastrous miscarriage brought about by that violence," will never have force enough to counteract that other phrase, written in a decree of the Supreme Power of Nicaragua dated May 6, 1857, which reads as follows: "A vote of thanks is granted to the Republics of Costa Rica, Guatemala, Salvador, and Honduras in recognition of the gratitude of Nicaragua for the services that those nations have rendered her as true friends and sisters."

This historical point having been rectified, I return to the principal ones.

Chapter XII.

THE GOVERNMENT OF SALVADOR WAS NOT AN ESSENTIAL PARTY TO THE TREATY OF LIMITS.

That the Government of Salvador was not a principal contracting party to the treaty of limits of April 15, 1858, is shown by the mere inspection of its text. It is enough to read its preamble to become convinced of this fact, and to reject at once as sophistical, violent, and badly brought, whatever may be said to the contrary.

Here are the words with which it was set forth in the beginning of the instrument, who were the contracting parties, what were the object and purposes of the treaty, what was the reason or "consideration" for its conclusion, and what determined the two Governments to stipulate what they did:

"We, José Maria Cañas, Plenipotentiary Minister of the Republic of Costa Rica, and Máximo Jerez, Plenipotentiary Minister of the Republic of Nicaragua, entrusted by our respective Governments with the duty of making a treaty of limits between the two Republics, which should set at rest the differences which have obstructed that best and most perfect understanding and harmony which must reign between them, for their common safety and prosperity; having exchanged our respective powers, which were examined by Hon. Señor Don Pedro R. Negrete, Minister Plenipotentiary of the Government of the Republic of Salvador, exercising the noble functions of fraternal mediator in these negotiations, who found them to be in good and due form, in the same way as we on our part did find sufficient, those which the same Minister exhibited; after discussing with the necessary deliberation the points to be settled, with the assistance and in the presence of the representative of Salvador, have hereby agreed to and concluded the following treaty of limits between Costa Rica and Nicaragua."

The simple reading of these words at once shows that those who agreed upon and celebrated the treaty were only the diplomatic representatives of Costa Rica and Nicaragua; that the diplomatic representative of Salvador did no more than attending and proceeding as fraternal mediator, exercising his good offices, examining the powers given to the negotiator, assisting the one and the other with his friendly and disinterested advice, and endeavoring to smother among them whatever germ of dispute might occur and endanger the peaceful relations of the two countries.

Nowhere does the treaty read that Salvador was one of the parties concurring to its formation. Nor could it read in this way, because the nature itself of the compact forbade it imperatively. If the subject to be disposed of was the dividing line between Costa Rica and Nicaragua, and not between Costa Rica and Salvador, nor between Salvador and Nicaragua, the intervention of Salvador in the treaty which would mark that line could not be even practicable. *De re tua non agitur* Salvador might have been told in reply to such an attempt on her part. And certainly that Republic would not have by any means attempted to force herself as a contracting party into a compact which did not concern her.

There is no doubt, nor can any be raised, about the fact whether the treaty does or does not say that the two contracting parties to it are Costa Rica and Nicaragua, and no one else. And when a thing is not expressed by words, there is at once the *prima facie* proof that it did not enter into the mind of the contracting parties. But if, through collateral argument, and through more or less strained interpretation, an attempt is made to read what is not written in the instrument, then it will be necessary to turn the eyes to the common law and look there in the light of its principles for the solution of the difficulty.

In his standard work on Contracts, Parsons said that the

circumstances of each case and the situation and relation of the parties must be examined and taken into account for the purpose of determining who is really interested, or, in other words, who are parties to the transaction. "The nature, and especially the entireness of the consideration," says the same writer elsewhere, "is of great importance to determine the nature of the obligation."[1]

What were the circumstances which surrounded the treaty herein referred to, what the situation or relation of the parties thereto, what the nature and entireness of the consideration which led to the adjustment and ratification of the compact?

Article I of the treaty explains all of this satisfactorily:

"The Republic of Costa Rica and the Republic of Nicaragua (that of Salvador is not mentioned) do hereby declare in the most express and solemn terms," so says Article I, "that if for one moment they felt disposed to combat each other for differences about limits and for other reasons, which each one of the high contracting parties (Costa Rica and Nicaragua, not Salvador) considered to be legal and a matter of honor; now, after repeated proofs of good understanding, of peaceful principles and of true fraternity, are willing to bind themselves, as they hereby formally do (Costa Rica and Nicaragua, not Salvador), to secure that the peace, happily re-established, should be strengthened each day more and more between the Government and the people of the two nations (the nations and Governments before indicated), not only for the good and profit of Costa Rica and Nicaragua, but for the happiness and prosperity, which, in a certain way (in an indirect or incidental way) redounds in favor of our sisters, the other Republics of Central America."

All of this is clear and admits of no misinterpretation or dispute. The two Republics of Costa Rica and Nicaragua were the ones which saw themselves profoundly divided by dif-

---

[1] Parsons on Contracts, Book 1, chapter ii, § 1.

ferent opinions in regard to their respective limits, and to the sovereignty stubbornly claimed by each one of them over certain determined territories. Both Republics were the ones which were about to wage war against each other and subsequently gave themselves mutual proofs of good understanding, fraternity, and peaceful principles. Both, also, were the ones who wanted formally to put an end to those questions and settle those disputes by means of a treaty which they concluded, ratified, exchanged, promulgated and carried out.

Who doubts, then, that if Salvador intervened in all of this, she did not do so, nor could she have done so, as an interested party, or in the capacity of a contracting party to the treaty, but simply, as it was the fact, as a fraternal mediator, a moderator of the discussion?

All the articles of the treaty, from the Ist to the IXth, inclusive, refer to nothing else than the question of limits, and the rights and duties of the two Republics of Costa Rica and Nicaragua, either over what was declared by them to belong exclusively to each country, or over what was stipulated that should be of common jurisdiction.

Could it be doubted, in view of all this, and in the absence of all mention that the Republic of Salvador was a party to the treaty, and, what is more, in the absence of all reason to mention her as such, that the said Republic had no interest in the matter, nor was an essential party to the treaty?

If the remote and eventual interest which is mentioned at the end of Article X should give Salvador the character of contracting party to the treaty, the same thing could precisely be said of Guatemala and Honduras, which are also sister Republics of Central America, and to which also, in a certain way, the non-disturbance of the peace on that soil proved beneficial. But this claim would be so absurd in itself that it has not occurred to any one nor admits of defence.

The conclusion to be reached from the silence of the treaty

in its nine fundamental articles—articles which dispose of all the questions pending, and give to them solution satisfactory to the two contracting parties—confirmed and corroborated by the study of its text, its history, and its circumstances, by the examination of the causes which induced its adjustment, and of the object which it had in view, the interests and advantages which it ought to produce, and in whose favor, clearly points out the answer to be given to this question, and is as follows: The Republic of Salvador was not one of the high contracting parties to the treaty of limits between Costa Rica and Nicaragua concluded April 15, 1858. Therefore, the want of the signature of Salvador in that treaty does not affect in the least the validity of the compact.

Chapter XIII.

THE GOVERNMENT OF SALVADOR WAS PRIMARILY A FRATERNAL MEDIATOR, AND SUBSEQUENTLY, AND IN REGARD TO ONLY ONE SECONDARY CLAUSE OF THE TREATY, GUARANTEEING PARTY OF THE EXECUTION OF THE SAID CLAUSE.

It has been said by the Government of Nicaragua that the Republic of Salvador, by virtue of the special guarantee spoken of in Article X of the treaty, became one of the contracting parties.

It is extremely singular that such an important matter as the determination of the question, who are the essential parties to a contract of any kind, and especially to an international agreement, should depend upon arbitrary interpretations, under which what is collateral and accessory changes its nature and converts itself into primary and principal, in all and for all.

Article X of the treaty says:

" The stipulation of the foregoing article (the one by which the two Republics bind themselves not to commit hostilities against each other on the Lake, or in the San Juan river, or in the port of San Juan, even in case of war) being essentially important for the security of the port and river against foreign aggression, which would affect the general interest of the country, the strict compliance therewith remains under the special guarantee which, in the name of the Government mediator, its Minister Plenipotentiary present, is ready to give, and does hereby give, by virtue of the faculties which he declares to have been vested in him for that purpose."

Neither the words of this article nor its spirit authorize the presumption of Nicaragua that the Government of Salvador became through it one of the principal contracting parties.

I need not enumerate particularly the acts and offices of

the Government of Salvador, in relation to this treaty, to cause the true and only character of its intervention to be established in a clear and uncontrovertible manner.

That Salvador acted only in the capacity of a generous and amicable mediator is revealed clearly, and without any effort, by the words of the preamble which were copied in the beginning of this part of my argument.

The diplomatic representative of Salvador intervened in the matter, and acted in it, as the preamble says, not as a party to the transaction, but "in the exercise of the noble functions of fraternal mediator in the negotiations."

And it was in that capacity, and in no other, as stated by his credentials, that the above said high officer constantly acted. So he himself said to the two Governments, both on his arrival at Managua and San José, and in all his subsequent steps.

It was in that capacity that the two contracting Republics admitted him.

It was, in fine, in that capacity that the two Governments recognized him when the moment of the exchange of the ratification arrived.

The act additional to the treaty of 1858 is, perhaps, the document which best establishes and determines the true position, the principal and only character of the Government of Salvador, in the negotiations between Costa Rica and Nicaragua and in the treaty of limits by which they culminated.

Here is that remarkable document:

"ADDITIONAL ACT.

"The undersigned, Ministers of Nicaragua and Costa Rica, wishing to give public testimony of their high esteem, and of their feelings of gratitude towards the Republic of Salvador and its worthy representative, Col. Don Pedro R. Negrete, do hereby agree that the treaty of territorial limits be accompanied with the following solemn declaration:

"The Government of Salvador having given to the Governments of Costa Rica and Nicaragua the most authentic proof of its noble sentiments and of its appreciation in all its value of the necessity of cultivating fraternal sympathy among all these Republics by interesting itself as efficiently and friendly in the equitable settlement of differences which have unhappily existed between the high contracting parties, and obtained this happy result through the Legation of both parties, owing in great part to the estimable and active offices of the Hon. Señor Negrete, Minister Plenipotentiary of that Government, who proved to be the right person to carry on its generous mediation, and has known perfectly well how to correspond to its intentions; and owing, also, to the important assistance which the learning and impartiality of the said Minister have enabled him to render in the discussion of all the matters concerning the subject, we, the heads of the Legations of Costa Rica and Nicaragua, in the name of our respective Governments, do hereby comply with the gratifying duty of declaring and recording here all the gratitude which the patriotism, learning, spirit of fraternity and benevolence characterizing the Government of Salvador justly deserve from them.

"In testimony whereof we have hereunto signed our names to the present instrument, which has been done in triplicate, in the presence of the Hon. Minister of Salvador, countersigned by the respective Secretaries of Legation in the city of San José, the capital of Costa Rica, on the 15th day of the month of April, in the year of our Lord, 1858.

"MAXIMO JEREZ.
"JOSÉ MARIA CAÑAS.
"MANUEL RIVAS,
Secretary of the Legation of Nicaragua.
"SALVADOR GONZALEZ,
Secretary of the Legation of Costa Rica."

The Government of Salvador was therefore a fraternal mediator, and nothing else.

I do not think it necessary to increase the volume of this argument by bringing authorities to prove what is by itself evident; that is, that the amicable mediator who intervenes between two parties, purely for the sake of humanity and mere generosity, without having any interest personal and direct in the matter, and without what is called in law consideration, cannot under any circumstances whatsoever convert himself by some kind of mysterious evolution into principal party to the case, into contracting party, and find himself, whether willingly or forcibly, for all the purposes of the compact, in the legal relation of one contracting party to another.

To attribute to Señor Negrete and to Salvador a real and direct interest in the treaty would be to ignore the nobleness and generosity of their action. It would be more than that; it would be to be ungrateful.

It is therefore unquestionable that the primary part of the Salvador Government, in regard to this treaty, was the part of a friendly mediator, and nothing else.

But it is claimed that the Government of Salvador, through the instrumentality of its minister, bound itself to guarantee the exact compliance with Article IX of the treaty. But this fact, although true, did not place Salvador in the position of principal party to the contract. Its having offered a guarantee to one of the stipulations specifically designated only placed that Government in the situation of a secondary or accessory party, exactly in the same condition as belongs in a common contract to the surety or guarantor who comes and guarantees the fulfilment of an obligation contracted by two private parties whatsoever.

The guarantee in international law and the suretyship in private municipal law are the same thing, and, according to their own nature, neither of them can never be more than an accessory contract.

"A guarantor," says Carlos Calvo,[1] "is the one who re-

---

[1] Dictionnaire de Droit International.

sponds either for his own act or for the act of another; the one who becomes surety for the obligation of another."

"Guarantee is the engagement contracted by the guarantor, and, in legal language, it is *an accessory* obligation destined to secure the execution of the *principal obligation*."

"Sometimes a third party becomes surety for the faithful compliance with a treaty."

Tribune Chavot, at the meeting of the 21st Pluviose of the 12th year of the French Republic, when the Code Napoleon was under discussion, expressed himself as follows:

"Suretyship is but an accessory of the principal obligation."[1]

Treilhard, Counsellor of State, at the meeting on the following day, said:

"Suretyship is a thing accessory to the principal obligation. * * * I have said that suretyship is something accessory to an obligation, and it cannot, therefore, exceed it. It would be contrary to the nature of things that what is accessory could exceed what is principal."

In accordance with this principle, Dalloz, the great interpreter of the French law, in the word Cautionnement (No. 928 of his standard work, Répertoire de la Legislation et de la Jurisprudence), says as follows:

"The extinction of the principal obligation carries with it the extinction of the suretyship, because the accessory cannot exist without the principal. The reverse does not, however, happen. *The suretyship can cease to exist without the principal obligation losing its force.*"

This doctrine is universal, and there is no human legislation which does not admit of it. It has been recognized and proclaimed since before the days of the great Roman jurists, whose immortal works have been the basis of the modern codes. And it is so universal as to constitute one of the most elementary principles of law.

---

[1] DALLOZ. *Répertoire*, word "Cautionnement."

The guarantee may disappear without affecting in the least the principal obligation. The force, validity, firmness of the latter does not depend at all upon the validity and firmness of the former.

If there are cases of exception to that principle they are rare and special; for instance, when the guarantee has been made *expressly* an indispensable condition for the subsistence of the contract. In this case, if the guarantee fails the whole compact also fails, because such was the *express* will of the parties; but in the case of the treaty herein referred to there is no occasion to think of that exception, and the general rule must be observed.

And as the question under consideration is, above all, a question of common sense, rather than quoting from authors and legal works I want to refer in support of my assertion to a fact of daily occurrence.

Titius lends to Sempronius one thousand dollars under the guarantee of Cajús. Cajus may fail and not pay. He may argue that the instrument witnessing the obligation is false. He may plead error, violence, fraud, minority, &c., &c. He may, in a thousand different ways, evade the fulfilment of the guarantee. But no matter what he does, Sempronius will always be indebted to Titius in the sum that the latter lent him, and it will never be lawful for him to evade the fulfilment of his obligation by alleging that the guarantee failed.

This is precisely the present case. Costa Rica and Nicaragua bound themselves by a treaty, and Salvador offered its guarantee but did not give it. There is no guarantee. But the obligations of Costa Rica and Nicaragua remain firm and unreleased. No one of the two parties can rightly refuse to comply with the compact under the pretext that there is no surety to respond for it.

The guarantee offered by Salvador was in truth such a secondary thing that the contracting parties did not wait for it for the purpose of carrying the agreement into effect. During the time in which it could or should have been given, no one of the two parties did anything to obtain it, and when the time passed neither of them entered the slightest protest. The treaty continued in observance for many years afterwards.

It was because the two high contracting parties acted in good faith and with the true intention of doing honor to their signature. The guarantee was not considered to be necessary. The Government of Salvador so also understood it as Señor Ayon himself says in his "Considerations:"

"But neither the Government, nor the Congress of that Republic (Salvador), approved of or ratified the stipulation, and it may be depended upon that neither the Legislatures nor the Cabinets, nor even the people of Salvador, ever remembered it again."[1]

The same thing happened in Nicaragua. Her successive Executives, Chambers, diplomatic ministers, tribunals, always complied faithfully with the compact, without thinking that there was a surety who might compel Nicaragua to comply with the duties which the treaty imposed upon her, or respond for Costa Rica.

The discovery was made by Don Tomas Ayon, and this not in the beginning of the diplomatic contention initiated by him against the treaty, but very long afterwards, when he was hunting for faults in the treaty and its articles, and when in each one of its requisites he imagined to find a a cause of nullity.

---

[1] Consideraciones sobre la cuestión de límites territoriales, entre las Repúblicas de Nicaragua y Costa Rica. Managua, 1872. Imprenta de "El Centro Americano."

Chapter XIV.

The Guarantee cannot be construed as a condition of the Treaty.

One of the best known principles of law is that conditions are not presumed. Therefore, in order to consider that a condition has been established, one of the two following circumstances is required:

Either that the text of the instrument witnessing the obligation clearly and explicitly says so, or that it is to be concluded, logically and necessarily from the spirit thereof, as the common and manifest will of both parties.

That in the present case no express condition exists is a matter of self-evidence, and needs no discussion.

The problem is to decide whether the condition exists by implication.

"Condition," says Pothier,[1] "is the case of a future and uncertain event, which may or may not happen, and on which the obligation has been made to depend."

Dalloz[2] says: "An obligation is conditional when it is made to depend upon a future and uncertain event, either by suspending it until the event happens, or affirming or rescinding it according to the happening or non-happening of the event."

"In the former case what depends upon the event is the existence of the obligation; but in the latter it is its efficiency. Condition is, therefore, a future and uncertain event upon which the legal bond constituting the obligation is made to depend; or, rather, it is a kind of restriction attached to the existence of a legal relationship in connection with a future and uncertain event."

---

[1] Oblig., No. 218–222.
[2] Répertoire, Art. Obligation, No. 1099.

This is also the opinion of Savigny.[1]

Examples: I make you a present of a house, provided that I draw the large prize in the next lottery; but the present will not be valid if within a year I receive new information about my son.

In the first part of the promise a future and uncertain event is established as a legal restriction upon the subsistence of the obligation; but in the second part another fact, also future and uncertain, is established as being the cause of the complete nullification of the contract.

The first condition is "suspensive," the second "resolutive."

Where, and when, or how, does Article X of the treaty of limits say that the effects of the agreement witnessed by it are to be suspended until the Government of Salvador gives the guarantee spoken of by it; or that the whole compact is to be nullified if such a guarantee fails to be given? No such a thing is said anywhere in the instrument. Nor how could it be said if even the article referred to does not require from the contracting parties themselves to guarantee each other the fulfilment of that special obligation; and when it plainly appears that the act of Salvador was one of mere liberality, neither asked nor demanded by either one of the contracting parties, and consisted only of a spontaneous and officious promise of assuming the duties of surety, which in the end was left undone?

All the circumstances, both preceding, simultaneous, and subsequent of the treaty of limits, combine together to show that the idea of rendering the guarantee of the Government of Salvador a condition for the validity of the treaty, and much less a *sine qua non* condition, never entered the minds of the high contracting parties.

In the first place, the guarantee did not refer to all the clauses and stipulations of the treaty, or to a considerable

---

[1] Droit Romain, Vol. 3, p. 126.

portion of them, or even to any of the essential portions of the same, but confined itself to only one point, to a certain extent foreign to the question of limits, which was the subject-matter of the treaty—a clause indeed which might have found a better place in a treaty of peace and amity between the two nations.

If the guarantee of Salvador would have referred to all the different stipulations of the treaty, or if at least the Minister of Salvador would have said that his Government guaranteed the stability of the frontiers such as marked out by the treaty, the pretension of the Government of Nicaragua that the guarantee implied a condition, without ceasing from being groundless, would seem, however, somewhat more tenable.

How can it be concluded that the instrument is in such a manner indivisible that if the accessory clause, which is the guarantee given in regard to a point also accessory, Clause IX, should fail, the whole of the compact also falls to the ground?

The principal stipulations of the agreement could certainly exist without needing the guarantee at all, and to such an extent this was true that the latter was not extended to them by the will and declaration of the contracting parties.

Had they thought otherwise, either none of the clauses would have failed to be guaranteed or the treaty would never have been carried into effect.

The indivisibility now claimed, far from being written in the text of the treaty, is plainly contradicted by it.

Of such small practical importance was and is really the guarantee herein referred to, that the Government of Nicaragua, as remarked before, did not think of it any more, and carried into execution the treaty as far as Nicaragua was concerned, and demanded from Costa Rica the full and faithful execution of the same whenever deemed advisable.

Should the omission of the guarantee have had the transcendental importance now claimed for it, it was natural that, during the 14 years elapsed between the signing of the treaty and the date in which, under the circumstances above explained, Secretary Ayon set forth before the Nicaraguan Congress the doubts which he is said to have entertained about the validity of the convention, some one of the Governments which Nicaragua had had in that time would have said at least one word to the effect of demanding that the guarantee should be carried out.

It can be understood how little importance was attached by Nicaragua to the omission of the guarantee offered by Salvador, by considering that when Secretary Ayon submitted to the Chambers his alleged doubts, he grounded his theory that the treaty was invalid, on the want of a second legislative ratification, and also on the supposed acknowledgment by the Secretary Don Agapito Jimenez that it was not firm; but he said nothing about the lack of the guarantee of Salvador.

It would have been surprising for Señor Ayon to have forgotten, under such circumstances as those then existing, this ground of nullity. Its omission shows the little importance that it had in the eyes of the Government of Nicaragua itself. This argument did not come to the mind of Señor Ayon until a long time afterwards; and as from the text of Article X of the treaty no possible inference can be drawn, even under the most strained and violent construction, that it contains a condition, whether suspensive or resolutive, Señor Ayon attempted to derive the said condition from other sources and by way of implication.

He resorted for that purpose to the legal doctrine and well known general principle that in the bilateral contracts the obligation of one of the parties is subject or subservient to the fact of the other party complying with its own obligations, and that, for instance, the seller of an article is bound to deliver it when the purchaser pays him the price, and that reciprocally the purchaser should pay the price before he becomes entitled to receive the article. But this doctrine has not, nor can it have, practical application to the present case.

Before invoking this doctrine against Costa Rica as a cause of nullity of the contract, it would be necessary to prove that Costa Rica ever failed to comply with the obligations contracted by it. And neither has this charge ever been made, nor can it be, since it has been an invariable principle of its politics to keep always faithfully its international engagements. And as Costa Rica never failed on its part to execute the treaty, Nicaragua cannot consider herself released from the obligations of the same.

Secretary Ayon says that Costa Rica bound herself to give the guarantee or suretyship of Salvador for the purpose of securing the faithful execution of Article IX of the treaty. Where is that written in the treaty? What it says is, that Salvador *guarantees* alone, and neither of the contracting parties gives the guarantee referred to.

And if the language of Article X is so forcibly strained as to make it read (what it does not) that the two Republics bound themselves to guarantee each other the faithful execution of that clause, the result would be, in good logic, that the fault is not of Costa Rica alone, but of both Nicaragua and Costa Rica, for which reason, as the fault was common, it cannot do any harm or benefit to either Government.

Señor Ayon argues that the clause was written for the special benefit of Nicaragua, and for the purpose of protecting her against surprises of Costa Rica through the unpopulated regions of the Lake and the San Juan river. But to maintain this proposition is tantamount to ignore Article X of the treaty, because its language plainly and intelligibly expresses that the promise that no hostilities should be ever made on the lake and the river was mutual, and that the obligation of complying with this promise was also mutual. How can it be ignored that Costa Rica, according to the treaty, is joint owner of the Bay of San Juan, and that it has the right of navigation on the San Juan river, and that it has therefore exactly the same interest as Nicaragua in securing that that route, which, in the future, will be its most important thoroughfare, should be sheltered from hostilities even in the unhappy event of a war with its neighbor?

The history of the treaty clearly says that the clause was written because the Bay of San Juan, the San Juan river, and the lake were an open road for the invaders of the Central American soil in 1855 and 1857. Struggles between Costa Rica and Nicaragua upon those places would offer foreigners an easy access to both countries to their common detriment.

If Nicaragua owns unpopulated and undefended lands on the banks of the San Juan river, the right bank of the same, or the portion thereof which belongs to Costa Rica, is no more populated or better defended ; and if it were possible to think, as Señor Ayon says, that Nicaragua was anxious to protect her undefended frontier against surprises on the part of Costa Rica, there is no reason to suppose that Costa Rica herself did not entertain the same idea, because the circumstances were equal for the two countries, and there was exactly the same possibility on the part of each one to open and carry on hostilities against the other on the places referred to.

No matter how strained the construction placed upon this mutual promise may be, it can never lead to the belief that the promise of guarantee made by a third party, Salvador, was an obligation on the part of Costa Rica in favor of Nicaragua, as it was indispensable to convert it into a condition in favor of one of the parties and against the other.

Granting even what is inconceivable, the most that can be admitted is that the guarantee was mutual or common. Señor Ayon says that it was not complied with ; but who failed to comply with it? Was it Costa Rica ? Was it Nicaragua? Either none, or both, failed ; and, if both failed, neither party can found on its failure an argument of nullity, because reason and common sense declare that whoever makes a complaint has to rest on the foundation that he has on his part faithfully complied with the obligation.

Even granting, *gratia arguendi*, that Costa Rica was bound to guarantee to Nicaragua that it should not be hostile to her, even in case of war, at the places marked by Article X of the treaty, and that, by an extremely one-sided view of the case, Nicaragua had not, on her part, the same obligation in favor of Costa Rica, still the alleged cause of nullity would not exist. At the most, there would be, in that extreme case, a proper matter for negotiation, or a temporary suspension of the effects of the treaty until the delinquent party, after being served with the proper notice, should comply with its duty.

Carlos Calvo says in this respect what follows:

" A treaty can be terminated before the period fixed for its duration when, besides the causes of modification or nullification just mentioned, one of the contracting parties refuses to fulfil its engagements, and gives thus to the other party implicitly the right of likewise freeing itself. * * * The non-execution may on the other side refer only to one clause relatively secondary (this would be the case with Costa Rica and Nicaragua in the present hypothesis), and may therefore not imply any intention of evading the other obligation of the treaty. In this case *there is not necessarily a complete and final rupture of the treaty, but there will be only matters for conferences and negotiations; or, in other words, a suspension of action until the reasons for refusing may have been considered and weighed in due form.*"[1]

When did Nicaragua ask Costa Rica to give the guarantee?

She never did, because on her own part she would have had to submit herself to the same burden.

The guarantee had been set aside, in fact, from the time of the making of the contract; and if it is now spoken of it is only because it furnishes one of those means to which the contending parties are accustomed to resort to under certain circumstances in support of untenable causes.

---

[1] Droit International, &c., Part 1, § 729.

Chapter XV.

EXAMINATION OF THE LATTER REASONS ALLEGED BY NICARAGUA IN SUPPORT OF HER THEORY THAT THE TREATY OF LIMITS IS INVALID.

It is said that the treaty of limits abridges the sovereignty of Nicaragua, deeply wounds her dignity, and causes great injury to her interests.

I have already transcribed what Gen. Don Joaquin Zavala set forth in connection with this point, and was assented to and confirmed by the Nicaraguan Secretary of State, Don Anselmo H. Rivas.

By the explicit confession of the Nicaraguan Government the validity of the treaty is not impeached because it lacks this or the other formality; but because it is alleged that it does injury to the interests of Nicaragua, and wounds her national pride, and abridges her sovereign rights.

But when or where has it happened that the interest of one of the contracting parties is a legitimate cause for the nullification of the compacts? There is no Code in the world which has ever sanctioned such an immoral principle; while, on the contrary, every law and statute ever enacted establishes that a contract once made and perfected is the law to which the contracting parties must submit on the particular matter which has been the subject of their agreement; and that neither of the said parties can be released from their respective engagements and exempted from complying with them except by mutual consent.

This principle governs the contractual relations both among private parties and nations. It would be tedious, and even offending to the common sense of humanity, to look for authorities in support of these views.

An equitable arrangement, secured by the mediation of a friendly government, whose offices have been accepted with gratitude, setting at rest a controversy which had been pending for many years—sometimes in quiet diplomatic discussion, sometimes little less than with arms in hand—never can be construed as an abridgement of the sovereignty, or as a wound to the dignity and pride of the nation which assented to it.

All nations adjust by settlements of this kind the differences which unavoidably arise among them, and by these arrangements they rather reaffirm their independence, and secure all the benefits which peace brings with it.

By the treaty of limits the Nicaraguan Territory, far from having sustained any kind of dismemberment, proved on the contrary to have been enlarged ; and this is shown by historical documents of incontrovertible strength, which I have quoted elsewhere. But supposing that this is not the fact, and that Nicaragua actually gave up a portion of more or less extent of her territory, who has ever said that such giving up brings with it the nullity of the compact by which it was witnessed ? A nation can never renounce her own independence as an individual can never alienate his freedom ; and the compact where such things were stipulated would be void in itself. But nations can renounce and give up, and they do so daily, a portion of their territory, without any attempt having ever been made, except the present one of Nicaragua, to nullify the agreement on this ground.

Should such a principle be admitted, there would be no nation who would acknowledge to be bound by international compacts affecting their frontiers. Mexico would come and ask for the nullification of the treaty of Guadalupe-Hidalgo, made by her with the United States in 1848. Guatemala would come also and claim that her treaty with Mexico, of 1883, is null and void, and the result would be, in fine, that the repulsive and famous dream of Hobbes, "the war of all against all," would be realized.

The principle which I maintain is so universally admitted that not even in case of war, in which force, it might be said, is the cause which elicits the consent, the invalidity of the compact cannot be claimed.

In connection with this, Dalloz says as follows:

"To show that these treaties (the unequal ones) are binding upon the contracting parties, it is enough to think that when two nations resort to war, they accept beforehand the consequences of their action. Each one on its part hopes to succeed against the other, and both must abide by the result. The one who cedes something would certainly, if victorious, have demanded the same thing, and the title so acquired would have been considered by it no less valid and permanent. If the title is good when in favor of one, it must also be good when in favor of the other."

"It is a matter of public interest that every agreement or compact should be held binding upon the parties who enter into it; and besides this there is another consideration which must be taken into account when the agreement or compact is a treaty of peace. This treaty is a compromise between the conqueror and the conquered, and a protection for the latter against the former because it affords the only way of escaping the law of might. The conquered party submits to sacrifices, but it has to abide by its promises, since otherwise the conqueror, being unable to rely on its faith, would be compelled to protract the war.

To secure the reign of order among the different states, it is absolutely necessary that their respective engagements and compromises should be held sacred.[1]

When nations (the same as private parties) think they have been wronged by the provisions of the treaties entered into by them, the way to obtain redress, suggested by reason and principle, is not to denounce them; but to enter into negotiations for the purposes of obtaining the desired change, always upon the impregnable foundation of the RESPECT OF THE PLEDGED FAITH AND THE COMPLIANCE WITH THE WORD GIVEN.

---

[1] DALLOZ. Repertoire, word Traité International, Art. 1, § 4, No. 127.

THIRD PART.

THIRD PART.

ANSWER TO THE QUESTIONS PROPOUNDED BY NICARAGUA IN REGARD TO THE RIGHT CONSTRUCTION OF THE TREATY OF LIMITS.

CHAPTER I.

WHETHER THE STARTING-POINT OF THE BORDER LINE IS MOVABLE AS THE WATERS OF THE RIVER, OR WHETHER THE COLORADO RIVER IS THE LIMIT OF NICARAGUA, AND WHETHER THE WATERS OF THE SAN JUAN RIVER CAN BE DEVIATED WITHOUT THE CONSENT OF COSTA RICA.

IN compliance with Article VI of the Convention of Arbitration concluded at Guatemala, and by telegram received at the city of San José, of Costa Rica, on the 23d of June ultimo, the Government of Nicaragua communicated with the Government of Costa Rica the eleven questions or points which the former considers to be of doubtful interpretation, and which are to be submitted additionally to the decision of the Arbitrator.

For Costa Rica there is not one single point in the treaty of limits which is not perfectly clear and intelligible, or the interpretation of which admits of any doubt. For this reason I do not submit to the consideration of the Arbitrator any question relative to this point, and shall have to confine myself to answer those which the Government of Nicaragua has propounded, and dispel any doubt which might arise therefrom.

But while it is true that the treaty is clear, it is also true that the doubts propounded by Nicaragua exhibit such subtlety and ambiguity as scarcely can be found elsewhere, the intention being transparent, that they have been formulated to evade, in a subsidiary way, the effects of the treaty of 1858, even in case that it should be held valid.

The interrogatories of Nicaragua are capable of admitting systematical arrangement and classification in relation to the different subjects to which they refer respectively; and so, in order to avoid repetitions and to present in its true light each one of these subjects, it has seemed to me advisable to somewhat modify the order in which the questions appear stated and form several groups which may be studied intelligently and more conveniently.

The first group of questions herein referred to consists of questions Nos. 1, 7 and 9, such as stated on pages 9 and 10, and read as follows:

"(1.) Punta de Castilla having been designated as the beginning of the border line on the Atlantic side, and finding itself according to the same treaty, at the mouth of the San Juan river; now that the mouth of the river has been changed, from where shall the boundary start?"

"(7.) If, in view of Article V of the treaty, the branch of the San Juan river known as the Colorado river must be considered as the limit between Nicaragua and Costa Rica, from its origin to its mouth on the Atlantic?"

"(9.) The eminent domain over the San Juan river from its origin in the Lake and down to its mouth on the Atlantic, belonging to Nicaragua according to the text of the treaty, can Costa Rica reasonably deny her the right of deviating those waters?"

I shall set forth at the outset that question No. 1 is ambiguous and admits of three interpretations, as it may mean either that the new mouth of the San Juan river is the Colorado river, into which a great part of the waters of the former have been emptied; or that the new mouth is the branch named Taura, also a large one during late years; or that it is the "Caño de Animas," which is nearer to the original mouth than the Taura and the Colorado rivers.

Owing to this ambiguity of the question, three different answers have to be given.

The San Juan river, which is the outlet (Desaguadero) of the Lake of Nicaragua, carries the waters of this lake to the Caribbean Sea through a course of about 150 miles, but in reaching a certain point, some miles distant from the coast in a straight line, forks itself in two branches, one of which runs towards the east, which is called the Colorado river, while the other, which is the trunk, continues towards the north and empties into the Bay of San Juan, not, however, without having formed two other branches at a short distance from the mouth, which are the streams named Taura and Caño de Animas.

The map which I accompany hereto, marked No. II, made in 1851 by Baron A. Von Bulow, shows the course of the San Juan river and the peculiar shape of its delta, divided into two islands, one between the San Juan and the Taura rivers, and the other between the Taura and the Colorado rivers.

The location and course of the new stream called Caño de Animas is also shown by Map No. XI appended to the "Report of the United States Nicaraguan Surveying Party, 1885, by Civil Engineer A. G. Menocal, U. S. N.," a copy of which I also append.

On the left side of the Bay, on the ancient mouth of the river, the port of San Juan del Norte, otherwise called Greytown, is situated, and on the right there is the strip of land, the extremity of which is known by the name of Punta de Castilla Point.

These geographical antecedents having been given, nothing is easier than rightly understanding Article II of the treaty of limits of April 15, 1858, and satisfactorily answering the three questions propounded.

Article II of the treaty reads, that the dividing line between the two Republics will begin at the extremity of Punta de Castilla Point on the mouth of the San Juan river, and that it will continue along the right bank—that is, the Costa Rican bank—of the same river up to a certain point three English miles distant from Castillo Viejo. Therefore it is plain that both Punta de Castilla Point and the whole delta formed by the San Juan and Colorado rivers are Costa Rican territory.

The question propounded by the Government of Nicaragua might, indeed, have been formulated in a plainer way, as follows: " Whether in spite that the treaty of limits of April 15, 1858, establishes that the starting-point of the border line between the two Republics on the side of the Caribbean sea is the extremity of Punta de Castilla Point, and that the frontier runs from there along the right bank of the San Juan river up to a point three miles before reaching Castillo Viejo, would it be permissible for Nicaragua to remove that starting-point and that frontier, and carry both to either Caño de Animas or the Taura river, or, better still, the Colorado river, which are within the Costa Rican territory and in the delta formed by the Colorado and San Juan rivers, for the reason that, subsequently to the treaty of 1858, the volume of the waters of the San Juan river has decreased, and because the Colorado river has become more copious, and because new mouths have been opened on the sea, always inside the delta belonging to Costa Rica?"

The rigor of logic demands that this question should be answered negatively. The three mouths of the Colorado, the Taura and the San Juan rivers, which now exist, also existed at the time in which the treaty was made. The three rivers then flowed to the Atlantic as now, and each one had its own separate and distinct mouth. What happened with them in 1858 is the same that happens at present, through a tract of many miles. And the limit ascribed by the treaty to the two Republics is neither the Colorado river, nor the Taura stream, nor the Caño de Animas, but the river or branch which was known at the date of the compact by the name of the San Juan river, at the extremity of the right bank of which Punta de Castilla Point is found.

The geographical point named in 1858, the mouth of the San Juan river, has not changed its position, although it may be that the volume of waters emptied through it into the ocean is now less than in 1858, and although it may be also that the waters of the Colorado river have increased or found new outlets through the Caño de Animas or any other opening.

Both legally and geographically each one of these points is different and independent of the other, as well as perfectly visible, and no one of the contracting parties can be allowed by its own will, and according to its own convenience, to take the one for the other.

In other words, the geographical point, which, in the treaty of 1858, was called the mouth of the San Juan river, has not changed in position, whatever the capricious course of its waters (which never have run on the same bed) might have been. The Bay of San Juan de Nicaragua, where Greytown is located, is now found in the same place where it always was, where it appears to have been by all the maps contemporary to the treaty; and the mouth of the Colorado river, much more to the south, is found now exactly on the same place as it was in the beginning, and the mouth of the Taura river is now also where it was. The geographical position of all these places remains the same as when the treaty was made, and the number of new mouths, or outlets, or openings, which may have been made afterwards is absolutely immaterial.

The work of nature has produced a diminution of water in the San Juan river, and a correlative increase in that of the Colorado river, and also new outlets or mouths; but this circumstance does not affect, nor can it affect, the geographical limit fixed by the treaty, which is perfectly clear and visible, as said before, and is not movable like the waters.

The point, or cape, named in the treaty of 1858 "Punta de Castilla," is, and has to be, the end of the line on the Atlantic side because the treaty says so; that "Punta de Castilla" is not, nor has it ever been, at the mouth of the

Colorado river, nor at the mouth of the Taura stream, nor at any bank of the " Caño de Animas," nor at any other place which Nicaragua may now be pleased to call the mouth of the San Juan river; but at the right bank of the mouth that the San Juan river had on the 15th of April, 1858, when the treaty of limits was concluded.

Supposing, *gracia arguendi*, that the Colorado river, the mouth of the Taura river, and the " Caño de Animas " were not, as they are, geographical entities different from the San Juan river, existing, and recognized to exist, when the treaty was made ; and, also, that the old bed of the San Juan river was left dry, and that the whole mass of the waters of that river flowed into the bed of the Colorado river, or emptied either through the mouths above named, or through some others unknown—even in that case it would be plain that " Punta de Castilla," the point, or cape, which existed in 1858, and the ancient bed of the San Juan river, the bed through which it flowed in 1858, shall continue to be the border line between the two nations.

International law does not allow any doubt upon this subject.

In 1856, Mr. Caleb Cushing, Attorney-General of the United States, was called to give his authorized opinion in regard to it.

A portion of the frontier between the United States and Mexico is marked by the Rio Grande or Bravo river, which is subject to frequent changes in its course, and often leaves its bed to empty into the Gulf of Mexico through other outlets. The opinion of Mr. Cushing was asked, on November 11, 1858, on the question, whether the border line between both countries changes together with the river, or whether it is stationary, and constantly remains at the place where the bed of the river originally stood, even if it is dry.

The answer of Mr. Cushing, which can be consulted on page 175 and the following, of Volume VIII of the Opinions of the Attorneys-General of the United States, is a complete, conscientious, and really masterly work. The doctrine explained by him was accepted and endorsed by the Government of the United States, and it is held to be an authority on the subject, in Vol. I of the Digest of the International Law of the United States of Dr. Wharton, Chapter II, § 30, page 96.

Mr. Cushing says:

"If, deserting its original bed, the river forces for itself a new channel in another direction, * * * THE BOUNDARY REMAINS IN THE MIDDLE OF THE DESERTED RIVER BED. For, in truth, just as a stone pillar constitutes a boundary, not because it is a stone, but because of the place in which it stands, so a river is made the limit of nations, not because it is running water bearing a certain geographical name, but because it is water FLOWING IN A GIVEN CHANNEL AND WITHIN GIVEN BANKS, WHICH ARE THE REAL INTERNATIONAL BOUNDARY."

"Such is," Mr. Cushing says further, "the received rule of the law of nations on this point as laid down by all the writers of authority." (See ex. gr. Puffend., Jus Nat., Lib. IV, cap. 7, sec. II ; Gundling, Jus Nat., p. 248 ; Wolff, Jus Gentium, s. 106-109 ; Vattel, Droit des Gens., Liv. I, chap. 22, s. 268, 270 ; Stypmanni, Jus Marit., Cap. V, n. 476-552 ; Rayneval, Droit de la Nature, Tom. I, p. 307 ; Merlin, Répertoire, ss. voc. alluv.)

"I might multiply citations to this point from the books of public law. But in order that either the United States or the Mexican Republic, whichever in the lapse of time shall happen to be inconveniently affected by the application of this rule, may be fully reconciled thereto, it seems well to show that it is conformable to the common law of both countries."

To prove that this is the law of Mexico, and of the countries of Spanish origin, Mr. Cushing quotes from Riquelme, Don Andres Bello and Don José Maria de Pando, as well as from the "Derecho Público" by Almeda.

"Don Antonio Riquelme," he says, "states the doctrine as follows:

"When a river changes its course, directing its currents through the territory of one of the two coterminous States, THE BED WHICH IT LEAVES DRY REMAINS * * * RETAINED AS THE LIMIT BETWEEN THE TWO NATIONS; and the river enters so far into the exclusive dominion of the nation through whose territory it takes the new course." (Derecho Internacional, vol. I, p. 83).

"Don Andres Bello and Don José Maria de Pando," Mr. Cushing continues, "both enunciate the doctrine in exactly the same words, namely:

"When a river or lake divides two territories * * * the rights which either has in the lake or river do not undergo any change by reason of alluvion. * * * If, by any natural accident, the water which separated the two States *enters of a sudden into the territory of the other*, it will thenceforth belong to the State whose soil it occupies, and *the land, including the abandoned river channel or bed, will incur no change of master*." (Bello, Derecho Internacional, p. 38; Pando, Derecho Internacional, p. 99).

Mr. Cushing quotes, furthermore, copiously from the Roman civil law, from the civil law of Spain, from that of Mexico, and from the laws in force in England and in the United States; and especially in regard to the latter from Bracton de Legg. Angliæ, from Blackstone's Commentaries, from Woolrych, and from Angel on Water-courses.

In addition to the opinion of Mr. Cushing, many others can be cited whose authority it is impossible to deny.

Sir Traver Twiss, Counsel for the Crown in the Great British Empire and Regius Professor of International Law in the University of Oxford, maintains the same doctrine, and supports it on the authority of Grotius and Martens.[1]

Grotius says:

"A river that separates two empires is not to be considered barely as water, *but as water confined within such and such*

---

[1] The Law of Nations. Oxford, 1861, page 208.

banks, and running in such and such a channel; therefore, the addition, subtraction, or such changes of its particles as allow the whole to subsist in its ancient form, allows the river to be considered as the same. * * * *If a river should have become dried up, the middle of the channel would remain as before, the boundary of empire between two nations.*"

Martens, in his "Précis du Droit des Gens," says:

"In case that a river should change completely its bed, the bed dried up would remain, dividing the two nations as the river divided them before."[1]

Calvo, in his famous "Traité du Droit international théorique et pratique," expresses himself as follows:

"When a river has opened for itself a new bed or channel through the neighboring lands, or when a lake has opened new outlets or divides itself into several branches, *the political frontier of the bordering states does not remain for that less fixed or established in the same places in which it was before.*"[2]

Bluntschli says:

"When the river completely abandons its bed to flow in another direction, *the ancient channel continues to be the dividing line.*"[3]

Woolsey, in his excellent "Introduction to the Study of the International Law," decides the question in the same way, and uses the following language:

"Where a navigable river forms the boundary between two states, both are presumed to have free use of it, and the dividing line will run in the middle of the channel unless the contrary is shown by long occupancy or agreement of the parties. *If a river changes its bed, the line through the old channel continues.*"[4]

Halleck, in his "International Law," Chapter VI, § 25, says as follows:

---

[1] MARTENS. Précis du Droit des Gens, § 39.
[2] Book IV, § 294.
[3] Le Droit Internationel Codifié, Art. 299.
[4] Woolsey, § 62.

"Where the river abandons its ancient bed and forms a new channel, or where a lake leaves its former banks and forms a new lake or a series of new lakes, *the boundaries of the states remain in the abandoned bed of the river or in the position formerly occupied by the lake.*"

And the American statesman who now presides over the Foreign Office of the United States, the Hon. Secretary of State, Mr. Bayard, has rested on these grounds, and maintained in regard to the Rio Grande, or Bravo, river, which marks for a long space the Mexican boundary, the following doctrine:

"It may be proper to add that it has been held in this Department that when, through the changing of the channel of the Rio Grande, the distance of an island in the river from the respective shores has been changed, the line adjusted by the Commissioners under the treaty is nevertheless to remain as originally drawn."[1]

(Mr. Bayard, Secretary of State, to Mr. Bowen, June 12, 1885).

It results from the above, that the first question propounded by Nicaragua ought to be answered, upon the authority of all writers on International Law, in the following way: The dividing line between Costa Rica and Nicaragua is the one marked by the treaty of 1858, and no other. This line starts from the cape, or point, named "Punta de Castilla," and runs along the right bank of the stream which at that date was known by the name of the San Juan river; and this will be the case, even if that stream, whether trunk, or branch, or river, would abandon its course, and the whole of its waters would empty into the Atlantic through the channels of the Colorado river, or the Taura, or the "Caño de Animas," or any other whatsoever.

Passing now to answer question No. 7, I have to say in the same way that the Colorado river can never be considered

---

[1] Dr. Wharton's Digest, Vol. I, Chapter II, § 30, p. 95.

as the boundary, or frontier, between the two nations, unless Article II of the treaty, which reads that said limit shall be the San Juan river, from Punta de Castilla up to a point three English miles distant from Castillo Viejo, is wholly wiped out or ignored. The said limit, besides being specifically established by the treaty, is, as it has been shown, according to the principles of law, and the universal practice among nations, permanent and unchangeable, even in case that the San Juan river should lose, what has never happened, nor probably will ever happen, the whole of its waters.

This conclusion is not modified, but, on the contrary, strengthened and confirmed by the language of Art. V of the treaty, according to which, and only temporarily and transiently, as long as certain circumstances, which afterwards disappeared, should exist, Nicaragua had the right to enjoy, in common with Costa Rica, not the sovereignty, because this belongs to Costa Rica, but the use and possession of the delta.

Article V of the treaty reads as follows :

" As long as Nicaragua does not recover the full possession of all her rights in the port of San Juan del Norte, the point named Punta de Castilla shall be used and possessed entirely and equally and in common by both Nicaragua and Costa Rica; and the whole course of the Colorado river shall be the boundary as long as this community of use and possession lasts. And it is further stipulated that as long as the said port of San Juan del Norte exists classified as free, Costa Rica shall not collect from Nicaragua port dues at Punta de Castilla."

The course of the Colorado river was given as limit by Article V of the treaty, only *during the precarious possession* allowed by Costa Rica to Nicaragua, and as long as Nicaragua should remain deprived of her port of San Juan del Norte, and by no means as a final and perpetual boundary between the two Republics, which was established by Article II of the treaty, when it was provided that it should run from Punta de Castilla along the right bank of the San Juan river up to three miles from Castillo Viejo.

The special circumstances referred to in Article V of the treaty of 1858 disappeared on the 28th of January, 1860, by the treaty concluded between Nicaragua and Great Britain, and is known by the name of the Zeledon-Wyke treaty. Nicaragua recovered under this treaty the sovereignty, use, possession, and enjoyment of the port of San Juan; and, ever since, the precarious possession of the Costa Rican delta, allowed by Costa Rica to Nicaragua, ceased to exist in fact and in law.

Article V of the treaty has not at present any practical application, and only belongs to history. But even admitting that the special circumstances which gave birth to it are still in existence, and that Nicaragua is not yet in full possession of the port of San Juan del Norte, and that her commerce is now, as it was in 1858, obstructed on the side of the Caribbean Sea, the alleged doubt of Nicaragua should always be not only absurd and unjust, but even an attack on the rights of Costa Rica. The most that Nicaragua could ask under those circumstances would be the use and possession in common, but never the ownership, or sovereignty, or an extension of territory, or change of the frontier, against the plain language of Article II of the treaty of 1858, which says that the San Juan river, not the Colorado, shall be the border line between the two Republics.

This doubt No. 7 is one of those which render the spirit of Nicaragua in the present controversy perfectly patent. Costa Rica, by an act of most special favor or graciousness, granted Nicaragua the use of Punta de Castilla as long as she would remain deprived by Great Britain of her own port of San Juan del Norte. And now, seventeen years after she was restored to the possession of that port, she comes and founds upon that favor a claim to the ownership of what she herself declared not to belong to her.

This question No. 7 is answered by itself. It carries with it the most emphatic negative.

As to the ninth question, that is, whether Nicaragua can change the course of the San Juan river, at any place between its origin in the lake and its mouth on the Atlantic, and whether Costa Rica can reasonably deny her the right to deviate the waters of that river, the answer seems to be very obvious.

It is to be remarked at the outset, that even if the said operations were permissible for Nicaragua, the location of the border line would not suffer thereby any change, because, as it has been shown, the said frontier would continue to be marked by the ancient bed, and would run, in the same way as before, along the right bank of the said bed, as stated in Art. II of the treaty of limits of 1858. But as the deviation of the waters, independently of all questions of limits, would cause Costa Rica to suffer considerable · detriment and losses of all kinds, not owing to the unavoidable action of nature through physical causes beyond the control of man, but owing to the deliberate will of Nicaragua, the question whether Costa Rica has the right to oppose such a thing appears to be almost inconceivable.

Art. VI of the treaty of limits of 1858 recognizes, in favor of Costa Rica, the "perpetual right of navigation" in the waters of the San Juan river, between the point within three miles of Castillo Viejo and the mouth of the river on the Atlantic Ocean; and although it is true that it was also stipulated that Nicaragua should have the sovereignty and eminent domain over the waters of the said river, said sovereignty and eminent domain are to be understood with the restriction that the right of perpetual navigation of Costa Rica imposes upon them. Nicaragua has the power to do in the San Juan river, by virtue of sovereignty, all that she may be pleased to do, provided that she does not abridge or destroy, through her action, the rights acquired by Costa Rica. Otherwise, the said rights which Costa Rica secured by the treaty, not gratuitously, but in exchange of and in compensation for other rights, that it had prior to the treaty and gave up by it, would become illusory.

This doctrine is well settled in municipal law. The one who has the direct ownership of one thing cannot render the condition of this thing worse, or injure the position of the other party which has the right of possession. The rights of the owner are limited by the rights of the *cestuy que use.*

In addition to this, and leaving aside all the former considerations, it will be easy to understand that when a country has for its boundary a water front as extensive as the Costa Rican bank of the San Juan river is, innumerable and considerable and legitimate interests of all kinds must necessarily have been created in the neighborhood of that stream, which it is indispensable to respect.

The vast and fertile northern territories of Costa Rica are now to a great extent owned and occupied by private parties, who, in acquiring them, had very specially in view their location near a navigable river, or adjoining to it, or to its affluents, and the propinquity to the place through which some day the interoceanic canal shall pass. Let it be said, therefore, if the waters referred to, such as they are at present, and as now kept by the hand of God, are, or are not, necessary for Costa Rica.

That necessity cannot be evaded or left unsatisfied only because Nicaragua may deem it advisable for her, whether in use or in abuse of her sovereignty, to force those waters into different channels.

If the deviation were due to natural causes, then it would be necessary for all parties concerned to submit to the loss sustained if the remedy was impossible; but, it being the act of the free and deliberate will of the neighboring nation, it would admit of but one construction, consisting in looking at that act as one of extreme hostility.

Woolsey, in his Introduction to the Study of International Law above quoted, clearly explains (§ 62) that such a deviation would be illegal, and that it cannot be recognized by law. The same doctrine is held by many other writers upon this subject, from whom I do not quote, not to give too much length to this argument.

In the United States, perhaps more than in any other country, by virtue of the blessing bestowed by Heaven upon them, among many others, of having so many and such copious rivers, and of the circumstance that many of them mark, as the San Juan river does between Costa Rica and Nicaragua, the dividing line between their several States, the matter now discussed has been studied carefully and settled justly, through an uninterrupted current of legal decisions.

It would be sufficient to cast a rapid glance at the standard work written by Angel, under the title of " A Treatise on the Law of Water-courses,'" to find there most abundant precedents in support of the doctrine which I maintain in this argument.

In Chapter IV, Sec. 2, of that book, devoted to the study of " the damage done by voluntary deviation " of the waters, innumerable decisions will be found rendered by the courts of Illinois, Connecticut, New York, Maine, Massachusetts, New Hampshire, &c., &c., all of them recognizing the legal principle, "*sic utere tuo ut alienum non ledas*," and subjecting to responsibility those who, for their own profit and to the detriment of others, divert from its ordinary channel the waters of a river.

In Chapter XI of the same book, devoted to the study of the eminent domain or sovereign rights of a nation in their relations with this particular subject of deviation of the waters and change of their distribution, the same legal doctrine is held to rule supremely, and is fully vindicated.

Among the great number of cases and authorities therein referred to, the one which relates to the Blackstone river, which divides the States of Rhode Island and Massachusetts, and the course of which had been changed, or ordered to be changed, by a law enacted by the Legislature of Rhode Island, to the detriment of existing rights and interests of Massachusetts, is particularly applicable to the point now under consideration. It was decided, in that case, that the State of

Rhode Island, or its Legislature, had no power to do such a thing.[1]

But the best proof which can be given of the fact that the doctrine herein held by me is the only legitimate and correct one will be found in the explicit sanction which Nicaragua herself has given to it.

By Article VIII of the treaty of limits of 1858 it was stipulated that, before entering into any contract of canalization or transit, Costa Rica should be consulted; and the reason of this provision was, as plainly stated in Article VIII, because of the "disadvantages that the transaction might produce" for Costa Rica. This was proper and just, as, also, was the stipulation that the opinion of Costa Rica should not be merely advisory and consultative, but an actual vote, when the disadvantages alluded to were such as "to injure" the natural rights of Costa Rica.

Natural rights, disadvantages, injury, necessity of consultation, the right of veto, if such can be said, have been acknowledged; and all of this means that Costa Rica has a perfect and indisputable right to oppose the deviation of the course of the San Juan river.

If Costa Rica has this right when the work to be done refers exclusively to canalization and transit, how can it be denied when the work to be done is the radical one of carrying the river elsewhere, and depriving Costa Rica of the long river front which she now enjoys?

---

[1] Angel on Water-Courses, chap. xii, p. 507.

Chapter II.

WHETHER MEN-OF-WAR OR REVENUE CUTTERS OF COSTA RICA CAN NAVIGATE ON THE SAN JUAN RIVER.

By the necessity of system, and following the plan initiated, I must now pass to occupy myself with question No. 8, propounded by Nicaragua.

This question reads as follows:

"*Eight.*

"If Costa Rica, who, according to Article VI of the treaty, has only the right of free navigation for the purposes of commerce in the waters of the San Juan river, can also navigate with men-of-war or revenue cutters in the same waters?"

In order that the language be precise, and that the meaning of the compact should not be modified by the introduction of a word, I must begin by calling the attention of the arbitrator to the fact that the word *only* which occurs in the question does not occur in Article VI of the treaty of limits.

That article simply reads in this way:

"But the Republic of Costa Rica shall have in the said waters the perpetual rights of navigation, from the above said mouth up to a point three English miles distant from Castillo Viejo, for the purposes of commerce, either with Nicaragua or with the interior of Costa Rica," &c.

Does this mean that Costa Rica cannot under any circumstances navigate with public vessels in the said waters, whether the said vessel is properly a man-of-war, or simply a revenue cutter, or any other vessel intended to prevent smuggling, or to carry orders to the authorities of the bordering districts, or for any other purpose not exactly within the meaning of transportation of merchandise?

The answer seems to be very simple, especially when the

fact is taken into consideration that, under no circumstances whatever, even in case of war, acts of hostility can be done by either of the two Republics against the other in the waters of the river, or of the Lake of Nicaragua, or the Bay of San Juan.

It seems to be beyond discussion that Costa Rica can navigate in the San Juan river with public vessels, which are not properly men-of-war.

It was stipulated in the treaty, to the benefit of Nicaragua, that Nicaraguan vessels could bring their cargoes to the Costa Rican bank of the river and unload them there; and this permission, or right, presupposes, necessarily, the correlative right of Costa Rica to watch its own banks by the only practicable means, which is the revenue police, during the whole course of the river navigable for Costa Rica.

If this only means of vigilance would not be permitted, the Costa Rican commerce would be deprived of protection and at the mercy of smuggling.

Within the meaning of the words, commercial navigation, both the revenue police, the carrying of the mails, and all other public services of the same kind are necessarily included.

In regard to men-of-war, there is no reason why they cannot be admitted upon the waters of the San Juan river.

Carlos Calvo, in his work already cited, Book IV, § 230, says the following: * * * "In principle, a port of free entry is considered tacitly as one accessible to the men-of-war of all nations, and, unless stipulated to the contrary, the free access granted to all merchant vessels is extended to war vessels of the friendly nations. This is a point upon which all writers of public law fully agree."

By analogy, this doctrine can be perfectly well applied to the navigable rivers; and if all the friendly nations have the right to navigate with men-of-war in the large rivers, why can the right of Costa Rica to do the same thing on the San Juan river be disputed by Nicaragua, who is separated from her only by the river ? How can that right be disputed when the fact is taken into consideration that before the treaty of 1858 Costa Rica was co-owner of the San Juan river, and that by the treaty itself Costa Rica reserved for herself the perpetual right of navigation in the same river, and that, in fine, the compact does not read that Costa Rica has the said right of navigation *only* for purposes of commerce, and for no other ?

And if the limitation of the rights of Costa Rica is to be derived from the alleged fact that the treaty only mentions commercial purposes, such an argument could be met at once with the assertion that the maxim, *qui dicit de uno negat de altero*, is only applicable when the thing affirmed excludes the other, which does not happen in this case.

Even in those very rare instances in which the navigation with vessels of war is forbidden, as it happens in the Dardanelles, the prohibition has not been made except by specia convention, in the absence of which it would be difficult for the Porte to close the Dardanelles or the Bosphorus against vessels of war.

Something similar to this happens in the Black Sea. By the treaty of Paris, of March 30, 1856, the neutrality of the Black Sea was declared exactly in the same way as the neutrality of the San Juan river, the port of San Juan, and the Lake of Nicaragua, as far at least as Nicaragua and Costa Rica are respectively concerned, was declared by the treaty of San José, of April 15, 1858. It was also declared in the former treaty that the Black Sea was open to the commerce of the world, and so are also the waters of the river, port, and lake above mentioned, at least for the two Republics.

The treaty of Paris forbade " formally and perpetually that vessels of war, whether of the bordering nations, or of any other whatsoever, should navigate in the Black Sea." But soon the necessity was recognized of establishing there some force to do the shore service ; and the same treaty provided the manner in which Russia and Turkey should enter into some agreement in regard to this point.

As it is known, there are now in those waters a certain number of steamers of no more than 800 tons burden, and some sailing vessels of certain dimensions agreed upon by both parties; but all of them men-of-war and belonging to the two nations.[1]

As remarked by Dr. Wharton, in his Digest, in reference to the work of Fauchille (Blocus Maritime, Paris, 1882), one thing is the neutrality of certain waters, and the prohibition for the nations who so stipulated it to commit hostilities against each other in the said waters, and another, and a very different thing, is to navigate in those waters with vessels of war.

So it is that Costa Rica and Nicaragua cannot wage war against each other in the San Juan river, but, nevertheless, they can navigate with men-of-war in the waters thereof.

And certainly Nicaragua is, perhaps, the nation who has proclaimed most loudly the distinction above referred to. She has concluded several treaties with different European nations, and has stipulated in them that the waters of the interoceanic canal, the waters of the San Juan river being included in them (if the canal is ever built) shall be neutral; but, nevertheless, she has permitted the said nations to navigate the said canal with vessels of war, and to station there armed forces for the purpose of protecting commerce and the interests of the foreign citizens or subjects of the contracting nations which might be in danger.

So it was stipulated with France, by Article IX of the treaty of the 11th of April, 1859; with Great Britain, in Article XXII of the treaty of February 11, 1860; and with the United States of America, by Article XXI of the treaty of June 21, 1867.

---

[1] Woolsey, § 61.
Dr. Wharton's Digest, chap. ii, § 40, p. 169.

Costa Rica might claim the same privilege granted to the three above-named nations, because, under Article IV of the treaty of August 14, 1868, between Nicaragua and Costa Rica, it was provided that everything granted to any nation whatsoever by either contracting party must be at once understood to be common to the other. This stipulation would give Costa Rica the right to place on the waters of the San Juan river, in the event foreseen, and for the purposes had in view by these treaties, all kinds of men-of-war.

But there is, after all, a fundamental consideration which is perplexing, not, certainly, on account of the decision to be given to the point in question, but owing to the difficulty of understanding how the Government of Nicaragua could ever consider this point of the treaty of limits of 1858 to be doubtful and admit of different interpretations.

All that I have said in this portion of my work in explanation of the facts and law which relate to the subject might be erroneous, badly brought, irrelevant, and absolutely inadmissible on general principles, and, nevertheless, it would be true that Costa Rica can navigate with men-of-war and other Government vessels on the waters of the San Juan river. It is Nicaragua herself who has solemnly granted that right by an article of that very same treaty which she alleges to be doubtful or capable of different interpretation.

"Costa Rica shall also be bound," says the second part of Article IV of the treaty, " owing to the portion of the right bank of the San Juan river, which belongs to it, * * * to co-operate in its custody; and the two Republics shall equally concur in its defence in case of foreign aggressions ; and this will be done by them with all the efficiency that may be within their reach."

It can be seen by these phrases, as plainly and transparently as they can be, that Costa Rica has not only the right but the duty, or to follow exactly the language of the treaty, the " obligation," not only of watching, guarding, and defending its own river bank, but of contributing to the custody and defence of the other bank belonging to Nicaragua.

If that duty should not be complied with *with all the* efficiency within the reach of Costa Rica, the latter nation would violate an obligation contracted in a solemn treaty, and Nicaragua might prefer against Costa Rica a well-grounded charge. And if this is the case, how can it be possible for Nicaragua to suppose that Costa Rica has no authority to navigate in the said river with Government vessels to be used in the police service of the locality, and in the custody of the two banks, and with regular men-of-war to be used in the defence, as efficient as possible, of the same banks in case of foreign aggressions?

No one can accomplish a purpose, unless he has the means to do it; and it would be against logic and reason to impose upon, either a man or a government, the duty of *guarding* and *defending* a place, and at the same time deprive the one or the other of the right of arming or preparing themselves for resisting in the proper manner the aggression foreseen.

"The right to a thing," says Wheaton, "gives also the right to the means without which that thing cannot be used." (Part III, chap. IV, § 18). "This is founded on natural reason, is accredited by the common opinion of mankind, and is declared by the writers."

Let it not be said that the authority to navigate with men-of-war is only confined to the special case of foreign aggression. The treaty does not refer to this case exclusively, but speaks also of guard or custody, which means watching, vigilance, and other things of permanent character and necessarily previous to actual defence. This, especially in a river, cannot be improvised at the very same instant that trouble arises; since, in order that it may be possible and efficient, a perfect knowledge of the locality, which cannot be acquired except by navigating the same river, is absolutely indispensable.

Much more so when it is well known that the navigation of the San Juan river encounters many obstacles, not only on account of its shallowness at certain places, but also owing to its rapids and other dangers. The defence of a river of this kind, without practical knowledge of all its peculiarities, rather than defence would be a sure surrender to the enemy of the elements brought into action to oppose it.

Let it not be claimed either that Costa Rica is relieved from the duty assumed by her of guarding and defending the river, nor that such duty has ceased or been abridged through the fact that Nicaragua denies to her the right to navigate said river with men-of-war; because the navigation of the San Juan river, which is the boundary between Costa Rica and Nicaragua, and is a boundary open and accessible to invasions by all kinds of enemies, was mentioned in the treaty, not simply for the benefit of Nicaragua, and as an obligation on the part of Costa Rica, but because it involves also a sacred right of the most vital importance for its safety and preservation.

CHAPTER III.

WHETHER COSTA RICA IS BOUND TO CO-OPERATE IN THE PRESERVATION AND IMPROVEMENT OF THE SAN JUAN RIVER AND THE BAY OF SAN JUAN, AND IN WHAT MANNER; AND WHETHER NICARAGUA CAN UNDERTAKE ANY WORK WITHOUT CONSIDERING THE INJURY WHICH MAY RESULT TO COSTA RICA.

A NEW group of questions comes now, consisting of those which in the list of Nicaragua are marked Nos. 4, 5 and 6, and read as follows:

"4. Nicaragua consented, by Article IV, that the Bay of San Juan, which always exclusively belonged to her and over which she exercised exclusive jurisdiction, should be common to both Republics; and by Article VI she consented, also, that Costa Rica should have, in the waters of the river, from its mouth on the Atlantic up to three English miles before reaching Castillo Viejo, the perpetual right of free navigation for purposes of commerce. Is Costa Rica bound to concur with Nicaragua in the expense necessary to prevent the Bay from being obstructed, to keep the navigation of the river and port free and unembarrassed, and to improve it for the common benefit? If so—

"5. In what proportion must Costa Rica contribute? In case she has to contribute nothing—

"6. Can Costa Rica prevent Nicaragua from executing, at her own expense, the works of improvement? Or, shall she have any right to demand indemnification for the places belonging to her on the right bank, which may be necessary to occupy, or for the lands on the same bank which may be flooded or damaged in any other way in consequence of the said works?"

Denying the historical truth of the statements made in the preamble of question No. 4, and the first of this group, and referring to those chapters of the first part of this argument, wherein I showed that Costa Rica had eminent domain and sovereignty on the waters of the San Juan river previous to the treaty of 1858, and taking only into consideration the particular point of the inquiry, I think that it is necessary before all to distinguish carefully what the treaty itself has taken pains to distinguish.

The right of Costa Rica on the Bay of San Juan is a right of sovereignty which she exercises jointly and in common with Nicaragua; and the right of Costa Rica in the San Juan river, from the mouth thereof on the Atlantic, to the point three miles from Castillo Viejo, which has been fixed, is the right of use and navigation. In the former case Costa Rica is joint owner; in the latter, Costa Rica is simply the *cestuy que use;* it being expressly stipulated by Article VI that the Republic of Nicaragua shall have exclusively the eminent domain and sovereignty over the waters of the San Juan river from its rise in the lake to its mouth on the Atlantic.

It is, therefore, plain that the answer to be given to the interrogatories of Nicaragua depends entirely upon the legal status in which Costa Rica finds herself, of joint owner in the one case, and of *cestuy que use* in the other.

It might be remarked with justice that the three questions of this group should be thoroughly eliminated from the present discussion because this refers only to those points of the treaty of 1858 which Nicaragua considers to be doubtful and upon which she desires to secure the authoritative and enlightened decision of the Arbitrator, while the points involved in those questions have nothing to do directly with the treaty of limits, nor are they doubtful, nor can they be considered other than pure effects of casuistry, the solution of which in reality should not be given beforehand.

It is plain, however, and so it is stated in the present answer in order that it may never be said that Costa Rica has evaded to make any reply, that if the sovereign rights which belong to Nicaragua over the San Juan river terminate on the right bank thereof, which is the Costa Rican, and that if her rights on the river itself are limited to the perpetual use or navigation, and to the other riparian rights acknowledged by law, the duty to keep the navigation of the said river free and unembarrassed, and of contributing to the expenses for that purpose incurred, is not, nor can it be, incumbent upon her.

It seems to be in the natural order of things that the obligation to make repairs and to keep the property in the condition in which it was when the use and possession thereof was granted to another party, and the duty to pay the expenses incurred thereby, should belong to the owner.

The Roman civil law, which in the matter of rivers has been generally adopted by all nations, as remarked by Halleck[1] and declared by Wheaton, who quotes the precedent established by Mr. Jefferson in his Instruction to the United States Minister in Spain, of March 18, 1792, settled this question finally[2] and explicitly.

The *jus utendi* does not involve the obligation to pay expenses for the preservation of the thing used, nor any other expenses alluded to in questions Nos. 4 and 5.

And the right of free navigation on a river which belongs to another power does not imply either in any way whatever, no matter how remote, the obligation to pay the expenses which the owner of the said river may be pleased to incur for its preservation and improvement.

Easements are rights which men have over things belonging to others; they are burdens weighing upon these things, whether by the will of the parties, or by the force of circumstances, and certainly it would be to disturb the order of law to demand from the possessor of the easement that he should assist the owner in paying the expenses required in the preservation and improvement of the property.

---

[1] Chapter VI, § 27.
[2] Wheaton, by Lawrence. Part II, Chap. IV, § 18.

Nothing would be easier than multiplying quotations from the Pandects, and from the Institutes of Justinian, in support of this doctrine, which is truly universal because of its wisdom and truth; and there is no nation in the civilized world that has not embodied it in its laws.

In Central America, as in England and the United States and everywhere else, the obligations which refer to the ownership are incumbent upon the owner; and the *cestuy que use*, or the possessor of any easement whatsoever, is not called to share those burdens unless by agreement especially entered into by him.

The civil law of Spain, which, until very recently, constituted the fundamental basis of the Nicaraguan law, as well as that of Costa Rica, has expressly declared this principle.

" But the one who has only the right of use over a thing," says King Don Alfonso the Wise, " as was stated in the preceding law, is not bound to do any of the aforesaid things in the property over which he has that use."[1]

Those things before said are, as it can be seen by perusing the said law, " to guard, preserve, repair, and improve " the property.

If the interpretation of the legal precept were different, the most lamentable confusion of things fundamentally different by their own nature, as are the rights of ownership and use, would take place. The former represents the plenitude of power, while the latter only represents restrictions or emanations thereof.

In reference to the Bay of San Juan, over which the rights of Costa Rica are sovereign, it seems to be unnecessary to state that the limitation or abridgment of the said rights cannot take place, whether directly or indirectly, except by an act of the will of Costa Rica, and with her consent.

The history of bordering nations, joint sovereigns of streams, straits, and bays, presents numerous cases fixing

---

[1] Law XXII, Title 31, Partida III.

the rule to be observed when some work is to be done or certain measures to be taken for the preservation or improvement thereof.

What has been done in those cases was always done by the will of interested parties, by means of treaties, and specially having in sight the concrete fact, the project of the work or improvement, its plans, the estimate of its expense, and everything else necessary to give a complete idea of the subject under consideration. It is in this way, and in no other, that both Costa Rica and Nicaragua have to act in regard to the Bay of San Juan; and Costa Rica has to reserve for itself its freedom of action until seeing practically and concretely what is intended to be done to improve that Bay and prevent it from being obstructed, and before that she cannot bind herself or contract engagements for the future, upon mere general propositions, or academical themes, more properly to be discussed in the law school than in an international arbitration.

If, in the opinion of both Republics, some work is to be done, and the particulars of the work are given in such a way as is proper for all public works, then it is through an agreement or a formal treaty, concluded in accordance with the respective Constitutions of the two countries, that the said work must be undertaken and carried into effect. The mutual interests of the two parties would be sufficient to facilitate the enterprise.

On the other hand, Nicaragua and Costa Rica find themselves in regard to this point exactly in the same position. Both are joint owners of the Bay, and either of them, when considering it necessary for their mutual interests to undertake a work for preservation or improvement, must submit the project to the other.

If the scientific studies required for the work, made by agreement of both parties, lead to a decision in favor of the advisability or necessity of the said work, the latter could be undertaken either at the expense of the two parties, in equal proportion, if both of them were benefited thereby equally and without delay, or on account of whichever party was in need of it, subject to indemnification by the other party whenever it should be willing to avail itself of the improvement. Such is the doctrine of equity, and the one which universally rules in matters of joint ownership.

Referring now to Interrogatory No. 6, I shall state positively that Costa Rica has the right to prevent Nicaragua from executing, at her own cost, the works to which she alludes, whenever undertaken without consideration of the rights which belong to Costa Rica, whether as *cestuy que use* of the river, or as joint owner of the Bay, or exclusive sovereign of the right bank of the San Juan river, and of the whole of the Colorado river, or of the other lands and waters of her territory.

Costa Rica can, therefore, prevent any place on the river bank which belongs to her from being occupied. And to prevent one thing from being done is something more than asking indemnification for the occupation and for the damages done in consequence thereof, whether through the flooding of the lands, or by destruction of the river front, or for any other reason.

Nicaragua cannot do any work either on the river or bay, whether for the improvement or for the preservation of the same, without first giving notice to Costa Rica and obtaining her consent. And as Costa Rica has the perpetual right of free navigation in the river, everything which may endanger or injure or modify or abridge that right is to be considered as an attack upon her property. *Sic utere tuum ut alienum non ledas* Costa Rica will always say and repeat to her sister and neighbor, Nicaragua. "Do not touch the river which is of common possession, nor the Bay over which the two parties are sovereign, without previous deliberation and agreement upon the full knowledge of the nature of the work to be accomplished."

In regard to the occupation of any part of the Costa Rican

territory, because it may be deemed necessary for the work of improvement, scarcely can it be understood how the idea that such a thing is possible has occurred to any mind. It is true that a sovereign can, by virtue of his eminent domain, appropriate for public use and for reason of public utility, within his own dominions, and subject to indemnify the owners, such property as may be required. But when or where has the doctrine been establised that such a power can be exercised extra-territorially ?

Who gives authority to a sovereign, no matter how absolute he may be within his own dominions, to appropriate for public use any property situated within the limits of the neighboring sovereign ?

The limit of the jurisdiction of Nicaragua is fixed by the line which runs along the right bank of the San Juan river, and from there to the interior of Costa Rica the land is inviolable for Nicaragua.

If, in consequence of some work surreptitiously done on the river or port, without the consent of Costa Rica, it should happen that some lands become inundated, whether absolutely or temporarily, or that the river-bed becomes dry and Costa Rica is deprived of her river front, the right of Costa Rica to demand the restoration of everything to the same condition in which it was before, and, furthermore, the proper indemnification for damages, does not admit of contradiction.

Chapter IV.

WHICH IS THE CENTRE OF THE SALINAS BAY?—IS COSTA RICA A PARTY TO THE GRANTS OF INTEROCEANIC CANAL WHICH NICARAGUA MIGHT MAKE? —WHAT ARE, IN THIS RESPECT, THE RIGHTS OF COSTA RICA?

The fourth group of questions, or doubtful points, propounded by Nicaragua embraces the interrogatories marked Nos. 2 and 3.

They read as follows:

" 2. How shall the central point of the Salinas Bay, which is the other end of the dividing line, be fixed?

" 3. Whether by that central point we are to understand the centre of the figure; and, as it is necessary for its determination to fix the limit of the Bay towards the ocean, what shall that limit be?"

True it is that Article II of the treaty of 1858 stipulates that the boundary towards the Pacific Ocean should be marked by drawing "an astronomical line" from the point therein named "to the central point of the Salinas Bay in the Southern Sea." But also it is true that nothing can be simpler than rightly construing these words.

The central point of the Salinas Bay, which, like the Bay of San Juan, belongs to the two Republics jointly and in common, as far as domain and sovereignty are concerned (Art. IV), cannot be more than one, especially when it is to be fixed by merely drawing a line, and, much more, an astronomical or air-line, regardless of valleys, mountains, or any other obstacles of any kind. That centre, the only one possible, has to be the geometrical centre, the one in which all the lines dividing the Bay into two equal parts cross each other. The place where this happens shall be the extremity of the boundary between the two countries.

This question, rather geographical and geometrical than of

international law, is extremely easy to decide. To determine the figure of the Bay there is no necessity to go beyond its limits and enter the ocean. It is enough to draw a line which, uniting the most protruding capes of its mouth, should, as it might be said, close it entirely; and then nothing would be easier and simpler than finding the centre of the polygon, no matter how irregular, in this way obtained.

And to do so, and do it well, no survey is now needed, because the United States of America have just published an excellent map of the Salinas Bay which renders the operation extremely simple. This map is the one published under the title, "Central America : West Coast of Nicaragua ; Salinas Bay ; from a survey in 1885 by the officers of the U. S. S. *Ranger*, Commander C. E. Clark, U. S. N., comdg."

The two questions herein referred to can have only one answer, and that is that the astronomical line, spoken of by the treaty, shall end at the geometrical centre of the figure, that is, at the point in which the greater and lesser axes cross each other ; and that the waters of the Bay, although divided into two equal parts by the astronomical line, and its prolongation towards the ocean, are common to the two Republics.

Now, it is time to refer to the last group of questions, which is the fifth, and embraces the tenth and eleventh interrogatories of Nicaragua. The language of these questions is as follows :

"10. If considering that the reasons of the stipulation contained in Article VIII of the treaty have disappeared, does Nicaragua, nevertheless, remain bound not to make any grants for canal purposes across her territory without first asking the opinion of Costa Rica, as therein provided ? Which are, in this respect, the natural rights of Costa Rica alluded to by this stipulation, and in what cases must they be deemed injured ?

"11. Whether the treaty of April 15, 1858, gives Costa Rica any right to be a party to the grants of interoceanic canal which Nicaragua may make, or to share the profits that Nicaragua should reserve for herself as sovereign of the territory and waters, and in compensation of the valuable favors and privileges she may have conceded?"

Whatever answer may be given to these questions must necessarily be prefaced by the statement that the stipulation contained in Article VIII of the treaty of limits does not explain the reasons, or causes, which induced the two nations to enter into it, of which the Goverment of Nicaragua has spoken in the preamble which it was willing to make to this interrogatory, and which the said Government says to have now disappeared; nor does it either allude to them even in the most indirect manner.

Article VIII reads as follows:

" Art. VIII. If the contracts of canalization, or transit, made by the Government of Nicaragua, before its having been given notice of the present agreement, should by any reason whatever become invalidated, Nicaragua binds herself not to enter into any other contract for the aforesaid purposes without first hearing the opinion of the Government of Costa Rica as to the disadvantages that the transaction might produce for the two countries, provided that the said opinion be given within thirty days after the receipt of the communication asking for it, if Nicaragua stated that the decision was urgent; and if the natural rights of Costa Rica are not injured, then the vote of Costa Rica shall be only advisory."

In other words, if the contracts which were made before the treaty of limits of April 15, 1858, became law, were in in force, then Costa Rica would have to submit to the accomplished fact, and respect in silence the stipulations made without its consent. But if for any reason whatever those contracts became invalidated, or inoperative, Nicaragua cannot enter into any new ones without first asking Costa Rica for its opinion, not only for the reason that its "natural rights" might be affected by the transaction, but also on account of the "disadvantages" which the transaction might produce for the two countries, that is, for Costa Rica and also Nicaragua.

And if it were urgently necessary that Costa Rica should give its opinion, then the opinion should be given within thirty days.

The vote, or opinion, of Costa Rica should be simply advisory when referring to "disadvantages" common to both countries; as, for instance, interests of race, language, religion, general commerce, &c.; but it will be "resolutive," that is to say, a real vote, as it must be necessarily, when referring to a "transaction" which does injury, or hurts, or alters, or modifies, or annuls, or ignores the natural rights of Costa Rica.

Nothing is said in this article, nor in any others of the treaty, in regard to the causes which induced the two countries to enter into the agreement. Nor can it be conjectured from the language of the agreement itself, that the circumstances under which it was entered into were transient and capable of disappearing, and that they have now disappeared, as it is claimed. Should it be possible for me, in view of the absolute silence of Article VIII, to engage in such a discussion as this, I should set forth that the presumption is that the circumstances under which the treaty of 1858 was concluded were fundamentally the same as now exist.

Why was it stipulated that Costa Rica should be heard before entering into any new grants of canal, or contracts of communication, or transit, and that its vote or opinion should be advisory when referring to the "disadvantages" that the transaction might produce for the two countries, and "resolutive," or a true vote, when referring to matters which might injure, or abridge, or ignore the "natural rights" of Costa Rica? Was it not because the sovereignty over the Salinas Bay, and the Bay of San Juan, belongs to it jointly, or in common with Nicaragua, and because the right bank of the San Juan river belongs to it exclusively, and is Costa Rican territory? Was it not because by virtue of these facts of permanent character, and of the perpetual right of use and navigation in the San Juan river, it was simply natural that nothing could be done capable of changing the status of all those things without first consulting the will of Costa Rica?

The one who has dominion over a bay, although his sovereignty may not be exclusive, but in union with another sovereign, has the right of being heard and of interposing his veto in a matter upon which may depend the changing of the form of the bay, or the drying up of the same, or making it more accessible to a foreign enemy; and such a right does not depend, nor can it depend, upon circumstances which exist to-day and disappear to-morrow. That right is the natural and legitimate result of complete dominion which constitutes sovereignty and does not need to be stipulated or explained.

The same has to be said of the river banks which correspond to Costa Rica from the mouth of the San Juan river going up to within three miles of Castillo Viejo. In regard to whatever project of canalization or of transit which might affect the rights of exclusive sovereignty which Costa Rica has over that portion of the right bank of this river, which may involve the possibility of diminishing the amount of its waters or of throwing them upon Costa Rica, thereby flooding some locality, or which might make the defence of the Costa Rican territory and the same river more difficult and burdensome, which Costa Rica is obliged to defend " with all the efficiency that might be within her reach," has necessarily and by virtue of the same nature of things to be consulted with Costa Rica. To act otherwise would simply be to invade the sovereign rights of that Republic.

These antecedents being established, and remembering that the laws of interpretation of the treaties are the same to be observed in the interpretation of contracts between private parties,[1] from which it is clear that there is no necessity to search for another meaning than that which its own words legitimately reveal, and which the legal necessities already recommended confirm, it will be easy to answer the two questions.

---

[1] Woolsey, § 118.

To the first, which is the one marked No. 10, I shall say positively that Nicaragua is bound not to make any grants of canal through her territory without first securing the consent of Costa Rica, in the terms, and in the way, and for the purposes, provided for in Article VIII of the treaty of April 15, 1858, and this not only because the said article is in force and has never been repealed or modified, but because, even in case that the said article should never have been written, the provisions thereof ought to be considered to be in existence as emanating from the dictates of reason and law. In other words, Article VIII of the treaty has not created the rights of Costa Rica and the correlative duties of Nicaragua in this respect; but the said rights and duties existed beforehand, and the treaty has done nothing else than express them.

Now, and in regard to the additional question, "Which are, in this respect, the natural rights of Costa Rica, alluded to by this stipulation, and in what cases they must be deemed injured?" I shall say, in the first place, that it is not reasonable to ask Costa Rica to formulate a complete catalogue of its natural rights in regard to this point, and to explain beforehand, through an almost prophetic effort of foresight, what are the circumstances through which those rights may be injured. And, in the second place, that those natural rights, and those circumstances capable to injure them, can be determined without difficulty when the concrete case rendering the investigation necessary presents itself.

It is well known that the natural rights of a man or nation, according to the excellent definition of Ahrens,[1] are those which constitute an indispensable condition, depending upon the will of another man or Government for the preservation and development, whether material, moral, or intellectual, of the individual or nation to which they refer.

That the river bank of Costa Rica remains such as it is; that

---

[1] Philosophie du Droit, chap. i.

its *statu quo* is not disturbed in consequence of a work of canalization; that Costa Rica does not become bounded by a dried up river-bed instead of a navigable river, or by a stream insignificant and without sufficient water for the purposes of navigation, commerce, and defence; that by a work of this kind a portion of the Costa Rican territory does not become flooded, and that the industries already created thereon, or which might be created in the future, become ruined, and the rights of the riparian owners nullified or ignored; that the "improvement" of the Bay of San Juan is not such as to injure the rights and interests of Costa Rica, and increase the burdens of its Government by rendering the duty of defending it, which the treaty imposes upon her, much more onerous or costly; all of this constitutes a natural right, perfect, demandable, irrefutable; and all that opposes the full satisfaction of that right, or renders that satisfaction more difficult, is and has to be considered as wrongful and invasive.

When the practical case should present itself no one doubts, nor can it be doubted, that Costa Rica and Nicaragua will agree with each other, since their rights are similar and substantially the same.

The eleventh and last question is nothing more than a repetition of the immediately preceding one, to which a kind of preamble or antecedent has been attached. The answer to be given to it has to be the same.

The Government of Nicaragua asks whether the treaty gives Costa Rica the right to be a party to the grants of interoceanic canal which that Government may make, and to share the profits which Nicaragua may reserve for herself as sovereign and in compensation of the valuable sacrifices made by her. And the answer is that Costa Rica has indeed the right to be a party to the grants of canal made since 1858, or which may be made in the future, and that, furthermore, that right is affirmed and recognized by Nicaragua herself in Article VIII of the treaty of limits.

As to sharing the profits and determining whether those which Nicaragua might reserve for herself are or are not, must or must not be, legitimate compensation for her sacrifices, these are precisely the questions which, among others, necessarily require the intervention of Costa Rica, and render the latter a legitimate party to the grants.

The letter and the spirit of Article VIII clearly show that everything in regard to this point will depend upon the special circumstances of the case. If the grant is of such a nature as to demand sacrifices on the part of Costa Rica, whether because her sovereign rights are injured or because other rights of a different nature belonging to her may suffer detriment, could ever Nicaragua pretend that such sacrifices should be gratuitous? Could she justly deny the right of Costa Rica to share the profits?

But this question is indeed premature. To resolve it properly, and even to avoid its coming up, the two Governments wisely stipulated that Nicaragua should not enter into any agreement of this kind without first listening to Costa Rica. Let this article be complied with according to its letter and spirit, and no difficulty of any kind will ever arise.

CONCLUSION.

CONCLUSION.

I HERE put an end to this argument and omit a general recapitulation, although it might be of some use, for fear of fatiguing too much the enlightened and benevolent attention of the Arbitrator.

The cause which I have defended is one of those which, on account of its notorious justice, needs no defence.

It was only in consideration of that justice, I must say so once more; it was only for the legitimate interest which Costa Rica has, and always had, in securing respect and inviolability for what has been covenanted, that she has maintained with firmness the validity of the treaty of 1858. Not by any means because she believes that the said treaty is favorable to her. When Costa Rica adhered to that compact she knew perfectly well that her ancient rights on the San Juan river became reduced by it to those of simple use; she understood without difficulty that, in moving away from the shores of the Great Lake, she also gave up her indisputable rights of community in it as a bordering State; and, therefore, she acted with the full knowledge that she was sacrificing her rights.

But the Costa Rican people, being eminently peaceful and abhorrent of having differences with their neighbors, thought it better to accept that settlement than to keep open for a longer time the old question of limits with Nicaragua—a perennial source of trouble for both Republics.

Exactly the same spirit now prevails in Costa Rica, and the very same reasons which induced her to act in 1858, cause her now to maintain the validity of the compact celebrated at that time, although the nullification thereof should produce the inevitable result of restoring the ancient frontiers of the Great Lake, the La Flor and the San Juan rivers.

Costa Rica never thought that the treaty of limits of 1858 was beneficial to her, and, if she shows herself earnest to maintain its validity, it is only for the sake of peace and tranquility, gifts which her children always held in high esteem, and always considered preferable to the possession of a strip of land, when no sacrifice of national dignity was required. Not once, nor twice, has the Costa Rican Foreign Office declared, in the most bitter part of the struggle, that the rescission of the treaty would be accepted by it, provided that Nicaragua should assume the responsibility of taking the initiative step, by which everything would be restored to its original condition; but this proposition was not entertained in Nicaragua, who, indeed, confuses the mind with her incomprehensible conduct, alleging, on the one side, the nullity of the convention of limits because she feels herself injured by it, while, on the other, refusing to accept the rescission of the compact when suggested to her.

The only explanation that this fact admits of is that the present question has been, for Nicaragua, a matter of domestic politics rather than an international affair—an idea which subsequent events have corroborated, because the treaty lately concluded at Managua, which put an end to the question, after having obtained the general approval of the country, and in spite of the support of the Administration which made it, was finally rejected through partisan interests and influences.

Those who act in this way do not realize how much harm they do to the real and fundamental interests of their own country. They do not understand that in reopening the question of validity or nullity of the treaty of 1858, which the Managua convention settled, the work of the interoceanic canal, the exponent of Central American patriotism, to which the United States of America looks with interest, and which is a work of universal importance, and by which both Costa Rica and Nicaragua will raise themselves to a great height, cannot but be embarrassed by differences which must be smothered on its account.

Fortunately, the end of such a disagreeable contention is near at hand. Soon the upright and learned Chief Magistrate of this great nation will say on whose side justice rests, and the Powers of both hemispheres will learn for their future guidance whether it has been judicious to maintain that an international compact, concluded by duly authorized plenipotentiaries, approved by the Chief Magistrates of the contracting States, ratified by the national representation of the two countries, exchanged in a solemn and special form, legally promulgated, communicated officially to all friendly nations, and executed and complied with in good faith for many years, is no more than blank paper, and has to fall before forensic subtleties, behind which the desire of breaking it appears concealed.

Costa Rica confidently relies upon the wisdom and righteousness of the Arbitrator. She trusts in the self-evident justice of her cause, and confidently expects a favorable decision. But should she be disappointed in this expectation, her deference and respect for the decision will be none the less.

PEDRO PÉREZ ZELEDÓN,
Envoy Extraordinary and Minister Plenipotentiary of Costa Rica.

WASHINGTON, D. C.,
October 27th, 1887.

DOCUMENTS.

DOCUMENTS.

No. 1.

Treaty of Limits between Costa Rica and Nicaragua, concluded April 15th, 1858.

We, Máximo Jerez, Minister Plenipotentiary of the Government of the Republic of Nicaragua, and José Maria Cañas, Minister Plenipotentiary of the Government of the Republic of Costa Rica, having been entrusted by our respective Governments with the mission of adjusting a treaty of limits between the two Republics, which should put an end to all the differences which have obstructed the perfect understanding and harmony that must prevail among them for their safety and prosperity, and having exchanged our respective powers, which were examined by Hon. Señor Don Pedro R. Negrete, Minister Plenipotentiary of the Government of the Republic of Salvador, exercising the functions of fraternal mediator in these negotiations, who found them to be good and in due form, as we on our part also found good and in due form the powers exhibited by the said Minister, after having discussed with the necessary deliberation all the points in question, with the assistance of the representative of Salvador who was present, have agreed to and adjusted the following Treaty of Limits between Nicaragua and Costa Rica.

ARTICLE I.

The Republic of Nicaragua and the Republic of Costa Rica declare in the most solemn and express terms that if for one moment they were about to enter into a struggle for reason of limits and for others which each one of the high contracting parties considered to be legal and a matter of honor, now after having given each other repeated proofs of good understanding, peaceful principles, and true fraternity, they are willing to bind themselves, as they formally do, to secure that the peace happily re-established should be each day more and more affirmed between the Government and the people of both nations, not only for the good and advantage of Nicaragua and Costa Rica, but for the happiness and prosperity which, to a certain extent, our sisters, the other Central American Republics, will derive from it.

Article II.

The dividing line between the two Republics, starting from the Northern Sea, shall begin at the end of Punta de Castilla, at the mouth of the San Juan de Nicaragua river, and shall run along the right bank of the said river up to a point three English miles distant from Castillo Viejo, said distance to be measured between the exterior works of said castle and the above-named point. From here, and taking the said works as centre, a curve shall be drawn along said works, keeping at the distance of three English miles from them, in its whole length, until reaching another point, which shall be at the distance of two miles from the bank of the river on the other side of the castle. From here the line shall continue in the direction of the Sapoá river, which empties into the Lake of Nicaragua, and it shall follow its course, keeping always at the distance of two miles from the right bank of the San Juan river all along its windings, up to reaching its origin in the lake; and from there along the right shore of the said lake until reaching the Sapoá river, where the line parallel to the bank and shore will terminate. From the point in which the said line shall coincide with the Sapoá river—a point which, according to the above description, must be two miles distant from the lake—an astronomic straight line shall be drawn to the central point of the Salinas Bay in the Southern Sea, where the line marking the boundary between the two contracting Republics shall end.

Article III.

Such surveys as may be required to locate this boundary, whether in whole or in part, shall be made by Commissioners appointed by the two Governments; and the two Governments shall agree also as to the time when the said survey shall be made. Said Commissioners shall have the power to somewhat deviate from the curve around the castle, from the line parallel to the banks of the river and the lake, or from the astronomic straight line between Sapoá and Salinas, if they find that natural land-marks can be substituted with advantage.

Article IV.

The Bay of San Juan del Norte, as well as the Salinas Bay, shall be common to both Republics, and, therefore, both the advantages of their use and the obligation to contribute to their defence shall also be common. Costa Rica shall be bound, as far as the portion of the banks of the San Juan river which correspond to it is concerned, to contribute to its custody in the same way as the two Republics shall contribute to the defence of the river in case of external aggression; and this they shall do with all the efficiency within their reach.

Article V.

As long as Nicaragua does not recover the full possession of all her rights in the port of San Juan del Norte, the use and possession of Punta de Castilla shall be common and equal both for Nicaragua and Costa Rica; and in the meantime, and as long as this community lasts, the boundary shall be the whole course of the Colorado river. It is furthermore stipulated that, as long as the said port of San Juan del Norte remains a *free* port, Costa Rica shall not charge Nicaragua any custom duties at Punta de Castilla.

Article VI.

The Republic of Nicaragua shall have exclusively the dominion and sovereign jurisdiction over the waters of the San Juan river from its origin in the Lake to its mouth in the Atlantic; but the Republic of Costa Rica shall have the perpetual right of free navigation on the said waters, between the said mouth and the point, three English miles distant from Castillo Viejo, said navigation being for the purposes of commerce either with Nicaragua or with the interior of Costa Rica, through the San Carlos river, the Sarapiquí, or any other way proceeding from the portion of the bank of the San Juan river, which is hereby declared to belong to Costa Rica. The vessels of both countries shall have the power to land indiscriminately on either side of the river, at the portion thereof where the navigation is common; and no charges of any kind, or duties, shall be collected unless when levied by mutual consent of both Governments.

Article VII.

It is agreed that the territorial division made by this treaty cannot be understood as impairing in any way the obligations contracted whether in public treaties or in contracts of canalization or public transit by the Government of Nicaragua previous to the conclusion of the present treaty; on the contrary, it is understood that Costa Rica assumes those obligations, as far as the portion which corresponds to its territory is concerned, without injury to the eminent domain and sovereign right which it has over the same.

Article VIII.

If the contracts of canalization or transit entered into by the Government of Nicaragua previous to its being informed of the conclusion of this treaty should happen to be invalidated for any reason whatever, Nicaragua binds herself not to enter into any other arrangement for the aforesaid purposes without first hearing the opinion of the Government of Costa Rica as to the disadvantages which the transaction might occasion the two countries; provided that the said opinion is rendered within the period of 30 days after the receipt of the communication asking for it, if Nicaragua should have said that the decision was urgent; and, if the transaction does not injure the natural rights of Costa Rica, the vote asked for shall be only advisory.

Article IX.

Under no circumstances, and even in case that the Republics of Costa Rica and Nicaragua should unhappily find themselves in a state of war, neither of them shall be allowed to commit any act of hostility against the other, whether in the port of San Juan del Norte, or in the San Juan river, or the Lake of Nicaragua.

Article X.

The stipulation of the foregoing article being essentially important for the proper custody of both the port and the river against foreign aggression, which would affect the general interests of the country, the strict performance thereof is left under the special guarantee which, in the name of the mediator Government, its Minister Plenipotentiary herein present is ready to give, and does hereby give, in use of the faculties vested in him for that purpose by his Government.

Article XI.

In testimony of the good and cordial understanding which is established between the Republics of Nicaragua and Costa Rica, they mutually give up all claims against each other, on whatever ground they may be founded, up to the date of the present treaty; and in the same way the two contracting parties do hereby waive all claims for indemnification of damages which they might consider themselves entitled to present against each other.

ARTICLE XII.

This treaty shall be ratified, and the ratifications thereof shall be exchanged, at Santiago de Managua within forty days after it is signed.

In testimony whereof we have hereunto subscribed our names to the present instrument, executed in triplicate, together with the Hon. Minister of Salvador, and under the countersign of the respective secretaries of Legation, at the city of San José, in Costa Rica, on the 15th day of April, in the year of our Lord 1858.

MAXIMO JEREZ.
JOSÉ M. CAÑAS.
PEDRO RÓMULO NEGRETE.
MANUEL RIVAS,
Secretary of the Legation of Nicaragua.
SALVADOR GONZALEZ,
Secretary of the Legation of Costa Rica.
FLORENTINO SOUZA,
Secretary of the Legation of Salvador.

ADDITIONAL ACT.

The undersigned, Ministers of Nicaragua and Costa Rica, wishing to give public testimony of their high esteem and of their feelings of gratitude towards the Republic of Salvador, and the worthy representative of the same, Col. Don Pedro R. Negrete, have agreed that the treaty of territorial limits be accompanied with the following declaration, namely:

"Whereas, the Government of Salvador has given to the Governments of Costa Rica and Nicaragua the most authentic testimony of its noble feelings, and of its high appreciation of the value and necessity of cultivating fraternal sympathy among these Republics, and has interested itself as efficiently as friendly in the equitable settlement of the differences which unhappily have existed between the high contracting parties, a settlement which has been secured by the two Legations, owing in great part to the estimable and efficient action of the Hon. Señor Negrete, Minister Plenipotentiary of the said Government, who proved to be the right person to accomplish the generous mediation for which he was appointed, and who has known perfectly well how to meet the intentions of his Government, and owing also to the important aid, to the learning and to the impartial suggestions of the same Minister during the discussion of the subject, we, the Representatives of Costa Rica and Nicaragua, in the name of our respective countries, do hereby fulfil the pleasant duty of declaring and recording here all the gratitude which we feel for the patriotism, high mindedness, fraternity, and benevolence characterizing the Government of Salvador.

In testimony whereof we have hereunto subscribed our names and signed this, in triplicate, in the presence of the Hon. Minister of Salvador, under the countersign of the respective Secretaries of Legation, in the city of San José, the capital of Costa Rica, on the 15th day of April, in the year of our Lord 1858.

MÁXIMO JEREZ.
JOSÉ M. CAÑAS.
MANUEL RIVAS,
Secretary of the Legation of Nicaragua.
SALVADOR GONZALEZ,
Secretary of the Legation of Costa Rica.

No. 2.

Decree of the Federal Congress of Central America in 1825, approving the annexation of Nicoya to Costa Rica.

The Federal Congress of the Republic of Central America, taking into consideration, firstly, the reiterated petitions of the authorities and municipal bodies of the towns of the district of Nicoya, asking for their separation from Nicaragua and their annexation to Costa Rica ; and secondly, that the said towns and people actually annexed themselves to Costa Rica at the time in which the political troubles of Nicaragua took place ; and thirdly, the topographical situation of the same district, has been pleased to decree, and does hereby DECREE :

ART. 1. For the time being, and until the demarcation of the territory of each State provided by Art. VII of the Constitution is made, the district of Nicoya shall CONTINUE to be separated from Nicaragua and annexed to Costa Rica.

ART. 2. In consequence thereof, the district of Nicoya shall recognize its dependence upon the authorities of Costa Rica, and shall have, in the Legislature of the latter, such representation as corresponds to it.

ART. 3. This decree shall be communicated to the Assemblies of Nicaragua and Costa Rica.

Let it pass to the Senate.

Given at Guatemala December 9, 1825.

[From the "Reseña Histórica de Centro-América," by Lorenzo Montufar, Guatemala, 1881, Vol. IV, p. 382.]

No. 3.

The state of things existing at the time of the labors of the Constituent Assembly is declared to be an extraordinary regime, wherein the constitutional rules in force under regular circumstances could be laid aside.

Session of the 30th of November.

* * * * * * *

There were present fourteen members, and absent Señores Lacayo and Machado on account of sickness, and Mejia, Salinas, Basilio, and Carazo for other reasons. * * *

Señores Baca and Chamorro (Don Pablo) said that they wanted to explain their negative votes to the decree of the 28th instant, and, the President having acceded to their wish, it is hereby recorded that the said gentlemen refused to vote in the affirmative because they understand that the faculty of exercising the acts which the decree refers to is included among the faculties of the legislative power, and that one thing is faculties of the legislative power and another thing faculties of legislation.

* * * * * * *

Señor Lopez made the following motion: " Whereas the election of justices desired to be made by this august body may find an insuperable obstacle in the scarcity of men properly qualified for such offices, I suggest to you that, before making the said election, you pass a resolution rendering the present members of this body to be eligible, *since the constitutional provision which excludes the members of Congress from serving in judicial offices* CAN ONLY BE UNDERSTOOD DURING AN ORDINARY REGIME."

The same Señor Lopez asked this to be declared urgent; and Señor Cesar, having made a previous motion that all questions referring to the faculties of the Executive Power should be first decided, and that the questions in regard to the judiciary should be postponed to another day, the motion of Señor Cesar was carried. * * *

The session was adjourned.

PEDRO ZELEDÓN,
Vice-President.
J. MIGUEL CARDENAS,
Secretary.
FRANCISCO JIMENEZ,
Secretary.

[From "La Gaceta de Nicaragua" No. 2, January 9, 1858.]

No. 4.

Communication from the Costa Rican Secretary of State—It shows the ardent desire of Costa Rica to settle finally and forever, the questions pending between it and Nicaragua, even at the sacrifice of its own rights and its national pride.

NATIONAL PALACE,
SAN JOSÉ, *December* 15, 1857.

To the Plenipotentiaries in Nicaragua :

I have had the pleasure to receive your very estimable communications of the 29th and 30th of November past, with inclosure, consisting of a copy of the letter addressed by both of you from the city of Rivas to the Secretary of Foreign Relations at Managua. I have also received your despatches dated at Rivas on the 9th instant, and inclosures marked Nos. 7, 11, 12, and 13, as well as copies of the treaty made by you on the 8th instant, and documents appended thereto.

His Excellency the President of the Republic having acquainted himself with the tenor of the ten articles of the agreement above named, and with the explanations contained in your despatches, has directed me to tell you both, in reply, as I have the honor to do, that only through the fatality of circumstances under which the Central American countries find themselves at present, owing to the recent filibustering invasion, he could have been moved to entertain and consider such stipulations as the ones referred to, which, while proving *that Nicaragua did not think of the dangers we all are now running, show also that she did not take into account the innumerable sacrifices that the Government and people of Costa Rica have made in order to cause their ancient rights, and their signification at the present day, to be recognized.*

Notwithstanding this, the undersigned will refrain from making any of those remarks which naturally spring up from the consideration of the terms on which some one of the conces-

sions of Nicaragua have been made, requiring in compensation thereof the sacrifice of such immense interests as are involved in the concessions of Costa Rica; but he will state, however, that from the moment in which the Costa Rican Government noticed the attitude taken by that of Nicaragua, and the character of the accusations made by the latter against the former, it firmly decided to abandon even those positions which had been conquered at the cost of Costa Rican blood, although without any intention to retain them, except during the period of the common danger. Under these circumstances, and acting always under the impulse of its peaceful ideas, and of its vehement desire of saving the independence of the Central American soil, the Government, setting aside and removing whatever obstacles might be found in its way, even at the cost of great sacrifices, has decided to refer the said treaty immediately to the consideration of the Congress of this Republic. There seems to be no doubt that the generous and noble feelings of the representatives of the Costa Rican people will induce them to sacrifice, as the Executive does, the rights herein involved, and ratify, even to the detriment of a just feeling of national pride, the treaty which you both have concluded; and with this Nicaragua is given a very significant testimony of the loyalty and disinterestedness of Costa Rica, and how highly it values the national Union and independence in the presence of the risks to which they are exposed.

As soon as the national representation of Costa Rica seals with its approval the said treaties, I shall have the honor to send them to you by messenger, it being understood that in the meantime the Constituent Assembly of Nicaragua will lend to them the same attention, IN ORDER THAT ALL THOSE QUESTIONS AS HAVE DIVIDED THESE TWO COUNTRIES BE FOREVER SETTLED, and the two countries themselves may, with entire freedom and liberty, attend to their preservation.

I have the honor to subscribe myself, with sincere expressions of high esteem and consideration, your obedient servant,

NAZARIO TOLEDO.

No. 5.

Communication showing the spirit of conciliation and fraternity which prevailed in the making of the treaty of limits.—The limits between Costa Rica and Nicaragua are, more than anything else, internal or domestic jurisdictional boundaries.

MANAGUA, *January* 18, 1858.

To the Secretary for Foreign Relations of the Republic of Costa Rica.

SIR: The treaty adjusted on the 8th of December ultimo, between the Commissioners of the Government of your Republic and the President of Nicaragua, General Don Tomás Martinez, was submitted to the Constituent Assembly of this Republic; and that august body, after giving the subject its most attentive meditation, decided that, in order to remove such obstacles as present themselves for its ratification, the negotiations of peace, amity, limits, and alliance between the two countries should be continued, so as to conciliate their respective interests and secure their independence. This will be shown to you by the terms of the decree, an authorized copy of which I have the honor to enclose.

* * * * * *

The limits between the Central American States are no more than limits dividing sections of one and the same State. More than barriers to opposite or conflicting interests, they have to be considered as internal or domestic jurisdictional boundaries. The States of Central America are no more than one people, whatever boundaries may be drawn to separate them from each other. And for this reason such questions as may arise out of this subject should never be carried to the extreme which has been attempted, unless some responsibility appears involved in it, which, affecting the interests of the one country, may react against the other. No difficulty appears to exist for the arrangement concerning reciprocal commerce, and that of foreign countries through the San Juan river; and as the maintaining their independence is a common desire of the two Republics, no obstacle appears to exist for combining for the mutual defence of that sacred right. My Government earnestly desires that *the people of both Costa Rica and Nicaragua may form a close unity*, and appear as if they were *only one people;* and in compliance with its duty, it is ready to appoint at once the proper Commissioners, who, in union with those whom your Republic may select, should give satisfactory conclusion to the pending negotiations. My Government expects that yours will be pleased to communicate to your own Commissioners such instructions as are required, for the reasons above expressed, as it has on its own part done to-day.

* * * * * *

GREGORIO JUAREZ.

[From the "Gaceta de Nicaragua," No. of January 25, 1858.]

No. 6.

Congratulation by the United States Minister for the near settlement of the differences between Costa Rica and Nicaragua.—Speech of Gen Mirabeau B. Lamar, Envoy Extraordinary and Minister Plenipotentiary of the United States in Nicaragua.

* * * * * * *

" May Your Excellency allow me to express, in conclusion, how gratifying it is for me that the storm of war which not long ago threatened this country and one of her neighboring sisters has vanished before the serene brilliancy of another policy much more to be desired ; *that Nicaragua and Costa Rica have put an end to their controversies, and that, as announced by everything, their old fraternal, peaceful relations are to be re-established upon solid foundations.* Who can say what may come out of such a happy event? It may, perhaps, conduce to the union of the two countries. And sometimes I have even thought that such a policy should necessarily promote the happiness of both. In my opinion such an example should be followed with great advantage by all the States of Central America, whose reunion under their former Federal Constitution would not only secure for them the benefits of peace, and strength, and dignity, but would place them on the same level as other important nations, rendering them able to compete with them in the prosecution of prosperity and glory. If Nicaragua, inspired by such feelings, should take the first step for the accomplishment of such a great enterprise she would win for herself a crown of immortal honor and the gratitude of all hearts which throb for the good of this country and the future progress of its people."

[From the *Gaceta de Nicaragua*, No. 7, February 13, 1858.]

No. 7.

Note of the Costa Rican Secretary of State showing the peaceful disposition of Costa Rica in regard to the question of limits.

SAN JOSÉ, *February* 15, 1858.

To the Minister of Foreign Relations of the Republic of Nicaragua :

I have had the honor to receive your estimable communication, dated at Managua, on the 18th of January instant, to which a copy of the Decree No. 19 of the 15th of the same month of January, enacted by the Congress of your Republic, was appended.

His Excellency the President of Costa Rica had flattered himself that all the questions which for such a long time had maintained two bordering and sister nations in disagreement, although for so many reasons they are called to form but one family, one nation, and to consolidate and combine their respective rights and prerogatives to save their own existence, overcome dangers and threats from outside, retain their political autonomy, and secure the accomplishment of their future destinies, were settled satisfactorily to both parties by means of the treaty of December 8, which this Government readily approved and which was ratified with no less readiness by the legislative body, showing by all this the self-denial which was required by circumstances, and overlooking the disadvantages and the great sacrifices which Costa Rica incurred for the sake of harmony, good friendship, and well understood interests of both Republics.

Nevertheless, if, as seen by your despatch and by the decree No. 19 of January 15, some obstacles have presented themselves, which from their magnitude, their nature, and their great political and social moment render it necessary to postpone the consummation of an act which in many respects involves the interests of the whole of Central America, and was intended to put an end to unfortunate territorial questions, my Government cannot ignore the weight of your arguments in support of the decree enacted by the Congress of your Republic, rejecting the treaty of peace and limits which had been concluded by the President, Don Tomás Martinez, and the Commissioners of Costa Rica.

My Government is pleased, however, to see the provision in the said decree to the effect that the negotiations should continue, and also the activity with which your Government has carried this provision at once into effect by appointing commissioners who, in union with such commissioners as be appointed by my Government, should discuss again and adjust a settlement of such vital interest.

You may be assured that Costa Rica earnestly and sincerely desires to preserve good understanding, friendship, and fraternal harmony with Nicaragua, and that it is therefore animated with the best wishes in favor of the peace of both countries, it being persuaded of the intimate connection, both in interest, happiness, and danger, which exists between them.

So it is that I can assure from this moment, and the Government of Nicaragua can depend upon it, that every consideration and respect will be shown in this Republic, with pleasure and earnestness, to the gentlemen that your Government may select for the important mission above alluded to.

His Excellency the President expects that the efforts which Nicaragua is going to make, the honorable and gratifying mediation of Salvador, exercised through its worthy Minister, Señor Negrete, who is already in this capital, and the exceedingly favorable disposition of my own Government, will give such results as will correspond to the interests to be dealt with and to the good name of the States which contributed to it.

Please accept the testimony of the distinguished consideration with which I subscribe myself your attentive servant,

NAZARIO TOLEDO.

No. 8.

Communication from the Secretary of State of Costa Rica, showing that the initiation of the treaty of 1858 was due to the friendly mediation of the Government of Salvador, and to overtures made by Nicaragua, subsequent to the repudiation by the latter of the treaty of 1857 which Costa Rica had approved of.

DEPARTMENT OF FOREIGN RELATIONS OF COSTA RICA,
NATIONAL PALACE,
SAN JOSÉ, *February* 16, 1858.

SIR: His Excellency the President of this Republic has officially received to-day His Excellency Don Pedro R. Negrete, Envoy Extraordinary and Minister Plenipotentiary of Salvador, who comes with the most important and gratifying mission to mediate in the question of territorial limits.

Although this Government has given repeated proofs of its desire to obtain a settlement, which with no less frequency has been made illusory; although its best wishes proved to be fruitless when it accredited a Legation, with ample instructions, to remove by an equitable settlement the only obstacle capable of hindering the relations and reciprocal interests of both Governments from being strengthened; although the rejection of the treaty of December 3d, was calculated to inspire diffidence and cause this Government to be more circumspect in entering into further negotiations; *notwithstanding all that, my Government, taking into consideration the friendly intervention of the Government of Salvador, and its efforts, both commendable and honorable, in favor of Costa Rica as well as Nicaragua*, and the fraternal manifestations of the worthy Salvadorean Minister, has not felt able to refuse a favorable hearing to the statements made by Señor Negrete on behalf of his Government, and therefore it finds itself *well disposed to listen to such propositions as may be made by the Government of Nicaragua*, hoping that on this occasion the efforts of Costa Rica and the sacrifices already made by her in different ways should not prove useless.

An answer to this effect has been given with pleasure to the Minister of Salvador, who, even before his official reception, had suggested that *a Legation from your Republic should be received here*, and declared that the place for the negotiation should be in this capital, since our Legation in your capital has been withdrawn.

I subscribe myself, with sentiments of the greatest consideration and respect, your obedient servant,

NAZARIO TOLEDO.

To His Excellency THE MINISTER OF FOREIGN RELATIONS of the Republic of Nicaragua, Managua.

No. 9.

Act of Exchange of Ratifications of the Treaty of Limits.

I, Tomás Martinez, President of the Republic of Nicaragua, and I, Rafael Mora, President of the Republic of Costa Rica, fully and competently authorized by the respective Congresses of Nicaragua and Costa Rica to perform the exchange of ratifications of the treaty of territorial limits, which was signed by Plenipotentiaries of both Republics and by one of Salvador as mediator power on the 15th of April instant, at San José, the Capital of Costa Rica, said Plenipotentiaries having been, on the part of the Republic of Nicaragua, General Don Máximo Jerez, on the part of that of Costa Rica, General Don José Maria Cañas, and on the part of Salvador, Col. Don Pedro Rómulo Negrete, having met at the city of Rivas, in Nicaragua, for the purpose aforesaid, have this day performed the exchange of the respective official instruments of ratification of the said treaty of April 15th, and drawn up and signed in triplicate, as we do now, the present act of exchange, which will be countersigned by the respective Secretaries of Foreign Relations of Nicaragua and Costa Rica, Lic. Don Gregorio Juarez and Dr. Don Nazario Toledo.

Done this 26th day of the month of April, in the year of our Lord 1858.

TOMAS MARTINEZ.
JUAN RAFAEL MORA.
GREGORIO JUAREZ,
Secretary of State for Foreign Relations.
NAZARIO TOLEDO,
Secretary of State for Foreign Relations.

[From the "Gaceta de Nicaragua," No. 15, May 8, 1858.]

No. 10.

Editorial of the Official Newspaper of Nicaragua on the Conclusion of the Treaty.—It shows the spirit of conciliation and fraternity of Costa Rica and Nicaragua.—Thanks given to the Government of Salvador for its friendly mediation.

PEACE BETWEEN NICARAGUA AND COSTA RICA.

The ancient question of limits between the two Republics, which has imposed so many sacrifices on both of them, and which so often has occupied their attention at a moment in which it was imperative for them to devote it to something else of a much greater character; that fatal difference, fruitful source of libellous publications, disgraceful to the dignity of the public press; that dispute, in fine, which, exciting the minds, often puts us face to face, ready to fight and to redeem with blood the wrong done, or alleged, appears now to have been, as it indubitably has been, *compromised in the most harmonious manner.* The stains which soiled the pages of the history of the two countries have been removed, and that fraternity which God established between their people, and which men attempted to ignore, has been promoted and fostered.

Up to this moment the Government has not yet any knowledge of the treaty concluded to this effect. It scarcely knows about it, anything else than *it was concluded on very equitable terms.* But this is enough to make it feel satisfied for the accomplishment of its expectations and the success of the labors lately undertaken.

True it is, indeed, that there is no question in this world which cannot be solved when there is a disposition to do so. Diplomacy has saved the human race from shedding as much blood as has been shed when it proved to be unable to exercise its empire.

A conviction, sufficiently founded, tells us that this time there will be no obstacle for the ratification of the treaty, both because *of the general desire that such differences be at least adjusted*, even by setting aside some right or another, and because, as it is reported, *the settlement has been* made in such a way as not to attack former engagements, and fully *satisfy the two peace-making parties*.

The Government officials who have been able to render themselves superior to the passions begotten and fostered in the course of the controversy; the persons who have intervened, or may in the future intervene, to seal the cordiality now coming into existence, and develop it to such a degree as is becoming to countries so intimately connected with each other, have crowned themselves with glory, and conquered for their native countries, not a new province won by force of arms, but peace, rest, fraternity, and the benevolence of a sister Republic, with which it has to run the same fate, since the interests which connect it with her are identical.

The Government of Salvador, by selecting such an intelligent and active representative as Colonel Don Pedro Rómulo Negrete to carry into effect its *generous mediation*, has given full evidence of the deep concern that it felt in the uncertain and dangerous condition of things between Nicaragua and Costa Rica, and has won, the same as its indefatigable representative, *the purest satisfaction of having done her sisters one of the most estimable benefits that could be expected.*

[From the "Gaceta de Nicaragua," No. 14, May 1st, 1858.]

No. 11.

Leave-taking of President Mora.

RIVAS, SAN JUAN DEL SUR, *May* 2, 1858.

To His Excellency DON TOMÁS MARTINEZ,
    President of Nicaragua.

SIR: The great objects of our meeting at Rivas having been so happily accomplished, I return to my country with feelings of satisfaction and contentment for the benevolent attentions kindly extended to me, both by Your Excellency, the various members of the Government, and some distinguished citizens of your Republic.

I congratulate myself for having had the good fortune of signing, with Your Excellency, the *compacts which put an end to all the causes of disturbance* which have affected the relations, both political and commercial, between our respective countries, and which will regulate them in the future and enable Nicaragua and Costa Rica to fight together against the pretensions of filibusterism, as well as to cement in the future our respective rights and liberties and the integrity and independence of the country. I congratulate myself, with so much more reason for all that, because the patriotic man who knew how to preserve the honor of the Nicaraguan people in the middle of difficulties and privations of all classes, always struggling with the common enemy, is the one who, with his signature, has sealed the peace and friendship of both peoples, and so secured happiness and greatness to Nicaragua.

Your Excellency can rely upon me for the carrying out of your programme of order and respect to the principle of legal authority. In this regard our ideas will always be in harmony. I return to my country contented, I say so again, making fervent wishes for the preservation of Your Excellency and for the greatness and happiness of the people of

Nicaragua, who, entrusting their destinies to Your Excellency, have given proof that they know how to reward merit.

Your true and loyal friend,

RAFAEL MORA.

[From the "Gaceta de Nicaragua," No. 15, May 8, 1858.]

No. 12.

Leave-taking of Señor Negrete.

LEGATION OF SALVADOR,
NEAR THE GOVERNMENTS OF NICARAGUA AND COSTA RICA.
No. 17.   MANAGUA, *May* 6, 1858.
To the Hon. Don GREGORIO JUAREZ,
 Secretary of State for the Department of Foreign Relations of the Republic of Nicaragua.

SIR: The important treaty of peace and limits between Costa Rica and Nicaragua, concluded at San José, having been consummated at the city of Rivas, on the 26th of April last, according to the record of the exchange of ratifications of that date, the undersigned Plenipotentiary of Salvador has the pleasure to inform you of his arrival in this capital for the purpose of cordially greeting the Nicaraguan Government, *congratulating it for the settlement of the grave questions* which were pending between it and Costa Rica, and giving notice of the withdrawal of this legation to the capital of Salvador, where it will report to its Government *the happy result obtained by the undersigned Minister in his dealings with the Republics of Nicaragua and Costa Rica.*

In taking his leave, it is exceedingly gratifying to the undersigned to set forth that his heart wishes with the greatest vehemence that the present social welfare of the Nicaraguan people, the domestic and foreign politics of her Government, and her well-founded hopes of improvement in every respect, be each day more and more improved and increased. Happy Salvador, if she succeeds in seeing Nicaragua great and prosperous! May the Supreme Ruler of Nations enlighten the august assembly now engaged in framing the political constitution of this Republic! May Divine Providence be bountiful in the assistance which the Government needs for the better ruling of the people whose destinies are commended to it! These are the wishes which Salvador will always make for Nicaragua, whom she considers as her sister, and whom she has defended.

This Legation, which acknowledges with gratitude the kind attentions and honors which the Nicaraguan people and Government have tendered to it, wishes, also, to record here, not only the said feeling, but also its fervent wishes that the Government may always find in the people a powerful support, and the people in the Government a paternal administration, such as is now seen in Nicaragua, with pleasure to Central America and satisfaction to the world.

Animated by this desire, the Minister of the Republic of Salvador takes leave of the Hon. Señor Juarez, and assures him of the high esteem with which he subscribes himself his most attentive and obedient servant,

PEDRO R. NEGRETE.

[From the "Gaceta de Nicaragua," No. 15, May 8, 1858].

No. 13.

Answer to the letter of leave-taking of Col. Negrete.—He is called apostle of peace.—Solemn and effusive expression of gratitude tendered to Salvador.

DEPARTMENT OF FOREIGN RELATIONS OF THE
SUPREME GOVERNMENT OF THE REPUBLIC,
MANAGUA, *May* 7, 1858.

To His Excellency Col. Don PEDRO R. NEGRETE,
Minister Plenipotentiary of the Government of Salvador near the Governments of Nicaragua and Costa Rica.

SIR: With the sublime satisfaction of an apostle of peace, Your Excellency returns to your country full of the noble pleasure of having succeeded in corresponding both to the confidence of your Government and the founded expectations of the Governments of Nicaragua and Costa Rica.

Thirty-four years of disagreement, or of badly disguised animadversion, were sufficient to give birth and strength to the most pernicious enmity between these two sister Republics; but the good-will of the Government of Salvador, and the prompt and most efficient action of Your Excellency at the most timely occasion, profiting by the favorable disposition in which the respective Presidents found themselves, succeeded in dispelling in one day the ominous clouds which for more than one-third of a century had been gathering.

My Government, deeply grateful to the Government of Salvador and to the person of Your Excellency, wishes to express its gratitude in the present despatch in order that it may enter into the immortal kingdom of history and be remembered by future generations.

My Government wishes for the Republic of Salvador the most perfect peace and harmony with the other nations of Central America, and all others with which it holds diplomatic relations, but if, unhappily, that peace and harmony should ever be disturbed, the Government of Your Excellency can always count upon the mediation of mine until reaching such success as desired.

His Excellency the President wishes you a happy voyage, and a long and prosperous life ; and I pray Your Excellency to consider my own sentiments to be identical to those I have just expressed in the name of the Chief Magistrate, whose organ I have the honor to be. I further pray Your Excellency to allow me to offer with great respect the consideration with which I subscribe myself, your humble and obedient servant,

GREGORIO JUAREZ.

[From the " Gaceta de Nicaragua," No. 15, May 8, 1858.]

No. 14.

Editorial of the " Gaceta de Nicaragua" subsequent to the official leave-taking of Señores Don Juan Rafael Mora and Col. Negrete.—The latter is promoted to the rank of General as a reward for his services.—The Nicaraguan people feel jubilant for the friendly relations between Costa Rica and Nicaragua.

INTERIOR.

The President and Ministers Juarez, Cortez, Jerez, and Negrete arrived in this city on the 4th instant highly satisfied all of them with the President of Costa Rica, with his Minister, Señor Toledo, and with all the persons who accompanied them.

Subsequently we have been informed that the latter returned to their country no less pleased with Nicaragua; and this reciprocity *cannot but fill us with joy, since we are satisfied that the hands which now have been grasped have not been grasped in vain, and that the promises of eternal peace and friendship which have been made are sincere, and due to such convictions and faith as are seldom seen to preside over treaties of peace and alliance among nations.*

Col. Negrete was rewarded by the Government with the commission of Brigadier-General, which he deserved for his services in the campaign against the filibusters, as well as for those which he has just rendered in his capacity of mediator between Nicaragua and Costa Rica. This gentleman returned to his country on the 6th instant, after having remained two days in this city.

Señor Jerez *left also for Leon to join his family and enjoy some rest after the arduous, but very useful, labors performed by him*, and as soon as possible he will return from there and place himself by the side of the Administration which so highly appreciates his services. * * *

[From the " Gaceta de Nicaragua," No. 15, May 8, 1858.]

No. 15.

Spirit of Concord which presided over the treaty.—Evident necessity and advisability that it should be concluded.—Faculties of the Government to approve it.—Final character of the treaty.—Identical position of Costa Rica and Nicaragua.

THE "GACETA."

It is at all times a duty to strengthen the sovereignty and independence of the nation, because it is upon these conditions that the life of the State depends. Among those disputes which either directly or indirectly affect said sovereignty and independence, those of limits are to be considered; *and for this reason their settlement is necessary to secure solid peace with the neighbors and remove the obstacles which might oppose the free development of commerce, industry, and progress, since it is well known that such disputes are a fruitful source of evils of the worst character.* Such questions promote uneasiness and alarm among the bordering people, give birth to rivalries, beget national hatred, and produce either a silent war of diplomatic hostilities constantly embarrassing the progress of the countries, or an open conflict in which muskets and cannons take the place which ought to have been reserved exclusively for reason and justice. When such differences arise, the bordering States contending with each other, although united by the contiguity of the soil and by the propinquity of their towns and cities, become so separated as to desire the complete destruction of each other.

Unfortunately, Nicaragua and Costa Rica had been for a long time laboring under the disadvantages of such dissensions without finding a way of settling their differences, which day after day grew greater and worse, and went as far as to initiate a fratricidal war, precisely at that moment in which the filibusters prepared themselves for a new invasion, and carry on their plans of robbery and extermination.

Reason and patriotism demanded all kinds of sacrifices to be made to re-establish harmony between two neighboring Republics threatened by a common enemy ; and reason and patriotism have triumphed at Rivas on the 26th of April instant, on which day His Excellency, the President of the Republic, Gen. Don Tomás Martinez, approved of and ratified the treaty of limits, celebrated by the Ministers Plenipotentiary of Nicaragua and Costa Rica, General Don José Maria Cañas, and General Don Máximo Jerez. His Excellency put an end to ancient and ruinous questions, settling them by a compromise, thus strengthening the bonds of fraternity which unite us together, and enabling us to meet, united, stronger, and mightier, the depredators of our country, who by their unexampled iniquities are the scandal of civilization.

The President of Nicaragua has ratified the Jerez-Cañas treaty, using the faculties which were vested in him by Legislative Decree, No. 22, authorizing him to do all that he might deem to be advisable for the defence of the sovereignty and independence of the nation. As the country cannot successfully undertake this defence, without unity of action on the part of all its members, it was necessary to eradicate completely every element which might prevent intimacy from being established, and would maintain discord between two sister countries. The mediation of Salvador has had much part in such a happy result, and it has been exercised with zeal, activity, and brilliancy by Don Pedro Rómulo Negrete, the Commissioner sent to that effect.

Henceforth, Nicaragua and Costa Rica will march in perfect harmony, and Central America will enjoy this benefit, which will certainly appall all those who took advantage of our dissensions in the same way as a rich mine is worked by avarice and ambition. Our readers will find elsewhere in this paper the full text of the treaty, *beginning of our concord, commencement of happiness and progress for the nation,* and by perusing it they will be convinced of the sincere patriotism of the two Presidents, Don Rafael Mora and Don

Tomás Martinez, who have shown their good-will for the salvation of Central America, and for securing that this beautiful portion of the world might march in peace to fulfill the high destinies to which it is called.

Having in view the same purposes, the two Presidents have adjusted in their interview at Rivas a treaty of commerce and alliance which satisfies the mercantile necessities of both countries and makes them combine in cases of war, whether filibuster or any other kind. They likewise signed another tripartite convention with the Minister mediator, in which the representatives of the three countries, namely, Salvador, Nicaragua, and Costa Rica, come closely together and secure their common efforts for the defence of the country in these calamitous times when in order to live it is necessary to be mighty and powerful.

Such a great benefit will in the future be derived from the timely and important visit that the President of Costa Rica paid to the President of Nicaragua at the City of Rivas. Both personages took leave of each other in the most perfect understanding, and both of them animated by the most philanthrophic sentiments in favor of the Republics whose destinies have been commended to their patriotic zeal.

[From the "Gaceta de Nicaragua," No. 15, May 8, 1858.]

No. 16.

The treaty of April 15, 1858, *is communicated to the friendly Governments as a happy termination of the protracted difficulties between Costa Rica and Nicaragua.*

No. 29.   DEPARTMENT OF FOREIGN RELATIONS
OF THE REPUBLIC OF COSTA RICA,
NATIONAL PALACE, SAN JOSÉ, *May* 12, 1858.

Mr. MINISTER: His Excellency the President of this Republic, being determined to employ all the means within his reach to *set at rest all questions pending with the neighboring Republic of Nicaragua, and finally settle all business pending between both* Republics, decided to make a trip to Nicaragua and pay a visit to the President thereof, General Don Tomás Martinez, settling thereby with him personally all the said questions and business, strengthening the bonds of union which naturally exist among the nations of Central America, and devising some means of strengthening that union and defending the territory and independence of the same whenever threatened. At the very moment in which His Excellency the President was preparing to leave this Republic, General Jerez presented himself at this capital as Envoy Extraordinary and Minister, sent by the Government of Nicaragua, this having been due in part to the patriotic zeal and solicitude of Col. Don Pedro R. Negrete, who, in his capacity of Minister mediator, had been accredited near the Governments of the two contending Republics, who had arrived at the moment in which the Assembly of Nicaragua had rejected the last arrangement celebrated at Rivas by Commissioners of this Republic. Señor Negrete, after having been received in public audience by this Government, and recognized in his diplomatic capacity, deemed it advisable to return to Nicaragua and urge the sending by her Government of the Commissioner whom it had offered to accredit. In consequence of all these steps a meeting could take place of ministers fully authorized to settle the pending questions, principally the one about territorial limits. It was in this way that the treaty of April 15, a competent number of printed copies of which I have the honor to enclose, could be celebrated; and *that treaty was ratified by His Excellency General Martinez, President of Nicaragua, in virtue of the full authority which the Constituent Assembly of that Republic had given him for that purpose.* The said treaty has been, therefore, and will continue to be, a substantial foundation of peace and union between these two bordering Republics, and it gave occasion to a subsequent treaty of peace, friendship, and commerce, which was celebrated at Rivas between the two Presidents of Nicaragua and Costa Rica, assisted by their respective Secretaries of State, a copy of which I have the honor to accompany to you, and which in due time will be submitted to the respective legislatures for the proper ratification.

Another treaty of defensive alliance was also celebrated at Rivas, and to it Don Pedro Rómulo Negrete, the Minister of Salvador, was a party; and, as this treaty is to be submitted to the Governments of Guatemala and Honduras, I have the honor to send to you an authorized copy of the same, as directed by Article IV of the same treaty.

Information received by the President of this Republic about a new filibustering expedition of certain importance and other pressing circumstances compelled him not to continue his voyage to the capitals of the other sections of Central America and postpone his visit to them until another more propitious occasion. In the meantime His Excellency feels exceedingly satisfied with the advantage which his visit to Nicaragua has produced, not only as far as these two Republics are concerned, but in regard to the common benefit of the whole of Central America, since this Government hopes that the great steps that have already been taken to secure the future welfare of the Central American States will not be in vain, and that, if the immense results which the said steps must produce are accomplished, they will respond to the securing of the integrity and independence of the territory, the salvation of its sovereignty and its liberties, and the prosperity which is incumbent to the fertility of its soil and its geographical position.

With such a happy opportunity, I have the honor to assure you the distinguished consideration, esteem, and respect with which I subscribe myself your attentive servant,

NAZARIO TOLEDO.

To His Excellency THE MINISTER OF FOREIGN RELATIONS of the Republic of Guatemala.

No. 17.

Validity of the Treaty.

No. 30.   DEPARTMENT OF FOREIGN RELATIONS
                      OF THE REPUBLIC OF COSTA RICA,
              NATIONAL PALACE, SAN JOSÉ, *May* 15, 1858.

Mr. MINISTER: I have the honor to reply to your estimable despatch of the 3d of April, the contents of which I communicated to His Excellency the President of this Republic. The feelings which animate your Government for the peace, unity, and prosperity of these bordering sister Republics are extremely worthy and proper in a Central American Government; and, fully agreeing with such generous sentiments, His Excellency the President of this Republic, wishing to take every step which might be *conducive to the final settlement of the questions pending between Nicaragua and Costa Rica*, decided to go personally to confer with His Excellency Don Tomás Martinez, the President of Nicaragua, and try not only to put an end to the difference between the two countries, but also prove by this example, the first one ever given in the political history of Central America, his cordial wishes for the good intelligence and intimate relations between the two neighboring countries. But in the moment of starting on the voyage already announced, General Jerez presented himself in this capital in the capacity of Envoy Extraordinary of the Government of Nicaragua, and in company with Col. Don Pedro Rómulo Negrete, who had the kindness to go from here to Nicaragua and act in this matter as mediator in representation of the Republic of Salvador. To all these patriotic steps it has been in part due that the treaty of the 15th of April was celebrated, and I have the honor to send to you with this note a sufficient number of printed copies thereof.

The visit which His Excellency the President of this Republic paid to Nicaragua on the 22d of April ultimo had the good effect, not only of causing the arrangement of all the pending questions between both Republics to be terminated, but also of strengthening the fraternal bonds which connect them together, and establishing on solid foundation peace, friendship, and commercial relations among their people. I have the honor to accompany herewith, as a consequence of the above-named steps, the treaty of defensive alliance celebrated between the two Governments, with the intervention of that of Salvador by means of its representative, Col. Don Pedro R. Negrete.

His Excellency the President of this Republic does not doubt that the said treaty will be accepted by your own Government, and also by that of Guatemala, and that the stipulations which it contains will serve as preliminary basis for other and more interesting agreements which may unite again the people of Central America and make them mighty in their union.

Availing of such a plausible occasion, I have the honor to subscribe myself your obedient servant,

NAZARIO TOLEDO.

To His Excellency THE MINISTER OF FOREIGN RELATIONS of the Government of Honduras.

No. 18.

The Constitution of Nicaragua declares that the Nicaraguan territory borders on the south by the Republic of Costa Rica. — The treaty of limits is raised to the character of fundamental law.

POLITICAL CONSTITUTION.

(Promulgated August 19, 1858).

CHAPTER I.

Of the Republic.

ARTICLE 1. The Republic of Nicaragua is the same which was, in ancient times, called the Province of Nicaragua, and, after the independence, State of Nicaragua. Its territory borders on the east and northeast by the sea of the Antilles; on the north and northwest by the State of Honduras; on the west and south by the Pacific Ocean; *and on the southeast by the Republic of Costa Rica.* The LAWS ON SPECIAL LIMITS FORM PART OF THE CONSTITUTION. * * *

ARTICLE 3. The territory shall be divided for the different purposes of the administration of the Government into such departments, districts, and sections as the Constitution and the laws provide for.

[From "La Gaceta de Nicaragua," No. 31, August 28, 1858.]

No. 19.

The value and force of the treaty of limits is recognized, and one of its provisions is thus carried into effect.

NATIONAL PALACE,
MANAGUA, *April* 13, 1859.

To the Minister of Foreign Relations of the Government of Costa Rica.

SIR: I have the honor to enclose for your information an authorized copy of the Convention made on the 12th instant between myself and Mr. Felix Belly, director of the enterprise of the canal in regard to provisional transit, and this I do, for the purpose of COMPLYING WITH THE ENGAGEMENT CONTRACTED BY THIS REPUBLIC WITH THE REPUBLIC OF COSTA RICA IN ARTICLE VIII OF THE TREATY OF LIMITS OF APRIL 15 OF LAST YEAR, in order that when the opinion of the Government of Costa Rica is given final action may be taken upon it.

I have the honor to offer to you the sentiments of consideration and esteem with which I subscribe myself your attentive servant,

PEDRO ZELEDÓN.

No. 20.

Costa Rica is recognized as a party to the contract of the Interoceanic Canal, and its acquiescence is asked to make certain modifications in it.

DEPARTMENT OF FOREIGN RELATIONS OF NICARAGUA,
NATIONAL PALACE,
MANAGUA, *April* 16, 1859.

Mr. MINISTER: As I have told you before, the contract about the canal, celebrated at Rivas on the 1st of May of the preceding year, was submitted to the ratification of the Chambers, which have granted it with the amendments and additions which appear from the authorized copy herewith accompanied. The Government, noticing THAT NICARAGUA, COSTA RICA, AND THE COMPANY ARE PARTIES TO THE CONTRACT, and that each one of them has to ratify it before it takes effect, and that the amendments and additions made by the Chambers have altered it in such a way as to require new ratification by the Congress of Costa Rica, and acceptance by Mr. Felix Belly; noticing furthermore that the contract has become unpopular, and that the amendments and additions made by the Chambers have given rise to odious interpretations;—deem it proper to confer with Mr. Felix Belly, and to enter with him into an equitable agreement, and granting him the temporary permission demanded by the situation for giving lodgings and occupation to his engineers, laborers, &c., in the San Juan river and the lake, all of which is reported to your Government in the meantime, IN ORDER TO OBTAIN FROM YOUR REPUBLIC THE RATIFICATION WHICH IS NECESSARY FOR CARRYING ON THE WORK.

The grantee left this city yesterday satisfied with the loyalty of the Government, and decided to wait for the above-named ratification.

In consequence thereof the Government has placed its EXE-

QUATUR to the contract as amended, and I have the pleasure to transmit to you a copy thereof for the purposes above indicated.

Another contract, relative to the steamer "Virgen," which the Company needs to charter, has been celebrated separately, and in due time it was submitted to the ratification of the Government.

The Company by faithfully and earnestly conducting the work will re-establish its lost credit, and if the transit is granted when that work is finished, all the interests will be conciliated.

I have the honor to offer the sentiments of my esteem and consideration.

PEDRO ZELEDÓN.

To THE MINISTER OF FOREIGN RELATIONS of the Government of the Republic of Costa Rica.

No. 21.

Official despatch acknowledging that the Nicaraguan territory ends at the Salinas Bay as declared by the treaty of limits of 1858.

[SEAL]. NATIONAL PALACE,
MANAGUA, *April* 27, 1859.

SIR: The Prefect of the Department of Rivas, under date of the 23d instant, said to the Government as follows: "I have positive information that IN A SMALL ISLAND AT THE GULF OF 'LAS SALINAS' WHERE THE TERRITORY OF THE REPUBLIC ENDS, a great deposit of iron and other metals, taken there by the filibusters during the time they were in this country, is to be found. That deposit was concealed under a large straw-roofed cabin which subsequently was burned by certain fishermen; and I have been assured that a Frenchman of Liberia arrived there awhile ago and carried away on board of some boats several tools which, when taken to his city, constituted loads for three beasts of burden."

"The public Treasury of Nicaragua suffered, no doubt, by this; and both for this reason, as well as for the reason *that said Island is on waters belonging exclusively to the State*, it corresponds to it to take knowledge of the facts."

His Excellency the President has directed me to request, through you, the President of your Republic, to order the authorities of Moracia to gather and safely keep the iron and other metals which may be found in the island of the Gulf of Las Salinas, in order that upon the proper notice and information of the expenses incurred in the operation my Government may make the proper indemnification of the latter and the transfer of the metal to where it may be proper.

Trusting that your Government will comply with the request herein made, I have the honor to renew to you the sentiments of esteem with which I am, your obedient servant,

PEDRO ZELEDÓN.

To THE MINISTER OF FOREIGN RELATIONS of the Government of Costa Rica.

No. 22.

The Nicaraguan Chambers direct Article VIII of the Treaty of Limits of April 15, 1858, to be complied with, and the Executive Power carries their decision into effect.

NATIONAL PALACE,
MANAGUA, *May* 7, 1859.

Mr. MINISTER: I have the honor to acknowledge the receipt of your estimable communication of the 27th of April ultimo, dated at Rivas, enclosing the decree issued by His Excellency the Captain General, President of the Republic of Costa Rica, approving in all parts the contract entered into in this city on the 12th of the same month, between this Government and Messrs. Felix Belly & Co., granting them exclusive transit through the San Juan river and Lake of Nicaragua to the Pacific, A CONTRACT UPON WHICH THE LEGISLATIVE CHAMBERS OF THIS REPUBLIC DECIDED TO HEAR THE OPINION OF THE GOVERNMENT OF COSTA RICA, AS REQUIRED BY ARTICLE VIII OF THE TREATY OF LIMITS ADJUSTED ON APRIL 15 OF LAST YEAR, BETWEEN NICARAGUA AND COSTA RICA.

The above-named contract will be submitted to the ratification of the Chambers as prescribed by the Constitution, because the Government has authority only for declaring the transit to be free and for granting it to companies under this and other basis established by the decree.

The loyalty and good understanding, which are due to the Government of Costa Rica and to the interested parties, impose upon me the duty to give you this information, and at the same time, I have the honor to subscribe myself,

Your attentive servant,

PEDRO ZELEDÓN.

To THE MINISTER OF FOREIGN RELATIONS of the Supreme Government of Costa Rica.

No. 23.

Official despatch showing the validity and strength of the Treaty of Limits, and the execution thereof by both Republics.

DEPARTMENT OF FOREIGN RELATIONS
OF THE REPUBLIC OF COSTA RICA,
NATIONAL PALACE, SAN JOSÉ, *May* 16, 1859.

Mr. MINISTER: *In compliance with Article VIII of the final treaty of limits between this Republic and yours,* and by note of the 13th of April instant, you have been pleased to transmit for the knowledge of this Government a copy of the convention of provisional transit celebrated between you and Mr. Felix Belly on the 12th of the same month.

The supreme Government of your country has been already informed that the Costa Rican Government has accepted as far as it is concerned the above-named convention; and now nothing new is to be added to said acceptance.

I remain, your attentive and obedient servant,

NAZARIO TOLEDO.

To His Excellency THE MINISTER OF FOREIGN RELATIONS of the Republic of Nicaragua.

No. 24.

Costa Rica a party to the contract of Interoceanic Canal approves modifications made thereto.

No. 45. DEPARTMENT OF FOREIGN RELATIONS
OF THE REPUBLIC OF COSTA RICA,
NATIONAL PALACE, SAN JOSÉ, *June* 27, 1859.

Mr. MINISTER: In answer to the remarks of your communication of the 7th of May ultimo, and in accordance with the contents of the note addressed to you on the 16th of May, No. 36, the undersigned has the honor, by order of the President, to transmit to you a copy of the decree enacted by the Congress of this Republic on the 22d instant, *approving the amendments and additions made by the Chambers of Nicaragua to the contract with the Atlantic-Pacific Maritime Canal,* made at Rivas on the 1st of May, last year.

You will be pleased to submit this decree to His Excellency the President of Nicaragua, and to accept the testimony of esteem and respect with which I subscribe myself your attentive and obedient servant,

NAZARIO TOLEDO.

To His Excellency THE MINISTER OF FOREIGN RELATIONS of the Republic of Nicaragua.

No. 25.

Despatch showing the validity and strength of the Treaty of Limits, and its execution.

No. 44. DEPARTMENT OF FOREIGN RELATIONS
OF THE REPUBLIC OF COSTA RICA,
NATIONAL PALACE, SAN JOSÉ, *June* 27, 1859.

Mr. MINISTER: Señor Don Máximo Jerez, on behalf of his Government, and IN COMPLIANCE WITH ARTICLE VIII OF THE TREATY OF LIMITS, transmitted from Punta Arenas the new contract of transit that he made in New York on the 6th of June instant with the Company, or branch thereof, which was formerly called "American Atlantic-Pacific Maritime Canal Co."

* * * * * * *

SALVADOR GONZALEZ.

To His Excellency THE MINISTER OF FOREIGN RELATIONS of the Republic of Nicaragua.

No. 26.

The Government of Nicaragua asks that of Costa Rica to remove its custom officers from the La Flor river, its former frontier, to the new limit fixed by the treaty of April 15, 1858.

[SEAL].
NATIONAL PALACE,
MANAGUA, *August* 3, 1859.

Mr. MINISTER: The Military Governor of the Southern Department has reported to the Government that the *Custom-House officers of your Republic on the Nicaraguan frontier* STILL CONTINUE STATIONED, AS THEY WERE BEFORE, AT THE LA FLOR RIVER, *exercising authority on all the extent of the Salinas Bay up to Escameca, where there is a military post of this Republic, and on the side of the lake as far as the Sapoá river opposite to Salgueros;* and that although the officer commanding that post has received orders to avoid all disagreement with the Costa Rican custom officers, as the latter interfere with the traffic, and *even have confiscated some articles at the La Flor river*, it is possible that some question affecting private interests may also require the action of the Government.

For this reason, *and considering that* THE FORMER LIMIT OF THE LA FLOR RIVER *lies this side of the middle of the Gulf of Las Salinas*, WHICH IS THE NEW ONE ESTABLISHED BY ARTICLE II OF THE TREATY OF APRIL 15, 1858 ; *and that Salgueros is not found on the straight line spoken of by the same article*, His Excellency, the President of the Republic, desiring to avoid a conflict which might injure private interests, *and also being disposed to establish on the frontier the proper vigilance to avoid smuggling*, which is done there to the great detriment of the interests of the Nicaraguan treasury, taking advantage of the franchise of commerce which the Province of Moracia and the port of Punta Arenas, of Costa Rica enjoy, has deemed it proper to call the attention of His Excellency the President of your Republic, as I do now through you, to the foregoing facts, and request him *to cause the action of its custom service to be reduced* TO THE LIMITS ESTABLISHED BY THE TREATY AFORESAID; and in case that this should be difficult, owing to the fact that the dividing straight line, which is the limit on that side, has not been yet actually drawn, to be pleased to appoint a surveyor, enjoying his confidence, who, in union with the one appointed by this Government, may proceed to locate the said line before private interests are further affected and the rigor of judicial action is resorted to.

I have the honor to reiterate to you the sentiments of my greatest esteem and consideration.

PEDRO ZELEDÓN.

To THE MINISTER OF FOREIGN RELATIONS of the Supreme Government of Costa Rica.

No. 27.

The Government of Costa Rica is invited to assist that of Nicaragua in improving the port of San Juan del Norte, almost destroyed by the deviation of the waters of the San Juan river into the bed of the Colorado river.

NICARAGUA DEPARTMENT OF FOREIGN RELATIONS,
NATIONAL PALACE,
MANAGUA, *December* 13, 1859.

Mr. MINISTER: The attention of the Government of Nicaragua has been forcibly called to the condition of the *port of San Juan del Norte, which has been filled up and almost rendered useless on account of the sand which has accumulated in it ever since its waters have abundantly flowed into the channel of the Colorado river;* and such a state of things must also demand the attention of Costa Rica, because the interest of the latter in this subject is not less felt, since by EXISTING TREATIES SHE HAS THE RIGHT *of navigation and free import from there.*

The inhabitants of the town named Greytown have made an effort to collect subscriptions and do such work as possible for the purpose of confining the waters to the channel of the Bay; and the Government, in spite of the scarcity of the public resources, is trying to raise money among the merchants of the Republic, and proposes to employ all the convicts of the State prison, more than 40 in number, to carry on that work, principally by closing, by means of palisades or other proper works, the communication between the San Juan and the Colorado rivers.

For such a purpose, and in the persuasion that Costa Rica will co-operate with pleasure in this work, I have been instructed to invite it to do so, and I hope that you will be pleased to set forth in your answer in what way such assistance will be rendered, it being preferable to a great degree that the said assistance be pecuniary, in order to provide for the support of the laborers and furnish them with tools and other implements.

I pray you, Mr. Minister, to submit all of this to His Excellency the President of your Republic, to communicate to me his decision, and to accept the sentiments of esteem and consideration with which I subscribe myself your very attentive servant,

PEDRO ZELEDÓN.

To THE MINISTER OF FOREIGN RELATIONS of the Republic of Costa Rica.

No. 28.

Nicaragua reminds Costa Rica of the duty imposed upon her by the treaty of April 15, 1858, *to defend her frontiers at San Juan and the Bolarios Bay.*

[SEAL]. NATIONAL PALACE,
MANAGUA, *September* 5, 1860.

Sir: Your Government must certainly be aware that William Walker has invaded Central America; and, as it is probable that that bandit may attempt some operation on the side of the river of San Juan del Norte, my Government has taken such steps as proper to protect that frontier and reinforce its military posts.

BUT AS ACCORDING TO THE TREATY OF APRIL 15, 1858, AS READ IN ITS IVTH ARTICLE, BOTH YOUR REPUBLIC AND THIS OUGHT TO TAKE CARE OF THE DEFENCE OF THAT LINE, my Government expects that your Government, in view of the threatening danger, WILL COMPLY WITH THE SACRED AND INTERESTING DUTY INCUMBENT UPON IT, by sending there such a force as may be necessary to protect the locality and repel the enemy if the invasion should take place through that point.

My Government thinks it proper to inform yours, furthermore, that another filibustering expedition, under the command of Henningsen, an old comrade of Walker, is now being organized in California, and that it is very probable that they intend to land at some of the ports on the Pacific coast, for which reason it is advisable that sufficient forces are sent to the SALINAS BAY, *the defence of which is also entrusted to the Government of Costa Rica.*

All of which I have the honor to communicate to you by order of His Excellency the President of this Republic, for the purposes above referred to, hoping that you will be pleased to communicate to me the decision that your Government may reach on the subject.

I avail myself of this opportunity to offer you my respects.

HERMDO. ZEPEDA.

To The Minister of Foreign Relations of the Supreme Government of the Republic of Costa Rica.

No. 29.

Execution of the Treaty of Limits.

SAN JOSÉ, *January* 25, 1861.

Mr. MINISTER: In order to send back the courier *ex professo*, whom you were pleased to send to this Republic, the President has directed me to tell you that, *as he has to consider the contract of transit in compliance with the stipulations of the Cañas-Jerez treaty,* he has decided that the Costa Rican Commissioner, who shall leave for your Republic within a very short period, should be the bearer of the said contract and of the decision thereon reached by this Government.

With this I leave your favor of the 10th instant answered, and I subscribe myself your obedient servant,

A. ESQUIVEL.

To His Excellency THE MINISTER OF FOREIGN RELATIONS of the Republic of Nicaragua.

No. 30.

The Nicaraguan Chambers direct the Executive to comply with Art. VIII of the Treaty of Limits of April 15, 1858.

NATIONAL PALACE,
GRANADA, *February* 25, 1863.

Mr. MINISTER: The contract of interoceanic transit, celebrated between the Government and Don José Rosa Perez, an authenticated copy of which I have the honor to accompany, together with the proposal upon the same subject made by Mr. J. E. Russell, having been submitted to the Chambers for ratification, THEY WERE PLEASED TO ABSTAIN FROM DOING SO, AND TO DECIDE IN COMPLIANCE WITH ARTICLE VIII OF THE TREATY OF APRIL 15, 1858, BETWEEN THIS REPUBLIC AND YOURS, THAT THE SAID DOCUMENTS SHOULD BE RETURNED TO THE EXECUTIVE IN ORDER THAT THEY, AS WELL AS ANY OTHER PROPOSAL WHICH MAY BE MADE, SHOULD BE SUBMITTED TO THE GOVERNMENT OF COSTA RICA FOR THE PURPOSE OF HAVING ITS OPINION ON THEM.

In compliance with the above decision, I have the honor to submit to you the said contract and proposal for the knowledge of His Excellency the President, and hope you will be pleased to communicate to me in due time his opinion on them.

I have the honor to subscribe myself your attentive servant,

PEDRO ZELEDÓN.

To THE MINISTER OF FOREIGN RELATIONS of the Supreme Government of Costa Rica.

No. 31.

*The strict compliance with the treaty of limits demonstrated.
— The Government of Costa Rica asks the rights vested in it
by Article VI of a contract of transit to be expressly secured.*

*To His Excellency the Minister of Foreign Relations of the
Republic of Nicaragua.*

SIR: With your estimable note of the 25th of February ultimo this department has received a copy of the contract of transit celebrated between the Government of your Republic and Don José Rosa Perez, and also the subsequent proposal of Mr. John E. Russell, all of which has been transmitted to this Government in order that it may express its opinion, AS PROVIDED BY ARTICLE VIII OF THE TREATY OF LIMITS OF APRIL 15, 1858.

I hastened to give information of your note to His Excellency the President of the Republic, who, after having carefully examined the documents referred to, has directed me to tell you in answer, as I have the honor to do, what follows:

Considering that, according to the above-named stipulation of the treaty of April 15, 1858, the vote of Costa Rica *is understood to be advisory in all matters which do not directly affect the natural rights of this Republic, nor those which emanate from her sovereignty, or the absolute rights of property, or of the common use that it has over certain places at the port of San Juan del Norte, the San Juan river, the Lake, and the Salinas Bay,* my Government has deemed it advisable, and trusts that your Government will consider it in the same way, that the opinion or vote should be extended to some other clauses of the contracts, although they do not directly affect the territorial interests of Costa Rica.

The spirit of Article VIII, and the reasons which were considered when it was enacted, were, if we are not mistaken, to provide for the preservation of the common interests in all cases which might produce complications with foreign countries, since it cannot be doubted that such questions affect and endanger the two Republics, and much more so under the influence of the events which take place in other points of Central America.

Under this point of view, and starting from the remark that the compact has been made with foreigners, whose claims, as shown by experience, may produce great evils and an intervention or invasion from abroad which would also threaten the neighboring countries, this Government is of the opinion that, in a contract of this kind, all stipulations which, by their consequences or by their language, may give occasion or pretext to disputes and to exaggerated pretension must be carefully avoided, and it is for this reason that I allow myself to call the attention of your Government to the following suggestions:

* * * * * * *

ARTICLE 8. *For the sake of clearness it seems advisable to make express mention of the Treaty of Limits of April 15, 1858, saving the rights which Costa Rica has by virtue of this treaty over the port of San Juan del Norte, the banks of the San Juan river, and the Salinas Bay, and the free navigation in all these waters, expressing that the exclusive privilege of the contractor will not prevent Costa Rica from establishing in the same waters steam navigation for the commerce with the tributary rivers of its territory, which empty into the San Juan river and the lake, and from exercising territorial sovereignty in all cases in which the transit company should be called to exercise some act of administration, use, or commerce within the territory of the said Republic, or subject to the laws and authorities of the same, as, for instance, in the case of Article 9.*

* * * * * * *

ARTICLE 17. In consideration of the intimate relations of friendship which exist between this Republic and yours, and of the advantages that the enterprise of transit has to derive from its frequent trade with the Costa Rican littoral, it seems to be equitable that the grantee should show in favor of citizens of Costa Rica, who would use for their commerce the means of transportation and communication of the company, and of those immigrants who would come in number of no less than 10 to settle in Costa Rica, the same liberality and the same franchises as granted to others.

If this Government should determine to send European mail by the way of San Juan del Norte and Sarapiquí, the grantee will carry the said mail subject to the postal conventions in force and in accordance with Article X of the project of contract, and XI of the proposal of Mr. Russell.

The ideas which I have the honor to set forth, are also applicable to the proposals made by the representative of Messrs. James M. Brow and George G. Hobson, of New York, it being understood that, in case your Government gives preference to the Russell-Perez contract, it will be necessary to render the language of the provision clearer and fuller in order to mark well the principal points of difference between them. In everything else it is to be supposed that the proposing party will accept the same basis as adopted in the former contract.

These are the remarks which this Government submits in regard to the contracts which the Nicaraguan Government has submitted to it; and now the only thing left to me is to assure Your Excellency that the above remarks have been made in the best spirit and looking exclusively at the common good. On the other hand, this Government is sincerely grateful for the sentiments which yours entertains in favor of the faithful and strict fulfilment of the compacts and for the confidence that it shows and the loyalty and righteousness of our relations with your Republic, our ally and sister.

I take advantage of this opportunity to subscribe myself,
Your very attentive servant,
FRANCISCO M. IGLESIAS.

APRIL 1, 1863.

No. 32.

The Government of Nicaragua asks for some forces to be situated at Sarapaqui (a confluent of the San Juan river, on the right bank).

GOVERNMENT HOUSE,
GRANADA, *April* 23, 1863.

Mr. MINISTER: Mr. Felix Belly, who has recommended himself so much by reason of his former action in Central America, has submitted to this Government a project of interoceanic transit and steam navigation in the interior of the Republic, an authorized copy of which I have the honor to enclose to you, *for the purposes of Article VIII of the treaty of April* 15, 1858.

With reference to your estimable despatch of the 1st instant, relative to the difficulties that lately arose between the Government and the Central American Transit Co., I must inform you, for the knowledge of your Government, that two agents of the said company, duly authorized by it to revalidate the contract which the Government had declared to be void, have just arrived in this city. Up to this date the Government has not deemed it advisable to listen officially to the proposals that they have come to make, its reasons to do so being, 1st, that they have not yet paid the sums due to this Republic as tolls for passengers; and, 2d, because the Government thinks that, if not all, some, at least, of the officers of the company are accessories to the piratical and filibuster outrage perpetrated on the 7th instant at the La Virgen Bay, on board the steamer *San Juan*, unfortunately in connivance with forces of Honduras and Salvador; but, as in the difficult situation in which Nicaragua finds herself at present it is possible for the company to do some violence to the rights of this Republic, the Government may perhaps be compelled by pure necessity to enter with it into some equitable arrangement of temporary character, but by no means final, which, while bridging over the difficulties of the present moment, enables the Government to do justice when the circumstances may be more propitious.

I do not think it to be inopportune in view of the current events to recommend to you and the Supreme Government of your country to cause some forces to be stationed at Sarapiqui to meet on that side any emergency that the same events might occasion there.

I take advantage of this opportunity to reiterate to you the just considerations with which I subscribe myself, your very attentive and obedient servant,

EDUARDO CASTILLO.

To the Hon. THE MINISTER OF FOREIGN RELATIONS of the Supreme Government of Costa Rica.

No. 33.

The Nicaraguan Chambers order one of the provisions of the treaty of limits of 1858 to be complied with.

ART. XI. Article XVII shall be stricken out, and the following shall be inserted in its stead :

" The present contract shall have no effect until accepted by Capt. Pim, and until the Governments of Guatemala and Costa Rica shall have given their opinion upon it ; and for that purpose the time for the *exequatur* is extended sixty days longer."

[Law of May 10, 1864. See pamphlet "Contrato de ferro-carril celebrado el 5 de Marzo entre el Honorable Sr. Ministro de Hacienda Lic. D. Antonio Silva, y el Sr. Bedford, C. T. Pim, capitan de la Marina Real inglesa, y ratificado por el Congreso de Nicaragua el 17 de Marzo de 1864. Managua. Imprenta del Gobierno, á cargo de A. Mejia, 1864."]

No. 34.

Validity and force of the treaty of limits.—Costa Rica does not accede to station forces at Sarapiquí on the ground that it is unnecessary.

DEPARTMENT OF
FOREIGN RELATIONS OF COSTA RICA,
SAN JOSÉ, *May* 26, 1863.

SIR: In taking possession, *ad interim*, of this department, my attention was called to your note enclosing a copy of the project of the contract of transit submitted to your Government by Mr. Felix Belly, and making some suggestions in regard to the advisability that the Government of this Republic should station some forces at Sarapiquí to meet there certain emergencies.

In regard to the Belly contract, you will allow me to call the attention of your Government to the timely remarks made by our common Minister at Washington in regard to the expiration of the contract celebrated with the American company in his despatch addressed to your department under date of the 28th of April, a copy of which was sent to this Government.

My Government thinks, therefore, that, for the present, and notwithstanding the good antecedents of Mr. Belly, the most prudent thing would be to refrain from making any new contract of transit and wait until the differences between your Government and the North American Company, in regard to the validity or invalidity of the contract, are settled; and this is all the more to be done, as it appears, according to the remarks already alluded to, that the probabilities of success are on the side of the American Company.

I hope that you will not see in these suggestions any thing else than the desire of carrying such an important business to success, as well as the interest that my Government has, in that your Government adopts the best means to terminate a matter which, like this, may have such important results.

In view of this it would be useless to enter into the substance of the Belly project, since this Government expects that yours will not take any step in the subject until all questions with the Transit American Company are settled. *Therefore, my Government, reserving for that occasion to give the vote secured to it by Article VIII of the treaty of April* 15, 1858, promises itself that your Government, before contracting new engagements, will do all that it can to bridge over the difficulties which it now encounters.

In regard to the suggestions made by you *on the advisability to station some forces at Sarapiqui*, I am directed to reply that as, fortunately, the danger which threatened your Republic on that side has already disappeared, the necessity of sending there any forces has also ceased to exist.

In transmitting the above to you I have the honor to subscribe myself,

Your very attentive and obedient servant,.

JULIAN VOLIO.

To His Excellency THE MINISTER OF FOREIGN RELATIONS of the Republic of Nicaragua.

No. 35.

Costa Rica protests against the occupation and deterioration of the Colorado river.

DEPARTMENT OF FOREIGN RELATIONS
OF THE REPUBLIC OF COSTA RICA,
SAN JOSÉ, *July* 15, 1863.

SIR: This Government having been informed that the Transit Company in Nicaragua *attempts to obstruct the Colorado river which runs within the territory of Costa Rica,* the President was pleased to direct the proper investigation to be made; and, as it appears from the report of the special committee appointed for that purpose, that the engineers of the above-named company sounded and marked the Colorado river, and have already prepared four useless schooners which they intend to load with sand and stones and sink in the said river in order to close it, His Excellency has directed me to address your Government and ask of it *to be pleased to prevent said purpose from being accomplished, since it is so extremely injurious to the interests of this country, and to give notice at the same time to the directors of the company aforesaid, that he is determined to prevent all usurpation of the territory from being consummated, and that the expenses to be incurred in the repairing of the damages caused by them in the river will be charged to those who caused them to be incurred.*

With distinguished consideration, &c.,

JULIAN VOLIO.

To His Excellency THE MINISTER OF FOREIGN RELATIONS
of the Republic of Nicaragua.

No. 36.

The Government of Nicaragua recognizes that the Colorado river and its mouth are in Costa Rican territory and belong to Costa Rica, and cannot be closed against the will of the latter.

GOVERNMENT HOUSE,
LEON, *July* 21, 1863.

Mr. MINISTER: Under this date I have written to the general agent of the company, and transmitted to the United States Minister residing in Nicaragua the following despatch:

"The Department of Foreign Relations of the Government of the Republic of Costa Rica has addressed to this Department, under date of July 15th, the following despatch: 'This Government having been informed that the Transit Company in Nicaragua *attempts to obstruct the Colorado river, which runs within the territory of Costa Rica*, the President was pleased to direct the proper investigation to be made, and as it appears from the report of the special committee appointed for that purpose that the engineers of the above-named company sounded and marked the Colorado river, and have already prepared four useless schooners which they intend to load with sand and stones, and sink in the said river in order to close it, His Excellency has directed me to address your Government and ask of it *to be pleased to prevent said purpose from being accomplished, since it is so extremely injurious to the interests of this country*, and to give notice at the same time to the directors of the company aforesaid that he is determined to prevent *all usurpation in his territory from being consummated*, and that the expenses to be incurred in the repairing of the damages caused by them in the river will be charged to those who caused them to be incurred.

"'With distinguished consideration I subscribe myself, your attentive and obedient servant,

"'J. VOLIO.'

" This Government had already received information that some old vessels had been bought by the company for the purpose of closing the mouth of the Colorado river, and noticed that this step would cause great injury to the town of San Juan del Norte on account of the violent accumulation of water at the mouth of the San Juan river which would be produced by it.

" On the other hand, the grant of transit made by the Government to the company is only temporary, because, in the opinion of the Government, the contract had expired; and it cannot see without suspicion that the said company seems to be bent upon making permanent works which ought to have been accomplished during the time fixed in the contract, and which now cannot take place under the provisional grant afterwards made.

" Under these circumstances I have been directed to tell you that THE CLOSING OF THE MOUTH OF THE COLORADO RIVER, WHICH RUNS IN THE TERRITORY OF THE REPUBLIC OF COSTA RICA, WHICH RESISTS THAT CLOSING, CANNOT BE PERMITTED, and that no other permanent work in the territory of Nicaragua not within the permission lately granted of provisional transit, under the trust and confidence of the United States Minister, can either be allowed.

" I have the honor to communicate it to you for your information, and subscribe myself your attentive servant,

" PEDRO ZELEDÓN."

And I have the honor to transmit to you the foregoing despatch for your information, and in answer to your despatch of the 15th instant above copied, assuring you that my Government will, on its part, always prevent any new work which may be attempted to be done upon 'the territory of your Republic.

I subscribe myself, with all consideration, your very attentive and obedient servant,

PEDRO ZELEDÓN.

To the HON. MINISTER OF FOREIGN RELATIONS of the Supreme Government of the Republic of Costa Rica.

No. 37.

Nicaragua recognizes still more solemnly that the Colorado river and the right bank of the San Juan river are Costa Rican territory.

GOVERNMENT HOUSE,
LEON, *July* 28, 1863.

SIR: In consequence of your estimable despatch No. 30, of the 15th instant, the proper communication has been addressed to the general agent of the company, stating that *the Government of Nicaragua does not permit him to do any work* IN COSTA RICAN TERRITORY, AS THE RIGHT BANK OF THE SAN JUAN RIVER AT THE CONFLUENCE OF THE COLORADO IS, nor to do any other work of permanent character in pursuance of the grant made in favor of the company only temporarily, for no more than three months. The same communication was transcribed to the Minister of the United States, who has under his care and trust the property of the company. The Government of Nicaragua therefore, far from countenancing said work, *relies upon Costa Rica to oppose it and prevent it from being consummated in its territory.*

I have the honor to say this to you in answer to your despatch above named, and subscribe myself your attentive servant,

PEDRO ZELEDÓN.

To THE MINISTER OF FOREIGN RELATIONS of the Supreme Government of Costa Rica.

No. 38.

The Minister of Nicaragua in Washington solemnly declares before the American Government that the Republic of Costa Rica borders on the interior waters of Nicaragua, and that its flag is the only one which, in union with the Nicaraguan flag, can float on said waters.

LEGATION OF NICARAGUA,
WASHINGTON, *Oct.* 7, 1863.

MOST EXCELLENT SIR:

* * * * * * *

On the other hand, I can assure Your Excellency that the present administration of Nicaragua DOES NOT FEEL DISPOSED TO CONSENT THAT ANY OTHER FLAG, EXCEPT HER OWN AND THAT OF COSTA RICA, AS A BORDERING STATE, SHOULD FLOAT IN THE NAVIGATION OF HER INTERIOR WATERS, *and that it considers that the use of the flag of the United States made by the Central American Transit Company, and even by the meanest laborers of the same, for the purpose of evading the orders and escaping the authority of Nicaragua, is an unauthorized abuse*, and that, it being persuaded that such an abuse can only produce complications, it will maintain its right, and will demand from the said company, or from any other company owing its existence to it, that it should root itself in the country and become, therefore, nationalized, according to the law of nations, and use pre-eminently the national flag, whenever one should be required within its jurisdiction, no other flag being admitted, except under exceptional circumstances and through courtesy.

* * * * * * *

LUIS MOLINA.

To His Excellency WILLIAM H. SEWARD,
&c., &c., &c., *Washington, D. C.*

[From "La Gaceta" of Nicaragua, No. 49, January 16, 1864.]

No. 39.

The Government of Nicaragua approves the declaration of its Minister at Washington, and commends him for his zeal and fidelity.

DEPARTMENT OF FOREIGN RELATIONS.

In consequence of the Executive Decrees of November 29th ultimo and March 2d instant, in which the contract of interoceanic transit was declared to be invalid, because the company had failed to comply with the indispensable conditions under which it had been granted, and in which the property of the said transit company, already belonging to Nicaragua by virtue of the stipulations of the same contract, was ordered to be taken possession of,—the company attempted to give rise to an international question, and by means of protests and affidavits of interested parties it attempted to surprise the Government of the United States, and falsely charged that when the said property was taken possession of, at the San Juan del Norte river and port, the flag of the United States hoisted upon each one of the company's establishments had been unworthily insulted.

His Excellency the Minister of Nicaragua at Washington, having been informed of those steps, and being zealous of the honor of the Republic and of the good understanding between his Government and the Government of the United States, engaged himself at once in causing an investigation of the facts to be made and communicated to that effect with His Excellency the Secretary of State of the North American Republic. The satisfactory result of this action is shown by the following communications, which the Government deems it proper to publish since they do due honor to the good faith and loyalty which govern the relations of the United States with Nicaragua, and reflect *no less credit* on the zeal and fidelity of our Minister at Washington.

No. 40.

The action of Don Luis Molina, Minister of Nicaragua in Washington, is approved and commended.—Executive Order rewarding the important services of Don Luis Molina, Minister Plenipotentiary of Nicaragua in the United States, and Mr. Mandeville Carlisle and Don Fernando Guzman.

THE GOVERNMENT,

In consideration of the extraordinary and important services of our Minister Plenipotentiary in Washington, Lic. Don Luis Molina, rendered in the question lately raised by the Central American Transit Company in the United States; and of the new contract which has been submitted to the approval and ratification of Congress; and also of the enlightened and valuable assistance rendered by Mr. Mandeville Carlisle, a lawyer, in the framing of the said contract; and also of the services rendered by Senator Don Fernando Guzman, in his trip to the United States for the same purpose, has decided to reward them as follows:

1st. His Excellency Don Luis Molina, Minister Plenipotentiary of Nicaragua in the United States, will be paid the sum of $10,000 in American gold.

2d. The lawyer, Mr. Mandeville Carlisle, will be paid $5,000 in the same money.

3d. Senator Don Fernando Guzman will be paid $2,500 in the same money.

The above said sums shall be paid by the company, as agreed between it and Señor Molina, as soon as the contract is ratified and the ratification is made known to the company.

Given at the National Palace of Managua on the 11th day of January, 1864.

MARTINEZ.

Countersigned:
    ZELEDÓN,
        Secretary of Foreign Relations.

[From the "Gaceta de Nicaragua," No. 49, January 16, 1864.]

No. 41.

Validity and strength of the Treaty of April 15, 1858.

NATIONAL PALACE,
MANAGUA, *January* 11, 1864.

To The Minister of Foreign Relations of the Supreme Government of Costa Rica.

SIR: *In compliance with the provision of the treaty in force between this Republic and yours*, and notwithstanding the information which you have already received from our Minister in Washington, Lic. Don Luis Molina, that this step had been foreseen and anticipated, I have the honor to transmit to Your Excellency a copy of the convention lately concluded between the said Minister under the proper instructions and powers from this Government, and the President of the Board of Directors of the Central American Transit Company, by which all questions lately raised by the said company against the decrees of this Government, nullifying the old contract and taking possession of the steamboats and other property which, under the same contract, had become the property of the Republic, have been settled and set at rest. This contract has been ratified by the Company, and is now subject to the approval of the Government and the ratification of Congress, to which the Government wishes to submit it, *together with the vote or opinion of Costa Rica and Guatemala*, in compliance with the respective treaties, as soon as it meets either in ordinary or extraordinary session. This Government cannot on its own part refrain from expressing that it has seen with extreme satisfaction that by means of this contract it has obtained the most which it desired in its instructions, and that the loyalty, efficiency, and ability of the worthy son of Nicaragua, entrusted with this negotiation and with the representation in

Washington of this Republic and of the Republic of Costa Rica, have been demonstrated.

I have the honor on this occasion of repeating to you the sentiments of esteem and consideration with which I subscribe myself your obedient servant,

PEDRO ZELEDÓN.

No. 42.

Validity and strength of the Treaty of Limits.

NATIONAL PALACE,
MANAGUA, *March* 19, 1864.

To the Minister of Foreign Relations of the Supreme Government of Costa Rica.

SIR: *In compliance with the provisions of the treaty in force between this Republic and yours,* I have the honor to transmit for the knowledge of your Supreme Government an authorized copy of the contract lately celebrated between the Secretary of the Treasury, as Commissioner appointed to that effect by this Government, and Mr. Bedford C. F. Pim, and approved by the Executive of Nicaragua, and ratified by the Legislative Power of the same, as shown by its text, which I do in order to obtain *the vote or opinion of your Government* required by said treaty.

With sentiments of high consideration, I subscribe myself your attentive servant,

R. CORTES.

No. 43.

The Government of Costa Rica orders an exploration to be made of its lands bordering on the San Juan river.

DEPARTMENT OF FOREIGN RELATIONS OF THE
REPUBLIC OF COSTA RICA,
SAN JOSÉ, *May* 26, 1864.

SIR: About two months ago, a committee consisting of Señores Nieves and Luis Serrano, Juan Florentino and Anastasio Quesada, started from the City of Alajuela, *for the purpose of exploring in the neighborhood of the San Juan river* the most convenient places to open a road between this Republic and Castillo Viejo. After waiting in vain for the return of that committee, information was received that when the said gentlemen reached Castillo Viejo they were arrested by the authorities of your Republic and taken prisoners to fort San Carlos.

My Government hopes, from the high sense of justice of that of your country, that if the said gentlemen did not give any legal reason to be committed to prison the proper orders would be transmitted to the authorities of the fort to restore them to liberty and facilitate their return to their country.

I avail myself of this opportunity to subscribe myself your attentive servant,

J. VOLIO.

To His Excellency THE MINISTER OF FOREIGN RELATIONS
of the Republic of Nicaragua.

No. 44.

New expedition to the banks of the San Juan river.

DEPARTMENT OF FOREIGN RELATIONS
OF THE REPUBLIC OF COSTA RICA,
SAN JOSÉ, *July* 31, 1864.

SIR: Following the suggestion that you were pleased to make in your estimable despatch of June 9th last, I have the honor to inform you of the approaching departure of a new *exploring expedition to the banks of the San Juan river for the purpose of locating the shortest road between the interior of the Republic and the waters of that river.* The said Commission has been provided with the proper passports.

According to all information up to this time received, the opening of a road to the above-named point is a very easy matter, and it will considerably facilitate, to the common benefit of both Republics, their commercial relations. It is, therefore, to be expected that the Supreme Government of your country, if so disposed, will be pleased to direct the authorities of Castillo Viejo and Fort San Carlos not to oppose any obstacle to any one who, for the purposes aforesaid, should approach those fortresses, whenever they exhibit their passports from this Government.

Taking advantage of this opportunity, I have the honor to reiterate to you, &c.,

J. VOLIO.

To His Excellency THE MINISTER OF FOREIGN RELATIONS of Nicaragua.

No. 45.

Nicaragua acknowledges that Costa Rica borders on the San Juan river.

NATIONAL PALACE,
MANAGUA, *August* 23, 1864.

To the Hon. Minister of Foreign Relations of Costa Rica.

SIR: I have had the honor to receive your estimable despatch of the 31st of July ultimo, in reference to mine of June last, and to a new *exploring expedition sent by your Republic to the banks of the San Juan river* for the purpose of locating a convenient road.

THIS ROAD MAY BE OPENED UP TO THE SAN JUAN RIVER WITHOUT GOING OUT OF THE TERRITORY OF YOUR REPUBLIC, ACCORDING TO THE TREATY OF LIMITS BETWEEN IT AND NICARAGUA; but it may be also · constructed, if shortness is principally consulted, in such a way that it touches the territory which this Republic reserved for itself for the proper defence of Castillo Viejo and its free communication with San Carlos. In the latter case a previous arrangement would be necessary between the two Governments.

It is for this reason that the arrival of the explorers to Castillo Viejo, or to any place whatever between it and San Carlos, *cannot be but accidental;* and in order that it may not cause alarm in those garrisons I have sent a copy of this note to the respective commanding officers thereof, and I hope that you will be pleased to communicate the same to the contractor to avoid all mistakes.

I am, with high consideration, your attentive servant,

P. ZELEDÓN.

No. 46.

Nicaragua promises that the interests of Costa Rica will be respected, and that its rights will suffer no detriment.

NATIONAL PALACE,
MANAGUA, *June* 13, 1866.

Mr. MINISTER: I informed His Excellency the President of this Republic of your despatch of May 25 ultimo, reiterating the statements of the communication addressed by your Department, under date of July 15, 1863, in relation to the work of the transit company, and for the purpose of preventing the latter from doing anything which might obstruct the Colorado river, or any of its branches, this reiteration being made because your Government has been informed that some work of this kind is now intended to be done by the above said company.

This Department has no knowledge that any work is being done in the sense above indicated, and therefore, under this very date, it has asked the authorities at both the port and river of San Juan del Norte for the proper report. With the result thereof the proper answer will be given to your despatch of May 25 ultimo, above named; but in the meantime *the Supreme Government of Costa Rica may rest assured that the Government of Nicaragua will respect the interests of Costa Rica, and will see that its rights are in no way injured.* This is the answer which I have been directed to give you, and I have the honor to reiterate to you the protests of my great esteem.

ROSALIO CORTES.

To the Hon. MINISTER OF FOREIGN RELATIONS of the Supreme Government of the Republic of Costa Rica.

No. 47.

Costa Rica protests against the deviation of the waters of the Colorado river belonging to that Republic.

DEPARTMENT OF FOREIGN RELATIONS
OF THE REPUBLIC OF COSTA RICA,
SAN JOSÉ, *June* 26, 1866.

SIR: The President of the Republic having been informed that the Central American Transit Company *attempts to obstruct the Colorado river or some of its branches, all of which run in the territory of this Republic,* in order to increase the volume of waters of the San Juan river, and *trusting in the promise that your Government made to the Government of Costa Rica on July* 21, 1863, in answer to the communication of the 15th of the same month, *protesting against that attempt,* has been pleased to direct me to address your Government, as I have the honor to do, *reiterating the statements of the said communication of July* 15, 1863, in order that, in due regard to the interests of both Republics, your Government *may be pleased to interpose its authority to prevent the said company from carrying out its purpose of injuring the right bank of the San Juan river, belonging to Costa Rica, or the Colorado river, or any one its branches.*

Taking advantage of this opportunity, it is pleasing to me to offer you the assurances of my esteem, &c.

J. VOLIO.

To His Excellency THE MINISTER OF FOREIGN RELATIONS of the Republic of Nicaragua.

No. 48.

Despatch stating that a sanitary cordon of Costa Rica has trespassed on the Nicaraguan frontier as established by the treaty of 1858.

OFFICE OF THE PREFECT
OF THE SOUTHERN DEPARTMENT,
RIVAS, *January* 8, 1867.

*To the Hon. Secretary of State
of the Government of Nicaragua.*

SIR: I have the honor to report that the Government of Costa Rica moved, no doubt, by the information that cholera had broken out in this Republic, has ordered a sanitary cordon to be stationed on the frontier. But in doing so the Costa Rican Government *has invaded the territory of this Republic by establishing a garrison at the place named El Naranjito, which is two leagues, or perhaps more, distant on this side from the dividing line* lately agreed upon by the two Republics.

This, in my judgment, is an attack upon our property which may create great difficulties, and for this reason I report it to Your Excellency, in order that Your Excellency may take such action as proper.

MAXIMO ESPINOSA.

No. 49.

Nicaragua asks that a sanitary cordon be moved back to the frontier established by the Treaty of 1858.

[SEAL]. NATIONAL PALACE,
MANAGUA, *January* 12, 1867.

Mr. MINISTER: I have the honor to enclose an authorized copy of a communication sent to this Department by the Prefect of the Southern Department. You will see by it that the officers commanding a picket belonging to the sanitary cordon established by your Government *have trespassed upon the dividing line* by situating their forces in Nicaraguan territory.

My Government hopes that yours will be pleased to issue the proper orders for the purpose that the above-named forces *vacate the points which at present they occupy in this country and station themselves on Costa Rican soil.*

No doubt is entertained that such orders will be issued with the promptness required by the case, because it is not to be presumed, in view of the sense of justice of your Government and of the good relations which exist between the two countries, that there is any desire to do any hostile act against Nicaragua.

With the assurances of my greatest esteem and consideration, I subscribe myself your attentive servant,

ROSALIO CORTES.

To the Hon. MINISTER OF FOREIGN RELATIONS of the Supreme Government of Costa Rica.

No. 50.

The Government of Costa Rica consents to move back its sanitary cordon to a point indisputably located within the limits established by the treaty of April 15, 1858.

DEPARTMENT OF FOREIGN RELATIONS OF COSTA RICA,
SAN JOSÉ, *January* 25, 1867.

SIR: I submitted to the President of the Republic your attentive official communication of the 12th instant, enclosing an authorized copy of the letter addressed to you on the 8th instant by the Prefect of the Southern Department, and stating that the officer in command of the sanitary cordon of this Republic trespassed upon the dividing line in stationing forces on Nicaraguan territory, and that your Government expects from the sense of justice of my Government and the good relations existing between both countries that the proper orders should be given to the above-named forces to vacate the aforesaid territory. In consequence thereof I have been directed to give you the following answer:

Although the place where the Governor of Liberia stationed the first sanitary cordon is not shown to belong to the territory of Nicaragua, because the dividing line between the two Republics is not yet actually drawn there, still it was sufficient that your Government should deem that point to be included within the limits of your Republic, to make my own Government, without entering into the merits of the question and for the sake of harmony between one and another people and of the sincere friendship of both Governments, to cause the sanitary cordon to be, as it has been, immediately withdrawn and established only on such places as indisputably belong to the territory of Costa Rica.

The wishes of your Supreme Government are thus complied with; and, in transmitting to you this fact, I reiterate, &c.,

J. VOLIO.

To His Excellency THE MINISTER OF FOREIGN RELATIONS of Nicaragua.

No. 51.

Costa Rica shows her disposition to enter into arrangements with Nicaragua to determine by mutual agreement what should be done in regard to communications on the Atlantic side.

DEPARTMENT OF FOREIGN RELATIONS OF COSTA RICA,
SAN JOSÉ, *November* 25, 1868.

SIR: This Department has received, together with your important despatch of the 7th instant, an authenticated copy of the report of the civil engineer of your Republic *who made the survey of the San Juan and the Colorado rivers*, and in due conformity with the wishes of your Government, I now transmit to you a true copy of the report upon the same subject which has been made by the engineers of this Republic.

You will see that both reports entirely agree upon the principal fact, and consider that San Juan is the place where a good port can be made with less cost and more advantages.

My Government will pay the greatest attention to such an important matter, and will readily enter into any arrangement which may be proposed to it beneficial to both Republics.

I reiterate to you the assurances of true esteem with which I am, &c.,

A. ESQUIVEL.

To His Excellency THE MINISTER OF FOREIGN RELATIONS of Nicaragua.

No. 52.

Contract Ayón-Chevalier.—Costa Rica is an essential party to the interoceanic canal.—The contract will be void if Costa Rica does not accept it.—Costa Rica will be invited to make in favor of the grantee such concessions in the Costa Rican territory as Nicaragua makes in her own.

The President of the Republic to its inhabitants, greeting:

Know ye, that Congress has decreed as follows:

The Senate and Chamber of Deputies of the Republic of Nicaragua

DECREE.

ARTICLE only. The contract of the Maritime Interoceanic Canal, celebrated in Paris on the 6th of October, 1868, by the Minister of Foreign Relations, Lic. Don Tomás Ayón, and Monsieur Michel Chevalier, a French subject, consisting of 59 articles, and an additional one, whose tenor is as follows, is hereby ratified in all its parts.

*   *   *   *   *   *   *

LIII.

The Republic of Nicaragua *binds herself to make every possible effort to obtain as early as practicable the adherence of the Republic of Costa Rica* to the present convention, in such a way that Costa Rica guarantees in favor of the grantee and in *her own territory, and in all that belongs to her*, the advantages stipulated by Articles VI, XIV, XV, XVI, XVII, XIX, and XX; the latter in combination with the XXI, XXIV, and XXV; the latter in combination with the XXVI, XXVII, XXVIII, and XXIX; the latter in combination with the XXX, XXXI, XXXIII, XXXIV, XXXV, XXXVI, XXXVII, XXXVIII, and XXXIX; the latter in combination with the XL, XLI, XLII, XLIII, XLIV, XLV, XLVI, XLIX, L, and LII, and also LVII, LVIII, and LIX following.

LIV.

The Republic of Costa Rica will be invited to treat the company in the same way as the Republic of Nicaragua does by the present Convention.

LV.

The Republic of Nicaragua reserves for herself to enter into arrangements with Costa Rica for the purpose of stipulating the advantages which Costa Rica will derive from adhering to the present Convention.

LVI.

If the Republic of Costa Rica should refuse her adherence, the present Convention shall be ipso facto *annulled.*

* * * * * * *

MICHEL CHEVALIER,
TOMAS AYÓN.

Given at the Hall of Sessions of the Senate, Managua, March 2, 1869.—P. Joaquin Chamorro, *President;* Vicente Guzman, *Secretary;* Pio Castellón, *Secretary.*

To the Executive Power. Hall of Sessions of the Chamber of Deputies, Managua, March 15, 1869.—S. Morales, *President;* P. Chamorro, *Secretary;* Miguel Robledo, *Secretary.*

Therefore, let it be executed.

GOVERNMENT HOUSE,
 MANAGUA, *March* 15, 1869.

FERNANDO GUZMAN.

A. H. RIVAS,
 Secretary of the Interior.

No. 53.

Editorial of the Nicaraguan "Gaceta" on the Ayon-Chevalier canal contract.—The San Juan river explicitly declared to be (1869) *in great part the frontier of Costa Rica. —The adherence of Costa Rica to the contract recognized to be indispensable.—Costa Rica is asked to grant in her territory what Nicaragua has granted in hers.—All of this presupposes the acknowledged validity of the treaty of limits.*

"*Gaceta.*"

THE CANAL CONTRACT AND THE REPUBLIC OF COST RICA.

The contract for the canalization of the Nicaraguan isthmus is already an accomplished fact. * * *

It is indubitable, therefore, that our canal contract has been made under the most favorable auspices.

The only thing that now remains to be done is that 'the Republic of Costa Rica co-operates in its accomplishment.

By Article XLIII of the canal contract the Republic of *Nicaragua binds herself to make every possible effort to obtain as early as practicable the adherence of the Republic of Costa Rica to the Convention*, in order that it may guarantee in favor of the grantee, within its own territory and in all that corresponds to it, the advantages that Nicaragua has granted.

And, in truth, it is so demanded by the topographic situation of the San Juan river and of the Lake of Nicaragua, which IN A GREAT PART SERVE AS A DIVIDING LINE BETWEEN THE TERRITORY OF THE TWO REPUBLICS.

Would our neighbor be willing not to oppose any difficulties to the realization of a project which has occupied us for so many years? Would it be willing to concur in this colossal work, which is of paramount necessity, and share besides the advantages which the same offers to it?

We do not doubt that the two Republics, whose citizens have often shed their blood in defence of the Central American independence on the fields of Rivas in 1856, will unite themselves to-day and co-operate in the opening of the canal, which offers such a vast horizon of prosperity for the two people whose interests are completely identical in this case.

If Costa Rica has to make concessions it has also to enjoy IN ITS OWN TERRITORY the same advantages as the vessels and commerce of Nicaragua, as is provided by the additional article of the Convention.

We trust that the sympathy and good sense of our neighbor, looking at things from the true stand-point, will adhere to the above said Convention, and we trust besides that the ability and wisdom of Don Mariano Montealegre, Envoy Extraordinary and Minister Plenipotentiary of Nicaragua, will secure the success of the mission entrusted to him by obtaining the adherence of the Costa Rican Government to the Articles of the Canal Convention which concern it.

Otherwise Article XLVI of the Convention reads clearly and inexorably : "IF THE REPUBLIC OF COSTA RICA SHOULD REFUSE HER ADHERENCE THE PRESENT CONVENTION SHALL BE, IPSO FACTO, ANNULLED."

Would this be the end of so many discussions, so much labor, so many expectations and hopes ? That is not possible.

[From "La Gaceta de Nicaragua," No. 17, April 24, 1869.]

No. 54.

The Government of Nicaragua asks the Government of Costa Rica to request the National Constituent Convention to modify certain articles of a treaty between the two Republics for the digging of an interoceanic canal.

SAN JOSÉ, *September* 2, 1870.

SIR: Señor Don Alejandro Cousin delivered to me your despatch of the 20th of August, asking *this Government* to request the National Constituent Convention to modify Article XXXVI of the Convention between Costa Rica and Nicaragua for the opening of an interoceanic canal, so as not to deprive the company of the right of appointing arbitrators for the settlement of the differences which may arise on this subject.

The National Convention organized itself on the 8th of August, and adjourned on the 25th of the same month.

It will reconvene as soon as the committee in charge of framing a project of constitution terminates its labors.

I can assure you that as soon as the Legislative Power reconvenes this Government will immediately make the request referred to by you.

I am, your very attentive servant,

MONTUFAR.

To His Excellency THE MINISTER OF FOREIGN RELATIONS of the Republic of Nicaragua.

No. 55.

Project of a road from San José de Costa Rica to San Carlos for the export of coffee through San Juan del Norte.— Costa Rica earnestly invited to co-operate in the restoration of the port of San Juan by uniting the waters of the Colorado river with those of the San Juan river.

THE " GACETA."

In number 41 of the "Debate," issued on the 28th of last month, an article full of important statements began to be published, showing the advisability that some means of communication towards the Atlantic should be opened through the route northwest of San Carlos.

The writer, resting on good calculations and on conclusive proofs, demonstrates that a road in that direction would offer Costa Rica considerable advantages, and facilitate the transportation of coffee from the places where it is raised to the port of embarkation.

We have noticed before this time the efforts made by the Government of that Republic to open a road to the northeast through the difficult and costly route of Limon. The estimates made for that enterprise contain, as was natural, heavy items, capable to be increased indefinitely, for the frequent and perhaps unceasing repairs which the road required, because it was to be built upon muddy ground, exceedingly hilly, and totally unprovided with the material necessary to do substantial work.

The Government of Costa Rica, having fixed the whole of its attention to finding the way of conquering the difficulties encountered by that enterprise, had not been able to notice that the San Carlos route was more accessible, more convenient to the commerce and agriculture of the country, more promising of good results for the section crossed by it, and

more profitable to all the localities where coffee is cultivated.
* * *

Coming back from our digression to the project of a northern road initiated by "El Debate," we can assure, upon inspection of the facts furnished by different surveys made at different times, both on the land as well as on the water-side, that the San Carlos route will be the easiest, the less costly, and the nearest to the principal points of the Republic.

From San José, which we consider as the central point, to Peñablanca, where the San Carlos river is reached and where a port can be established under favorable conditions of salubrity and sufficient area for a town, there are only eighteen leagues; from there to the confluence of the San Juan river there are no more than twenty leagues, counting in this measure the windings of the stream; and from there to the port of San Juan del Norte there are eighteen more leagues; so that between this port and San José there is a total distance of fifty-eight leagues. This is much less than the distance between the same port and the Nicaraguan towns on the lake shore; since from San Juan del Norte to Rivas there are sixty-three, and to Granada sixty-seven, leagues. To the capital there are seventy-eight; that is to say, twenty leagues more than the distance to the capital of Costa Rica. *It is, therefore, plain that Costa Rica has more interest than Nicaragua and is more benefited than she by the improvements of the San Juan river and of the port of the same name.*

The San Carlos river does not offer any obstacle of any kind, but, on the contrary, presents great facilities to navigation after Peñablanca is reached; because, as it has no other tributaries than the Arsenal river, the Rio Blanco river, and a few streams of small importance, carries sufficient water of its own to render the danger of scarcity or dryness in summer rather remote. The bottom of the river is generally sandy, at least in the navigable part, and it has no rapids nor rocks obstructing the way; and, if it is true that there are in it some irregular currents, still this does not constitute any danger nor difficulty for steamboats properly built for that purpose. The banks on both sides are high, showing an average altitude of from ten to twenty feet—sufficient to prevent overflows. The adjoining lands are endowed with a wonderful fertility for the cultivation of sugarcane, indigo, cocoa, and all the fruits of our climate.

The improvements in the port of San Juan del Norte and in the lower part of the river, sufficient to overcome all obstacles, absolutely depend upon the restoration of the branch named Colorado river. The incorporation of one with the other, wholly or in part, will not cost much. Some estimates have been made of the cost which such a work would require, and the amount reached scarcely exceeds $60,000 or $80,000. The conveniences of the port are proverbial, even now, and certainly will increase with the increase of the water and the restoration of the port to the condition in which it was a few years ago. * * *

It would, therefore, be desirable that the two Governments, listening to the voice of common interest, should enter into the proper arrangements to improve, at the cost of both Republics, the port of San Juan del Norte and the lower part of the river. A great writer of the last century said that the utility of one nation depended precisely upon the ruin or retrograde condition of its neighbor; but he was execrated by his contemporaries for being the propagator of pernicious maxims. Will it be possible for any one in this century to think that it is right to lessen the advantages of a neighbor, even to the detriment of his own interest? Let us hope that there is no such person, and that the Governments, laying aside all narrow-minded sentiments, will combine to promote the prosperity of both nations.

[From the "Gaceta de Nicaragua," No. 38, September 17, 1870.]

No. 56.

Remarks made by the Government of Costa Rica to the Government of Nicaragua when the latter submitted to the Nicaraguan Congress its so-called doubts in regard to the validity of the treaty of limits of 1858.

[SEAL]. SAN JOSÉ, *February* 1st, 1870.

SIR: I have read with deep sorrow that part of the message addressed by Your Excellency to the Nicaraguan Congress, wherein the treaty of limits between Costa Rica and Nicaragua of April 15, 1858, is discussed.

That passage of Your Excellency's message reads literally as follows:

"Article II of the Constitution of November 12, 1838, which was the one in force at the time in which the treaty of limits was adjusted, declared that the territory of the State of Nicaragua was exactly the same as the territory which the Province of Nicaragua had been. This Province, before the independence, embraced the whole territory of Guanacaste.

"Article 194 provided that, for the amendment of or addition to any article of the Constitution, it should be required among other formalities that the said amendment or addition should be approved by the two-third vote of the Senators and Members present, and that, after securing this vote, neither the amendment nor the addition should be considered as forming a part of the Constitution, as all laws on limits are, until sanctioned by the next Legislature."

"The same formalities are established for similar cases by Article 103 of the present Constitution."

"The treaty of limits, in which Nicaragua, abrogating Article II of her Constitution, generously ceded to Costa Rica a large portion of territory, which she has possessed quietly, both before and after the independence, required for its validity to have been sanctioned by the next Legislature. It was approved by the Assembly of 1858; but that was not enough. It ought to have been approved, also, by the Congress of 1859, because the two Legislatures were considered by the Constitution as if they were two co-ordinate legislative bodies, the approval by the first being only of initiative character and lacking legal force without the approval of the second, exactly in the same way as the action of one Chamber in the enactment of a law means nothing if the other Chamber does not act accordingly."

"The said formality having been omitted, the treaty of limits lacks legal force, and therefore Costa Rica has no right to demand its execution, because, according to the principles of the law of nations, treaties are void and inoperative through the omission of any requisite which, according to the Constitution of the State, was necessary for its consummation."

"The Government of Costa Rica has acknowledged that this is the condition in which the above said treaty finds itself, because in Article VI of a convention made on the 12th of July, 1869, between the Plenipotentiaries Don Mariano Montealegre and Don A. Jimenez, about the cession of the waters of the Colorado river for the purpose that they should be thrown into the San Juan, a convention of which, in due time, I gave you the proper information, it asked Nicaragua to ratify the treaty of limits with Costa Rica, and to agree to submit to the arbitration of the Government of the United States of North America all questions arising out, either of the said treaty, or of the execution of the convention just spoken of."

"Costa Rica, in asking Nicaragua to ratify the treaty of limits in which the latter State ceded to the former a large extent of its territory as preliminary for allowing the waters of the Colorado river to be thrown into the San Juan, looked as if pretending that Nicaragua first should give it the whole thing, and subsequently take back a portion of it. It is useless to repeat here the obvious reasons which you had in view for rejecting the convention."

"In order to avoid perplexities in the course of this business, the Executive requests your Honorable Body to define well the rights of the Republic in the matter of limits with Costa Rica before undertaking works or devising plans for the improvement of its ways of communication on the northern side."

This grave subject being now under discussion in the Chambers of your Republic, I think it my duty to present to Your Excellency some remarks, and request that, if deemed proper, they be transmitted to the Congress of Nicaragua for their consideration.

The Constitution of your Republic, promulgated on the 12th of November, 1838, as Your Excellency yourself recognizes, did not say anywhere that the territory of Guanacaste was part of Nicaragua. It confined itself to indicate that the territory of the State was the same as belonged to it when a Province.

In reference to this I must state that Guanacaste, in the time of the Spanish Government, always was under the immediate jurisdiction and control of Cartago; and that the Spanish Cortes, when they promulgated the Constitution of 1812, decided that Guanacaste should be incorporated in Costa Rica for the purposes of electing deputies both for the Cortes and for the provincial deputation or assembly.

I must say further, that according to the charter of the Colony of Costa Rica, the King of Spain appointed Don Diego Artieda y Chirinos to be the first Governor and Captain-General of this Province, marking as limit for the same the San Juan river on the Atlantic.

But there are other conclusive reasons founded upon documents of subsequent date in support of the treaty of limits.

It was approved by the Government of Costa Rica and Nicaragua.

It was ratified by the Congresses of Costa Rica and Nicaragua.

The ratifications of the treaty were duly exchanged, and

the treaty was promulgated in both Republics as the law of the land in regard to limits.

Thirteen years have elapsed since that publication, and all the Legislatures which have met during that period have looked at that treaty as the basis of the relations between both countries.

The Legislature of Nicaragua approved the treaty of peace and amity concluded on the 30th of July, 1868, taking for granted that the limits between both Republics were settled.

The present Constitution of Nicaragua, subsequent in date to the treaty, says, in its Article I, that the laws on limits make a part of the Constitution.

The treaty herein referred to is a Nicaraguan law on limits, and a law of the highest importance. Therefore it is an integral part of the Constitution of Nicaragua, according to its own literal language.

Under these circumstances, the august Chambers of your Republic would need, before declaring the treaty of limits to be invalid, to be invested with all the power which Your Excellency says to be indispensable to amend the Constitution of your country, in addition to all other circumstances prescribed by international law to invalidate a treaty signed, approved, ratified, exchanged, promulgated, and executed during 13 years.

Your Excellency refers to a project of Convention celebrated on the 21st of July, 1869, between the Plenipotentiaries Don Agapito Jimenez and Don Mariano Montealegre.

Article VI of the said project alluded to by Your Excellency says: " The Government of Nicaragua ratifies by this convention the treaties which it has celebrated in regard to limits with the Government of Costa Rica."

I do not understand what was the reason why the Costa Rican Plenipotentiary acceded to subscribe to such an article, included in a project which was relative to a matter entirely independent of all question of limits; but I understand very well that the said article does not prove at all that the treaty of limits is not valid.

Señor Montealegre, Plenipotentiary of Nicaragua, came to suggest that Costa Rica should allow the waters of the Colorado river to be carried into the San Juan.

He recognized the validity of the treaty of limits, and requested that the waters of the Colorado river be granted to his country, and the request was granted by the Costa Rican Plenipotentiary, who assented, furthermore, to the enactment of Article VI above copied.

But the said project of convention, including its Article VI, was not ratified by the Congress of this Republic; and, therefore, it has no more force and strength than if it were simply blank paper.

To have some right to argue against Costa Rica on the ground of the said convention, it would be necessary for the convention to have become a law, which never happened.

Now, by virtue of the discretionary faculties vested in the President, His Excellency has the power to ratify public treaties; but His Excellency has not only refused to ratify the convention referred to, but has been pleased besides to decree that it is invalid and void.

Be pleased to accept the consideration with which I have the honor to assure Your Excellency that I am your most attentive servant,

MONTUFAR.

To His Excellency THE MINISTER OF FOREIGN RELATIONS of Nicaragua.

No. 57.

Remarks of the Government of Costa Rica in refutation of the doubts entertained by the Government of Nicaragua on the validity of the treaty of limits.

[SEAL]. SAN JOSÉ, *July* 22, 1872.

SIR: The estimable despatch of Your Excellency, addressed to me on June 30, is now in my possession.

Your Excellency is pleased to set forth in it that it is not the intention of your Government to move for an immediate decision in the matter of limits, but to explain what the Government of Nicaragua has considered to be an undue and wrongful act of an officer of this Republic. * * *

Your Excellency goes on repeating what has been said in support of the opinion that the treaty of limits is illegal; insists upon declaring that what is called " Desaguadero " in the Royal Cedula of Aranjuez is not the San Juan river; affirms that several Cedulas and geographers, and tradition, show that they are two different things; says that the grant made by the King of Spain was on condition of conquering the territory spoken of in the Royal Cedula, and that no one will dare to maintain that the conquest was ever made, and ends by asking a frank explanation in regard to the action of the chief of the customs service.

Your Excellency will allow me to say that in your despatch of May 22 you did not confine the discussion to the matter of customs service alone, but extended your remarks to something else. Your Excellency said that the *statu quo* ought to be preserved until the treaty of April 15, 1858, is declared to be valid or invalid; and further said that this *statu quo* must be understood as follows: Nicaragua exercising the free navigation of the Colorado river and using all the places yielded to Nicaragua by the treaty of limits, so that the *statu quo*, according to Your Excellency, is and must be that

Nicaragua possesses the whole thing as absolute lord and master.

Your Excellency expressed in the same despatch that, after the validity of the treaty is admitted, it will be necessary to proceed to make the survey, and added that Nicaragua had granted Costa Rica a vast territory adjoining the right bank of the San Juan river.

In the presence of these statements it was necessary for my Government to say all that is contained in the note of June 10th.

Even in this despatch I cannot refer exclusively to the customs service question, because Your Excellency does not do so, but insists on discussing the question of limits and the validity of the treaty of April 15, 1858.

In this respect Your Excellency will allow me to say that historian Juarroz describes the limits of the Nicoya district as follows:

"It is bounded on the west by the 'corregimiento,' or 'Alcaldia Mayor' (territory under the jurisdiction of a mayor or local governor) of Sutiava; on the south by the Pacific Ocean; on the northeast by the Lake of Nicaragua; and on the east the boundary runs along the limits of Costa Rica."

The same thing says Alcedo in his Dictionary published in 1788.

The Most Illustrious Señor Don Francisco de Paula Garcia Pelez states in his "Memoirs" that the kingdom contained five Governments, namely, Guatemala, Nicaragua, Costa Rica, Honduras, and Soconuzco; and nine "Alcaldias Mayores," namely, San Salvador, Chiapas, Tegucigalpa, Sonsonate, Verapaz, Suchitepiquez, Nicoya, Amatique, and the mines of Zaragoza.

In the well-known "Report" on the Kingdom of Guatemala, made by Engineer Don Luis Diez de Navarro, in 1754, the following words are found: "On the 19th of January, 1744, I reached the mountain of Nicaragua, which is a very rugged one, where the province of that name ends, as

I have explained in my first trip, and I entered the jurisdiction of Nicoya, which, although an 'Alcaldia Mayor,' separate from the Government of Costa Rica, is reputed to belong to the latter province.

The same author further says as follows : " The capital of said province (Costa Rica) is the city of Cartago, and its boundaries and jurisdiction are as follows : On the Northern Sea from the mouth of the San Juan river to the 'Escudo' of Veragua in the Kingdom of Tierra Firma."

The La Flor river was the dividing line between Sutiava and Nicoya, as shown by the land titles and by the practice observed from time immemorial in the administration of the local government of both districts.

Three years after the independence Nicaragua had to suffer the scourge of civil war, because of the disagreement which has afflicted her so much between Leon and Granada, Managua and Masaya.

Costa Rica, on the contrary, constituted itself peacefully and with the greatest tranquility.

The Nicoya district did not want to follow the fate of Nicaragua, and be agitated by discord, but decided to belong to Costa Rica ; and Costa Rica accepted this decision in 1825, with the consent and approval of the Federal Congress.

When the Central American Union was dissolved each state retained the limits which it had at that moment, and this is the *uti possidetis* on which their rights rest at present.

In consequence of this, Nicoya formed an integral part of Costa Rica until the year 1858, in which the treaty of limits was signed.

By this treaty Costa Rica receded from the La Flor river and withdrew as far as the Salinas Bay.

The line which the treaty guarantees for Costa Rica is one which rests upon the firm ground of possession for many years.

Furthermore, in the apportionment of the foreign debt, the share of Costa Rica included the portion which corresponded to the territory now spoken of.

Costa Rica also recognized such a portion of the colonial domestic debt as corresponded to the same territory.

The Aranjuez Cedula describes the limits of Costa Rica by saying, from the mouth of El Desaguadero to Veraguas.

Your Excellency says that the San Juan river is not the same stream called Desaguadero in the Cedula referred to. But in the despatch of the 10th of June I had the honor to tell Your Excellency what follows:

" It is very important for all nations to fix their limits with foreign countries, and the dividing lines between their provinces. For this purpose, whenever practicable, ranges of mountains, rivers, lakes, or seas are always looked for. In the councils of the King of Spain this well-known truth was taken into consideration, and in marking the limit between Costa Rica and Nicaragua the most striking and natural possible line, that is, the San Juan river, was chosen."

To this remark Your Excellency has not been pleased to give any answer.

According to historian Juarroz, the southern bank of the San Juan river was reputed to belong to Costa Rica, and this proves that the San Juan river is the same which was formerly called Desaguadero.

The ancient names of the rivers which empty into the San Juan on the Costa Rican side prove the same assertion. The river which runs near Castillo Viejo is called on the old maps " Rio de Costa Rica."

To maintain that the " Desaguadero " is not the same San Juan river, Your Excellency has referred to " Cedulas," geographers, and tradition ; and Your Excellency will allow me to say that neither those Cedulas have yet been produced, nor the names of those geographers have been given.

In regard to tradition, Your Excellency knows very well that it is founded on a chain of competent writers, who, for an uninterrupted series of years or centuries, record as certain some facts witnessing an uniform belief in their existence.

I do not know of any such series of writers serving as

foundation to the tradition which Your Excellency speaks of; and on the contrary the writers from whom I have allowed myself to quote demonstrate not only that there is not the absolute agreement of belief in favor of the opinion which Your Excellency maintains, but that on the contrary there is a current of belief in a sense entirely opposite.

Your Excellency says that the grant made by the King of Spain, in favor of Artieda Chirinos, was on condition that he should conquer all the territory spoken of by the Aranjuez Cedula.

But, Mr. Minister, Pedrarias had began the conquest of that territory before Artieda Chirinos. The latter continued it, and his successors consummated it. So one of the above-named writers sets forth, quoting from the Decades of Herrera and from other authors.

So that even if the rights of Artieda would have been conditional, the condition was complied with.

Furthermore, Costa Rica promulgated its fundamental law in the year 1825. By it (Article XV) the mouth of the San Juan river was designated as the limit with Nicaragua, and the neighboring Republic did not make any claim against this designation.

The Congress of Central America accepted the Costa Rican Constitution, and the federal authorities respected it until the compact of the union was dissolved in 1839.

The treaty of limits is objected to on the ground that constituent Congresses do not ratify treaties; that the Constituent Assembly of Nicaragua which ratified our treaty acted as if it were an ordinary Congress; and that this being so it had no power to change the fundamental laws of Nicaragua in regard to limits.

This argument, Mr. Minister, only deserves examination because the person who makes it has just been the Secretary of Foreign Relations of Nicaragua, and is Lic. Don Tomás Ayón.

The Congresses or Assemblies are the powers in which the

faculty of enacting laws is vested. There are two classes of laws: one the fundamental or organic, and the other the secondary or municipal.

The series of fundamental or organic laws constitutes what is called the Constitution. And the collection of secondary or municipal laws, which receive different names according to the category to which they belong, form what is called the municipal law of each country.

The Constitution is the foundation and basis of all municipal laws, and to enact or frame it more power and more authority is needed than for framing or enacting municipal laws.

Constituent Assemblies are the supreme legislative power, and they can enact and frame not only organic laws but also statutes of other kinds for which less power is required.

The different Constituent Cortes which have been held in Spain are good proof of this well-known truth.

The Constituent Assembly of France did not only proclaim the principles of 1789 and the basis of the Constitution, but also abolished the tithes, took measures against nobility, and promulgated decrees of other kinds.

The other Assemblies which have met on the French soil have likewise enacted both fundamental and municipal laws.

The English Parliament, which is an ordinary legislative power, has also the faculty to amend laws of organic character, which is tantamount to exercising both legislative and constituent authority.

No objection can be founded, as far as treaties are concerned, on the fact that in England the ratification thereof belongs to the Crown, because this ratification by the Crown is not sufficient when the laws of England are modified by the treaty.

The Treaty of Utrecht between England and France was not carried into effect, because the English Parliament refused to pass the bill introduced on it giving sanction to the modification made by said treaty to the English laws on navigation and commerce.

In England Parliament has to take cognizance of all treaties by which Great Britain is bound to pay any sums of money.

Without going outside of the Central American limits, we find Constituent Powers to have enacted municipal laws or statutes and approved of treaties.

The treaty between Costa Rica and Guatemala of March 10, 1848, was ratified in the latter Republic by a Constituent Assembly, and, nevertheless, no one of our public writers has ever said that that treaty was null because Constituent Bodies cannot ratify public treaties.

Señor Ayón, in his capacity of Secretary of Foreign Relations of Nicaragua, sent a despatch to this Department, under date of August 20, 1870, asking that the Constituent Congress of this Republic should approve of certain modifications made to a treaty. And from this it is to be concluded that, while Señor Ayón, as Secretary of State, believed that Constituent Congresses have the power to ratify treaties, as a writer of pamphlets affirms, however, that they have no such power.

Constituent Congresses which have authority to enact organic laws, which is the greatest power, certainly have authority to enact municipal laws or statutes, which is the least.

Constituent Congresses lack only the power to enact those municipal laws or statutes when their convocation clearly and explicitly stated that their only power was to frame the Constitution.

In that case the people elected their representatives for that purpose, and for nothing else.

But the Constituent Assembly of Nicaragua, which ratified the treaty of limits, was not convoked exclusively to frame the organic law, and this ex-Secretary Ayón himself takes pains to explain in his pamphlet of the 10th of July instant.

But even if the said Assembly would have had only the power to enact organic laws, it would also have had the power to ratify the treaty of limits under the doctrines which the Department of Foreign Relations of Nicaragua holds to be correct.

Your Excellency says that all provisions about limits belong to the category of organic laws; and, therefore, under this doctrine, a constituent assembly is precisely the one which ought to have approved the treaty, because constituent powers are those which can enact organic laws.

The subtle distinction made by Ex-Secretary Ayón that the Constituent Assembly of Nicaragua which ratified the treaty did so as an ordinary assembly and not as a constituent power cannot satisfy any one.

That Assembly was vested with the august constituent power, the first and the highest of all, a power which is never delegated, nor could it delegate; and all its acts ought to be considered as performed in such a high capacity.

I believe, Mr. Minister, that it is entirely useless to officially continue this discussion because there is no authority which can settle the controversy. If there were a tribunal of arbitration to which the matter could be referred, then it would be proper to submit to it exhaustive arguments on the subject; but there is no such a tribunal in existence, nor has the Republic of Nicaragua been pleased to suggest its establishment.

It is of no use to state and prove that the treaty of limits was made by Plenipotentiaries fully authorized and competent to do so; that it was approved by the Governments of Costa Rica and Nicaragua; that it was ratified by the Congress of Costa Rica and by the Constituent Assembly of Nicaragua; that the exchange of ratifications took place; that the treaty was solemnly published as the law of the land concerning limits; that it has been carried into effect and obeyed and respected for 14 consecutive years, during which it has been used by the Congresses of Nicaragua as the basis of their deliberations, inasmuch as the true reason to oppose the treaty is, as explained to our Minister in Managua by General Zavala, competently authorized by the Government of Your

Excellency to discuss this subject, not because the said treaty lacks any indispensable solemnity for its validity, but because it is believed to be injurious to the interests of Nicaragua.

This assertion of General Zavala has been corroborated by the Nicaraguan press, which has gone as far as saying that the repudiation of the treaties, when injurious, has prevailed in all nations when able to cause them to prevail; that Napoleon III nullified the treaties of 1815; that Germany broke the treaty by which Richelieu had taken from her Alsace and Lorraine; that Russia has asked to be exempted from the obligation contracted in the treaty of Paris, and that Austria will break also the Villafranca treaty.

But, Mr. Minister, if I should propose to enter, to-day, into the analysis of this question, I would show that neither Napoleon III, nor Germany, nor any one of the nations which you refer to, has ever said, " We do not respect that treaty, because it is injurious to us; we do not respect it, because we were compelled to sign it."

What has often happened is, that the circumstances and interests of the nations having been modified, the pre-existing conventions have had to be modified also, either by mutual consent or by force; but, in this condition, neither Costa Rica nor Nicaragua find themselves.

In my despatch of the 10th of June, it was gratifying to me to set forth that at the time in which the treaty was signed Costa Rica did not overpower Nicaragua; that it was a friendly nation, a sister which had come to her territory to assist her in her war of independence and render her efficient aid against an enemy who had proclaimed, on her soil, slavery and death.

The disastrous discord between Leon and Granada, and the bitter opposition between the parties which called themselves Legitimists and Democrats, attracted to Nicaragua the filibuster invasion. And when that Republic was invaded the Costa Rican people shed their blood and spent their fortunes to save Nicaragua from foreign domination.

Costa Rica took possession of the steamers of the lake and of the San Juan river, carried its flag in triumph up to Punta de Castilla, prevented the filibusters from entering the great fluvial way, and put an end to the exterminating war which afflicted Nicaragua.

Your Excellency will allow me to say that I cannot understand how these acts of redemption can now be made the basis of a charge against Costa Rica and the foundation for the statement that the treaty is null, without considering that the invalidity of the same will, no doubt, bring new calamities upon the two sister and bordering Republics. * * *

Mr. Minister, the above-made statements are explicit, very explicit indeed. They explain that the customs service is authorized only for the purposes herein designated, and for nothing else; and that, therefore, the action of the officers thereof will be approved by the Government of Costa Rica, when circumscribed to the limits set forth in the paragraph above copied, and disapproved when extended to more than allowed by the language of the same paragraph.

The practice among nations, and the writings of the authors on public law, show to us that the free navigation of the rivers is obtained by conventions made with the states through the territory of which they pass. It was by treaty that the free navigation of the Rhine was obtained. It was by treaty that, in the latter part of the last century, the free navigation of the Scheldt river was obtained. It was by treaty also that the free navigation of the Elbe, the Po, the Danube, the Mississippi, the St. Lawrence, the La Platta, and the Amazon rivers was also obtained. This universal practice must serve Costa Rica as a guide in regard to the free navigation of the Colorado river, so much the more so as this river is found in all its extent within the Costa Rican territory.

The writers of public law agree, in regard to this kind of rivers, in the doctrine that the state to which they belong can legislate in regard to them as they may deem best.

Costa Rica, taking the most liberal point of view possible,

provided, by Article XII of its Constitution, that foreigners may exercise their industry and commerce, own real estate, purchase and manage the same, navigate the rivers, and freely exercise their religion. Under this provision all Nicaraguans can navigate the Colorado river with no more limitations than those prescribed by the revenue laws to prevent smuggling.

These revenue laws are limited to what I explained to you in my despatch of the 10th of June, and which I have repeated in the present; and beyond that they do not go.

In order that the interest of Costa Rica may not suffer detriment and that Nicaragua is not injured, and that the freedom of navigation on the river is not interrupted, it would be advisable to resort to some means suggested by mutual consent. His Excellency the Chief Magistrate of this country will hear with pleasure anything which the Government of Nicaragua should suggest in this respect, because what he wishes is a peaceful and friendly adjustment.

I believe that the Government of Your Excellency feels itself animated by the same sentiments; and in this confidence I have the honor to repeat that I am, Your Excellency's most obedient servant,

LORENZO MONTUFAR.

To His Excellency THE MINISTER OF FOREIGN RELATIONS of
    the Republic of Nicaragua.

No. 58.

Costa Rica declares that it will keep its custom-houses, and maintain its sovereignty over the whole territory which according to the treaty of 1858 belongs to it, unless other limits are not established by mutual agreement or arbitral decision.

SAN JOSÉ, *December* 3, 1875.

Mr. MINISTER: I have the honor to acknowledge the receipt of the official communication which you were pleased to send me under date of November 3 ultimo, which did not reach me until the 30th. * * *

You will allow me, Mr. Minister, in referring to the subject-matter of your despatch, to set forth that the custom-house force, because it is nothing else, referred to, is not a part of the military forces of this Republic, and it is the same and even smaller than the one which in former times the Government of Costa Rica used to keep stationed either at the mouth of the San Carlos river, or on the Sarapiquí, or the Colorado river, or Punta de Castilla; and as neither its establishment nor its preservation on any of those points can be considered as a wrong done to Nicaragua, or an abridgment of her territorial rights, my Government sets forth that in the use of the rights that the treaty of April 15, 1858, gives it on that territory, and within the limits by the same treaty prescribed, it will exercise such acts of dominion and sovereignty as may be proper as long as by decision of an Arbitrator, to whom it has offered to submit the question of the validity of the same treaty, the invalidity of that instrument is not declared, or as long as by an act of the same Arbitrator, or by mutual agreement of the two Governments, other boundaries are not marked out.

With the greatest consideration I renew to you my respects, and subscribe myself your attentive servant,

VICENTE HERRERA.

To His Excellency THE MINISTER OF FOREIGN RELATIONS of the Republic of Nicaragua.

No. 59.

Costa Rica protests against the non-compliance on the part of Nicaragua of Article VIII of the treaty of limits.

NATIONAL PALACE,
SAN JOSÉ, *June* 26, 1886.

To His Excellency the Minister of Foreign Relations of Nicaragua, Managua.

SIR: The courteous despatch of Your Excellency of the 31st of May ultimo, in reference to Nos. 21 and 23 of the official "Gaceta" of your Republic, has reached my hands, together with the said newspaper.

In the latter one it appears published as a law of this Republic the contract of a maritime interoceanic canal, celebrated by your Government with the "Provisional Company of Interoceanic Canal," organized in New York.

His Excellency the President, well-informed of that important document, has directed me to answer Your Excellency as follows :

While it is true that by Article XXIII of the contract, *the dividing line established by Article II of the treaty of April* 15, 1858, *between this Republic and yours has been respected*, it is also true that the provisions of Article VIII of the same treaty has not been complied with. Said Article reads : "ARTICLE VIII. IF THE CONTRACTS OF CANALIZATION OR TRANSIT WHICH HAVE BEEN CELEBRATED BY THE GOVERNMENT OF NICARAGUA, BEFORE IT HAD KNOWLEDGE OF THIS TREATY, SHOULD FOR ANY REASON WHATSOEVER PROVE TO BE WITHOUT FORCE, NICARAGUA BINDS HERSELF NOT TO ENTER INTO ANY OTHER AGREEMENTS TO THE SAME EFFECT WITHOUT FIRST LISTENING TO THE OPINION OF THE GOVERNMENT OF COSTA RICA AS TO THE DISADVANTAGES THAT THE TRANSACTION WOULD PRODUCE FOR BOTH COUNTRIES, PROVIDED THAT THE SAID OPINION IS GIVEN WITHIN 30 DAYS SUBSEQUENT TO THE RECEIPT OF THE COMMUNIcation asking for it, should Nicaragua have stated that the decision was urgent; and if the natural rights of Costa Rica are not injured by the transaction the opinion will be advisory."

Besides this it appears, as being almost an impossibility, that the building of the canal under the conditions agreed upon fails to affect the territorial rights of Costa Rica, since Costa Rica owns, in common with Nicaragua, the Bay and port of San Juan del Norte, and has also in common the free navigation of the river of the same name, and exclusively from the mouth of the river in the Atlantic up to a point three miles this side of Castillo Viejo, the right bank, and the Colorado river.

Great is the confidence that my Government reposes in the high sense of justice of the Government of Your Excellency, for which reason it is impossible for it to think that the non-compliance with Article VIII has been due to the evil purpose of violating the faith of a treaty and of breaking faith with this Republic which is the most intimately connected with Nicaragua in family relations, interests, and destinies, and, at the same time, with justice and honor.

My Government expects, with good foundation, that the cause of the action referred to is to be found elsewhere, and that it does not involve injury, nor does it prevent the omission noticed from being corrected.

But as long as such explanations as are competent from the enlightened Government of Your Excellency do not give the fact alluded to its correct meaning, the fact itself is to be declared inadmissible.

Costa Rica does not consent to it, not because it is moved by material interests which it willingly would sacrifice for the sake of another greater and more important benefit for the whole of Central America, as the canal in question is, a work of which the Costa Rican press has occupied itself with great enthusiasm, and in which my Government has always been ready to co-operate in all earnest, but because its honor and dignity so demand it, and the honor and dignity of a nation are above everything else.

My Government expects that the Government of Your Excellency, without any injury to its own sense of self-respect, since to recognize the rights of others is never wrongful, will find the means that the rights of Costa Rica remain respected, and that the harmony which now exists between both Republics and which may exercise such beneficial influence on their common future does not suffer detriment. But as long as the above said omission is not corrected in some pertinent way, my Government sees itself compelled to protest against the validity of the canal contract concluded in Managua on the 25th of May ultimo, without previous audience of Costa Rica and in violation of the article above copied of the treaty of April 15, 1858.

May Your Excellency be pleased to submit the above to His Excellency the President of your Republic and accept the distinguished consideration with which I subscribe myself, your most attentive and obedient servant,

JOSÉ MARIA CASTRO.

No. 60.

The explanations of Nicaragua as to the non-compliance with Article VIII of the treaty of limits are accepted.

DEPARTMENT OF FOREIGN RELATIONS OF THE
REPUBLIC OF COSTA RICA,
NATIONAL PALACE,
SAN JOSÉ, *September* 10, 1886.

SIR: This Department has received the courteous despatch of Your Excellency, dated on the 23d of July ultimo, in answer to mine of the 21st of June instant, wherein I had protested against the validity of the canal contract celebrated between Nicaragua and the Provisional Company of Interoceanic Canal, organized in New York.

The explanations given by Your Excellency in regard to the causes which prevented the Supreme Government of your Republic from complying with the provisions of Article VIII of the treaty of April 15, 1858, are satisfactory to the Government of this Republic. So it was desired by this Government, which was sorry to find that national dignity opposed an obstacle to its wishes under other aspects of being propitious to a contract of such vital importance for the whole of Central America.

Without prejudice to what I have stated, and referring to the idea enunciated by Your Excellency, that the validity of the treaty of April 15, 1858, has not been recognized by Nicaragua, I must tell Your Excellency that, although in the opinion of my Government the said validity rests upon indestructible grounds, and admits of the best defence, it deems it better not to discuss at present the said question, both because of the unpleasant feelings to which it has given rise at other times, and *because this Government will readily accede to the rescission of the aforesaid treaty, and agree that things come back to the state in which they were before April 15, 1858, provided that the Government of Your Excellency is the one which suggests such a thing*, since Costa Rica does not want to take the initiative in the matter.

I avail myself of this opportunity to reiterate to Your Excellency the protests of high consideration with which I subscribe myself, your obedient servant,

JOSÉ MARIA CASTRO.

To His Excellency THE MINISTER OF FOREIGN RELATIONS of the Republic of Nicaragua, Managua.

DOCUMENT No. 61.

Opinion of the historian of Central America, Dr. Don Lorenzo Montufar, at present the Secretary of State of the Republic of Guatemala, in regard to the treaty of limits between Costa Rica and Nicaragua.

This high body (the Central American Congress) never took further action upon this subject (the secession of Nicoya), and the Federation was dissolved, Guanacaste remaining united to Costa Rica. Nicaragua never showed herself satisfied with this diminution of her territory, but never thought it advisable to raise an army to obtain the recovery of what she thought to be her property. The whole question became reduced to diplomatic missions, or pamphlets, or printed sheets, more or less offensive. The Walker war caused the Central American people to understand that this everlasting discord between two countries, equally interested in maintaining the independence proclaimed in September, might become utterly injurious to all.

Through the action of the other Governments, and especially of the Government of Salvador, a treaty of limits was resorted to to settle the question.

The treaty was made and signed by the Plenipotentiaries Gen. Don José Maria Cañas and Gen. Don Máximo Jerez. This treaty was ratified, exchanged, and promulgated as law of limits. Subsequently there have been questions in regard to its validity. It is necessary to give an idea of the question of limits between Costa Rica and Nicaragua, not with the particularity of details with which both Governments have treated it in their messages, their official notes and their reports, and the respective legislative bodies, because this would be to increase too much the size of the present volume, but as laconically as possible. The importance of this question depends upon the hopes frequently entertained that an international canal will be finally opened. From the times of the conquest a passage from sea to sea across the American continent was looked for. Magellan found the straits that bear his name, but his discovery does not satisfy the aspirations of the world because it is very near Cape Horn. The eyes of the intelligent have fixed themselves sometimes on the Darien, sometimes on Tehuantepec or other places more or less adequate, and sometimes on the Isthmus of Nicaragua. The Spanish Cortes advocated the latter idea. There is in favor of it, not only the limited extent of the Isthmus, but also the existence of two lakes, namely, the one of Granada and the one of Managua. The project is to cause the vessels to reach the Lake of Granada through the San Juan river, and from there to pass into the Pacific Ocean. Two means have been suggested for that: one consisting in cutting the ground between the Lake of Granada and the Pacific Ocean, and the second consisting in canalizing the Tipitapa river, take it to the Managua Lake, and from there open a canal to the Southern Sea.

The enterprise is vast, but many engineers and a great number of scientists have thought it practicable; and there have been Nicaraguan patriots who have sometimes imagined that the vessels were already passing from one ocean to the other.

Those who believe the great canal to be practicable feel a great interest in the demarcation of the dividing line between Costa Rica and Nicaragua, because the share that Costa Rica will have in the canal will depend upon it.

The historian Juarroz, in speaking of the Costa Rican territory, says: "Its boundaries on the Northern Sea are from the mouth of the San Juan river to the Escudo of Veragua, and on the south from the Alvarado river, dividing line of the Province of Nicaragua, to the Boruca river, end of the Kingdom of Tierra Firma."

Don Felipe Molina says the same thing; but the testimony of Molina may with reason be impeached, because, when he wrote, he was in the service of Costa Rica, and, therefore, he had an interest in securing the triumph of the cause entrusted to his defence, not only for the benefit of Costa Rica, but for his own reputation.

But the testimony of Juarroz is unimpeachable. Juarroz wrote in Guatemala, and had no reason of any kind to feel any more affection for Costa Rica than for Nicaragua. He based his statements upon the documents he had before his eyes, and these completely authorize his assertions.

Philip II, King of Spain and of the Indies, signed at Aranjuez the commission of Don Diego de Artieda y Chirinos as Governor and Captain-General of the Province of Costa Rica, and marked as the limits of his command from the mouth of the Desaguadero (outlet), which is the San Juan river, to the Province of Veraguas, and from the limits of Nicaragua on the Nicoya side to the valleys of Chiriqui.

The limits between Costa Rica and Nicaragua being the Desaguadero (outlet), it is indubitable that Costa Rica has a part in the interoceanic canal, because it is precisely through that outlet that the vessels are to be introduced from the Atlantic into the Lake of Granada. But no part belongs to Costa Rica on the navigation through the lake, because the Salto or Alvarado river serves as a limit.

An event came to favor Costa Rica, and this was the annexation of Guanacaste, whose limits extend to the La Flor river. By virtue of this annexation the boundary between Costa Rica and Nicaragua was the Great Lake and the whole San Juan river.

The Federal Congress approved the annexation, but not finally. The approval was temporary, until Congress, in use of its powers, should fix the limits of each State. But the Federation was dissolved and the limits were never fixed.

Nicaragua claimed several times the restoration of Guanacaste, but Costa Rica refused to surrender it. This claim gave occasion to several acts of the people of Guanacaste favoring their annexation to Costa Rica; and the Quijano attempt of 1836 shows that they were very well pleased with their new allegiance.

The unceasing agitation created by the disagreement of both Governments gave occasion to fear that the interest of the whole of Central America might be endangered. The filibuster war caused this danger to be serious and perceptible; and as soon as the war ended the Government of Salvador sent to Costa Rica, upon agreement with Nicaragua, General Don Pedro Rómulo Negrete, in the capacity of Envoy Extraordinary and Minister Plenipotentiary, to propose some settlement. Gen. Negrete affirmatively stated afterwards, that he had instructions to declare war against the State which would refuse to put an end to the question by means of a treaty.

The Government of Nicaragua sent to San José Gen. Don Máximo Jerez as her Plenipotentiary; and Don Juan Rafael Mora, then President of Costa Rica, conferred full powers on Gen. Don José Maria Cañas, who had distinguished himself so much in the war against the filibusters. Then the Cañas-Jerez treaty was signed, and its Article II reads as follows:

"The dividing line between the two Republics, starting from the Northern Sea, shall begin at the end of Punta de Castilla, at the mouth of the San Juan de Nicaragua river, and shall run along the right bank of the said river up to a point three English miles distant from Castillo Viejo, said distance to be measured from between the exterior works of said castle and the above-named point. From here, and taking the said works as centre, a curve shall be drawn along said works, keeping at the distance of three English miles from them in its whole length until reaching another point which shall be at the distance of two miles from the bank of the river on the other side of the castle. From here the line shall continue in the direction of the Sapoá river which empties into the Lake of Nicaragua, and it shall follow its course, keeping always at the distance of two miles from the right bank of the San Juan, all along its windings, up to reaching its origin in the lake; and from there along the right shore of the said lake until reaching the Sapoá river where the line parallel to the bank and shore will terminate. From the point in which the said line shall coincide with the Sapoá river, a point which, according to the above description, must be two miles distant from the lake, an astronomic straight line shall be drawn to the central point of the Salinas Bay on the Southern Sea, where the line marking the boundary between the two contracting Republics shall end.

By this article both Republics yielded somewhat in their pretensions. The Costa Rican territory is not limited by the whole course of the San Juan river. It begins at the mouth of this river, follows its right bank up to a point this side of Castillo Viejo, and three miles distant from its fortifications. The Costa Rican territory does not reach the lake, but deviates from it, as expressed by the treaty. It does not either reach the La Flor river, but remains limited to the centre of the Salinas Bay.

Nicaragua, on her part, abandoned also many of her pretensions. Now, her territory does not reach the Salto or Alvarado river, but is limited to the Salinas Bay and the line drawn by the treaty.

This treaty was made by two plenipotentiaries competently authorized; it was approved by the Government of Costa Rica and by the Government of Nicaragua; it was ratified by the Congress of Costa Rica and by a Constituent Assembly of Nicaragua; the ratifications thereof were exchanged within the time designated in it; it was promulgated after the exchange and published as the law of limits in the official newspaper of Nicaragua. Costa Rica communicated the treaty to the foreign diplomatic body accredited near its Government, and also to its diplomatic body abroad. Nicaragua also communicated it to the Nicaraguan and the foreign diplomatic body, and all the friendly nations considered it as an accomplished and unimpeachable fact. For several years several legislative bodies of Nicaragua enacted laws fixing jurisdictional limits, taking it for granted that the treaty was valid. The lapse of seven years gave it greater strength. During that whole period not a single word was uttered officially against the treaty.

But after the lapse of more than seven years, Lic. Don Tomás Ayón, Minister of Foreign Relations of the Republic of Nicaragua, deemed it advisable to send a message to the Legislative body, objecting to the validity of the treaty.

This came to pass as follows: In 1868 the Government of Nicaragua, tired of the delays of certain companies in the opening of the canal, entered, in Paris, into a contract with Monsieur Michel Chevalier, through the same Señor Ayón. Chevalier was well acquainted with the Cañas-Jerez Treaty, and thought that it was absolutely indispensable to respect it, and required as a *sine qua non* condition that Costa Rica should adhere to the agreement. So it was stipulated; and the Government of Costa Rica adhered, and its Congress ratified the agreement.

Señor Ayón had been dazzled by the official position of Chevalier. He thought that for a Senator of the Empire of Napoleon III nothing could be difficult, and that the Emperor had an interest in the canal, both for the sake of extending his influence in the New World and also for the purpose of accomplishing a certain scheme which had been suggested to him and which he accepted while he was imprisoned at the Castle of Ham. But circumstances had changed. The Emperor of the French was preoccupied with European affairs, and a sad disappointment had shown him that his supposed omnipotence did not extend to the world of Columbus. Chevalier could not get the funds required for such a vast enterprise, and although with his contract in his hands he applied to the great capitalists of Europe, and looked for stockholders and partners, he only received attentions and fair words, but nothing positive. It may be said that he went from door to door asking for protection, and that none was given him.

All of this was perfectly well known, both in Costa Rica and Nicaragua, but Chevalier was always laboring under delusions, and imagined the great enterprise to be accomplished under his auspices. These delusions he unceasingly transmitted to Señor Ayón, who, having returned to his country from Europe, could not see, on account of the distance, the difficulties encountered by Chevalier, the repulses which he constantly met, and the hopeless prospects that the canal should be ever built under that contract. And he went as far as to call unpatriotic all those who did not share his delusions.

The Government of Costa Rica, well informed by its agents abroad of the true situation of Chevalier, understood that the contract, under those circumstances, instead of doing any good was really injurious to Costa Rica, to Nicaragua, to Central America, and to the whole world, because as long as it was in existence no further negotiations could be attempted either with the United States, which was the nation called by nature to do the work, or with any other country.

The Costa Rican Executive happened to be invested with unlimited powers, and, after having meditated carefully upon the subject, considering it under all its aspects, it decided to declare that the Ayón-Chevalier contract, as far as Costa Rica was concerned, had become inoperative. This declaration made a great sensation among the few Nicaraguans who still shared the delusions of Señor Ayón, and caused them to endeavor to destroy the Cañas-Jerez treaty, with which, if obtained, they would be able to enter into canal negotiations without the intervention of Costa Rica.

Señor Ayón does not deny that the treaty was made by legitimate representatives of both countries; nor that it was approved by both Executives; nor that it was ratified by the Congress of Costa Rica and the Constituent Assembly of Nicaragua; nor that the ratifications thereof were exchanged in due form; nor that the treaty was solemnly promulgated in both countries as the law on limits; nor that the two contracting parties respected it and constantly complied with its provisions for more than seven years without any objection or opposition. Señor Ayón does not deny anything of the kind; but he grounds his objection on another foundation. He says that the organic law of Nicaragua which marked the limits of the state included the territory of Guanacaste; that the Cañas-Jerez treaty marks different limits and therefore modifies and amends the Nicaraguan Constitution; that the Constitution, then in force in Nicaragua, provided that no amendment or change could be made in it by a decree of a Legislature without the ratification thereof by another subsequent Legislature; that the Cañas-Jerez treaty was ratified by one Legislature, but that it was not even submitted for approval to the next one; and that, therefore, there is *in radice* a cause of nullity.

The Legislative body of Nicaragua did not take any action upon the subject; and the question remained undisposed of.

Costa Rica has replied to Señor Ayón stating that the Congress which ratified the treaty of Nicaragua was not an ordinary Congress but a Constituent Assembly, having the most competent authority to reform the Constitution and to make a new one; that if the said Assembly was convened for the purpose of framing the organic law of the state, no reason can be alleged to deprive it of the right to mark the boundaries. It has also been said that even in case that the Assembly, instead of being a constituent body would have been an ordinary Congress, the treaty would not be void, as claimed by Señor Ayón, for the reason that several Nicaraguan Legislatures, one after another, took it as valid, firm, and unimpeachable, and enacted laws according to its provisions, and established jurisdictional limits in conformity with its text.

The Costa Rican Government always maintained upon these grounds the validity of the treaty, and it may be depended upon that if the question should be submitted to the arbitration of a power friendly to both contracting parties, no nation in the world would declare the treaty to be null upon the arguments and doctrines of Señor Ayón.

Certain Executive tendencies have sometimes been felt in Costa Rica, although unsupported by the general opinion of the Costa Rican people, in favor of the invalidation of the treaty, in order to secure, through this action, that the boundary should be again the whole of the right bank of the San Juan river from Greytown to San Carlos, and from the Lake of Nicaragua to the La Flor river, as it has been believed to be the limit marked by nature.

If these views should prevail, and the treaty should be set aside, the questions between Costa Rica and Nicaragua would become again very grave and uncertain. But if the difficulty is confined simply to the determination of the question, whether the Cañas-Jerez treaty is or is not valid, there cannot be any doubt in law as to the verdict which would be rendered. And so the two Republics understand since they have combined to respect the limits such as marked by the treaty.

No. 62.

Extracts from the "History of Nicaragua from the Remotest Times to the year 1852*," written by order of General Don Joaquin Zavala, President of the Republic, by Señor Dr. Don Tomas Ayón. Vol. I. Granada: Printing office of El Centro Americano,* 1882.—*The author of said history gives the name of Desaguadero to the San Juan de Nicaragua river.*

From Book 3, Chapter I:
"There being no necessity to stop in the Province of Nicaragua, that is to say, in the territory which is now the Department of Rivas, he proceeded from Granada to Tinabita City without stopping at Masaya, which was a great and populous city. Before leaving he took a brigantine, which he caused to explore the *Great Lake, until finding its outlet* (*the San Juan*), but the brigantine could not go farther than this outlet, because there were many rocks and two great rapids."

From Book 3, Chapter III:
"In compliance with royal instructions, he engaged himself in enlisting sufficient force to go, under the command of Captain Gabriel de Rojas, to discover the outlet (Desaguadero) of the Lake of Nicaragua, and found there a town. This enterprise was considered by the King of Spain as a most important one, because, after careful explorations of the land and the lake, he wanted to establish through the said outlet the communication between both oceans, and find thereby the shortest route to the Spice Islands."

From Book 3, Chapter II:
"Knowing the interest which the court felt in finding the route to the Moluca Islands, several persons addressed the King, and set forth that, as the natural straits of communication between the Atlantic and the Pacific Oceans had not

been found, they desired to call his attention to one of the four routes which suggested themselves to establish communication between both oceans. *The first of these routes was the outlet (the Desaguadero) of the Great Lake of Nicaragua, through which large vessels went up and came down, although it has still some dangerous rapids, and by opening a canal through the few leagues of land between the lake and the Pacific Ocean it would be easy for all vessels to reach that ocean.* The second through the Lagartos river, also called Chagres, which rises at about 5 or 6 leagues from Panamá, where a canal could be opened in order to connect the river with the ocean. The third, by the river of Vera Cruz or Tehuantepec, through which the Mexican merchants used to navigate with their merchandise from one sea to the other. And the fourth, the passage from Nombre de Dios to Panamá, where it is assured that there is no great difficulty to open a road, although there are some mountains. They also set forth that between the Uraba Gulf and San Miguel there were only 25 leagues, and that, although the difficulties to open a canal there would be great, the power of the Kings of Castile was still greater. They said, further, that the advantages of the work were indisputable since a third part of the distance to the Moluca Islands could be saved in this way, with the advantage that the voyage could be always made within dominions of Spain, without interference on the part of the Portuguese, and avoiding expense and labor."

From Book 4, Chapter IV:

" They said that from the Lake of Granada to the port of San Juan del Sur, there were only 3 leagues of land, and that with little labor and cost cars could go from the town of Nicaragua (Rivas) to that port; *that the frigates and the other men-of-war used to pass from the same lake, through the river of El Desaguadero, to Nombre de Dios on the Northern Sea, where there was a port which was considered to be the largest and the best yet discovered;* and that for these reasons it was advisable to order that the commerce with the Southern Sea should continue to be made by the way of El Desaguadero, saving thereby great expenses and trouble which were encountered at Nombre de Dios by those arriving from Spain and those who, coming from Peru and other lands, proceeded to Spain. They remarked also that the climate of Nombre de Dios was very unhealthy, and that the greatest part of the Spaniards arriving there died, and that those who escaped death were left in the greatest destitution on account of the extreme poverty of the land."

From Documents appended to the Book.

"Item. Your Majesty will know that between the Lake of this city and the port of San Juan of the Province of Nicaragua on the Southern Sea there are no more than 3 leagues by land, so that, with very little labor and expense, cars can go from the town of Nicaragua to the port of San Juan; and *from the Lake of this city to the Northern Sea the frigates and the men-of-war which leave this place go by water to Nombre de Dios. by the river of El Desaguadero, which empties in the Northern Sea, where there is a port, the greatest and the best yet discovered.*

"For the reasons and causes aforesaid, and according to what we have seen here and experienced, it seems to us that if Your Majesty is pleased to order that the commerce with the Southern Sea continues to be carried on through this outlet (Deste Desaguadero), a great many fatigues and expenses, which are encountered and incurred at Nombre de Dios by those coming from Spain or going there from Peru and other countries, would be saved; all of this, without counting that the greatest part of the Spaniards who come to Nombre de Dios and the city of Panamá, get sick and die. And, as living is so expensive there, those who escape death become so poor that they scarcely have means to continue on their voyage."

No. 63.

Organic Laws of Costa Rica in regard to limits with Nicaragua.

Decree of "Basis and Guarantees" of March 8, 1841.

ARTICLE 1.

SEC. 2. The territory of the State (Costa Rica) is comprised within the following limits: On the west, the La Flor river and the continuation of its line along the shore of the Lake of Nicaragua and the San Juan river, down to the mouth of the latter on the Atlantic Ocean; on the north, the same ocean from the mouth of the San Juan river to the Escudo de Veragua; on the east, from the last named point to the Chiriqui river; and on the south, from the last named river along the coast of the Pacific Ocean, up to the La Flor river.

Constitution of April 10, 1844.

ARTICLE 47. The State recognizes as the limits of its territory the following: On the west, beginning at the mouth of the La Flor river on the Pacific Ocean, continuing along the course of said river, the shore of the Lake of Nicaragua and the San Juan river, until the mouth of the latter on the Atlantic; on the north, the Atlantic Ocean from the mouth of the San Juan river down to the Escudo de Veragua; on the east, from the last named point to the Chiriqui river; and on the south, from the mouth of this river to the mouth of the La Flor river. But the border line on the side of the State of Nicaragua will be finally settled when Costa Rica shall be heard in the national representation, or when in default of this hearing the affair is submitted to the impartial decision of one or more States of the Republic.

Constitution of February 10, 1847.

ARTICLE 25. (It is exactly in the same language as that used in the Constitution of 1844.)

Constitution of November 30, 1848.

ARTICLE 7. The limits of the territory of the Republic are those of the *uti possidetis* of 1826.

Constitution of December 27, 1859.

ARTICLE 4. The territory of the Republic is comprised within the following limits: On the Nicaraguan side, those fixed by the treaty concluded with that Republic on April 15, 1858; on the side of New Granada, the limits of the *uti possidetis* of 1826, subject to what may be determined by subsequent treaties with that nation; and on the other two sides by the Atlantic and Pacific Oceans.

Constitution of April 15, 1869.

ARTICLE 3. The limits of the territory are the following: On the north, the Atlantic Ocean; on the south, the Pacific Ocean; on the side of the United States of Colombia, those of the *uti possidetis* of 1826; and on the side of Nicaragua, those established by the treaty of April 15, 1858.

No. 64.

Failure of canal negotiation with the Government of the United States, owing to the fact that Nicaragua refused Costa Rica intervention in it.

[From Message of the President of the United States to the Congress of the Nation].

Towards the close of the last Administration negotiations were earnestly conducted here with Nicaragua relative to a ship canal. The result thereof, however, did not prove successful because the pretensions of the Nicaraguan Government were not acceptable.

"*As the canal through the Nicaraguan route must probably have to pass along a portion of the San Juan river, over which Costa Rica claims to have jurisdiction, it was advisable to celebrate a treaty with the latter Republic as well as with Nicaragua in regard to this point. To this end the proper instructions were transmitted to the American Minister in Central America; but he has reported that Nicaragua was unwilling to negotiate, especially in connection with Costa Rica.*"

[From the "Gaceta de Nicaragua," No. 37, July 26, 1879.]

THE END.

ERRATA.

Page.	Line.	Reads—	Should read—
15	9	If, as I confidently hope,	If, as I confidently hope, upon grounds which cause me to entertain a profound conviction,
21	14	Rio Grande river.	Rio Grande.
22	2	1573.	1576.
23	19	" correjidor."	" corregidor."
24	4th line of notes.	² PERALTA.	PERALTA.
24	8th line of notes.	² Archivo.	² Archivo.
25	5	Ujarras (Curredabat), Asserri, la Villeta,	Ujarraz, Curridabat, Aserri, la Villita,
25	16	Potosi.	Potosí.
25	18	Diria, Dinomo.	Diriá, Diriomo.
25	19	Naudasmo,	Nandasmo,
25	20	Nisidiri,	Nindirí,
25	21	Subtiada.	Subtiaba.
33	8	1541.	1561.
33	13	TIERRA FIRMA	TIERRA FIRME.
36	30	Perera.	Pereyra.
37	2	Laens.	Saenz.
37	11	British Cyclopædia.	Encyclopædia Britannica.
42	21	easily enter it.	easily enter it.²
42	1st line of notes.	Package.	File.
43	11	According to that treaty the right bank of the river, from its origin in the Lake up to a point three miles from Castillo Viejo, belongs to Nicaragua.	According to that treaty, a strip of land three English miles wide, on the right bank of the river, from its origin in the Lake, to a point three English miles from Castillo Viejo, around which the boundary describes an arc of a circle, the fortress serving as centre, which ends three miles below, on the water's edge, belongs to Nicaragua.
56	3	April 18.	April 15.
56	29	Minister.	Commissioner.
61	9	ratified.	approved.
62	17	article 149.	article 194.
65	17	1853.	1854.
65	25	the organic law of 1853,	the laws of organic character passed by the Assembly of 1854.
66	19	1853.	1854.
69	14	1853.	1854.
76	11	1851.	1857.
86	6	Trevelyn	Trevelyan
88	14	in Central America.	to Nicaragua.
116	9	negotiator	negotiators

ERRATA—*Continued.*

Page.	Line.	Reads—	Should read—
124	22	928	298.
141	5	150	90
141	8	east	right
144	29	1858	1856
157	17	specia	special.
158	29	Article IX	Article XIX.
187	18	is concerned,	is concerned, as Nicaragua is by treaties,
193	6	November	November 8, 1857
208	4	RAFAEL MORA	JUAN RAFAEL MORA
215	36	Rafael Mora	Juan Rafael Mora
231	25	*straight line*	*straight line established between the same limit and the limit on the northern side*
235	4	Bolarios	Bolaños
242	3	Sarapaquí	Sarapiquí
254	31	Nicaragua	Guatemala
268	18	Article XLIII	Article LIII
269	19	Article XLVI	Article LVI
271	13	northwest	northeast
272	34	Arsenal	Arenal
280	26	Pélez	Peláez
280	30	Suchitepiquez	Suchitepequez
281	9	Firma "	Firme "
291	5	1886	1880
294	7	1886	1880
297	34	Firma "	Firme "
305	29	Chapter II	Chapter IV
307	25	Deste	deste

www.ingramcontent.com/pod-product-compliance
Lightning Source LLC
Chambersburg PA
CBHW030740230426
43667CB00007B/790